Emily Cruwys Sharland, John Henry Norman

Coin of the Realm: What it is?

Talks About Gold and Silver Coins

Emily Cruwys Sharland, John Henry Norman

Coin of the Realm: What it is?
Talks About Gold and Silver Coins

ISBN/EAN: 9783744759434

Printed in Europe, USA, Canada, Australia, Japan

Cover: Foto ©ninafisch / pixelio.de

More available books at **www.hansebooks.com**

COIN OF THE REALM: WHAT IS IT?

OR,

TALKS ABOUT GOLD AND SILVER COINS.

WITH A FEW PRACTICAL LESSONS

BASED ON

"NORMAN'S SINGLE GRAIN SYSTEM"

(Written expressly for Boys and Girls)

BY

EMILY CRUWYS SHARLAND.

ALSO, AS AN

APPENDIX,

AN EXCHANGE CALCULUS, FIVE PAPERS, AND A MEMORANDUM ON MONEY, WITH VALUABLE AND ORIGINAL TABLES,

BY

JOHN HENRY NORMAN.

PRICE TWO SHILLINGS.

LONDON:
WATERLOW & SONS LIMITED, LONDON WALL.
1888.

EXTRACTS OF LETTERS RECEIVED BY MR. NORMAN, IN COMMENDATION OF MISS SHARLAND'S AND HIS WORK.

From the Hon. H. R. LINDERMAN, *Director of Mints, U.S.A., May 25th,* 1875.

"The receipt of your favour of the 13th instant was a great pleasure to me. I had read with much interest the valuable tables in reference to weights of coins, exchanges, &c., received from you in the early part of the year. It is, I think, to be regretted that the statistics, &c., contained in those tables could not be placed more generally before the public. There appears to be a wide-spread ignorance, or disregard of the fundamental principle which underlies international exchanges, and hence the value of contributions like yours, in which the principle referred to (pure metal against pure metal) is so clearly stated."

From Professor Dr. A. SOETBEER, *Göttingen, May 16th,* 1887.

"I am very much obliged to you for the printed matter you kindly sent me, *i.e.*, 'Single Grain System.' I have taken notice of them with great interest."

Extract from THE BANKERS' MAGAZINE, *June,* 1887.

"Everyone should be encouraged to work out the system, especially the young, for the information may prove of much value to them in going through the world."

From Professor ERWIN NASSE, *Bonn, June 4th,* 1888.

"I have read with great interest the pamphlet you were kind enough to send me. Your method of comparing the weights of fine gold and silver contained in the coins of different countries has pleased me very much."

From H. J. Chaney, Esq., *Keeper of the Standards of Great Britain, June 27th*, 1888.

"The answers given by the children to the questions on money asked by Miss Sharland are really surprising, for they evince powers of mind and application which could hardly be expected in children so young. The success has its origin in the able chapters on money which Miss Sharland had prepared for the children. In these chapters the actual relation between the standard of monetary measure in different countries is based on the simple unit, a grain of standard substance; and so all the technical overloading, always met with in the literature of this subject, is quite swept away. The child has only a simple factor before him, and by successive gentle steps he has been taught to apply that factor to unravelling so many knotty problems in exchange and value. It has given me very great pleasure to read papers which you have sent me, and I shall be glad at any time to receive further information on the important and interesting question of monetary values."

From F. H. Senior, Esq., *September 8th*, 1888.

"I am sure every one who has read Miss Sharland's papers must have been very greatly pleased and owes his best thanks to her for the admirable exposition of your system."

From Professor Dr. W. Lexis, *Gottingen, September 17th*, 1888.

"I think that your 'Single Grain System' is most useful for all practical purposes, and simplifies very much the whole exchange calculus."

From Alex. L. Glencross, Esq., *September 28th*, 1888.

"Miss Sharland's chapters on "Money" are most instructive and most ingenious. They cannot fail, I am sure, to make boys and girls not only take an interest in but to make a hobby of the subject."

from Wm Graham Sumner Prof.
Pol. Econ. & Soc. Sci. Yale Coll USA
Author of "A Hist. of American Cur-
-rency" 1874 "Pol & Soc Science" 1885.
Dated 9-1-89 =

"The doctrines in "Coin of the realm &c" are entirely unimpeachable & are well stated."

from Mr Posey S Wilson. Washington USA Dated March 10th 1889.

COIN OF THE REALM: WHAT IS IT?

"When once people understand the relation which the foreign exchanges bear to domestic exchanges and that purchase & sale is essentially the weighing out of so much these metal against other commodities, it will be as if darkness on a traveller's way had passed away & day came."

[illegible]

I hear that there are not 20 men in the USA legislatures who could answer Mrs [illegible] 15 questions p. 116.

Appendix

I Address to the general reader. 131

II An antidote to Bi-Metallism. 136

III On the cause of the fall in the Gold price of silver, & of prices generally in the British Isles since 1873. 141

IV Mr Norman's writings on monetary subjects since 1883. 152

V The present & prospective positions of the universal currency dilemma. 153

VI Monetary Standards, money & monetary systems. 177

VII An American view of Bi-Metallism. 184

VIII Norman's Exchange Calculus. 186

IX — " — Single Grain System A

X Tables (3) of weights & values of coins & money of account. B

XI The Exchanges upon a scientific basis.

[illegible] C

Dedicated by Permission

TO

MRS. FAWCETT.

PREFACE.

MANY persons are fond of collecting coins. They spare no pains in hunting up the history of every fresh specimen that they are fortunate enough to add to their collection; and a most interesting and instructive form of amusement this is. But so few collectors of coins carry their researches up to the present date! so very few persons know anything concerning the coinage of their own day beyond its *shopping value.*

I hope to induce my young readers to confess, after reading the following pages, that "Money" is not so dry a subject as they have hitherto believed it to be; and I feel sure that among the great number of boys and girls who nowadays delight in mastering difficult arithmetical problems, some will be found who will enjoy the practical application of Mr. J. H. Norman's *Single Grain System*, fully explained in the second series of this work.

It is strange that almost all authors of geographies describe the religion, language, physical conditions, products, and manufactures of the countries about which they write; whilst the history of the standard and token coins circulated in those countries has hitherto been omitted. The addition of this latter subject would prove of great value to all students intending to follow a commercial career, or to travel in foreign lands; and I trust that some day the monetary systems of the countries that possess a standard currency will be taught in schools *with geography.*

I am indebted to many resources for the information given in the following chapters; more especially to the late Professor Jevons' delightful work, "Money"; to Blackie's "Popular Encyclopædia," or Conversations Lexicon; also to Mr. Alexander Watts' "Lump of Gold"; and to the report of the Director of the Mint, U.S.A., for the year 1885.

For the benefit of those who are sufficiently interested in the "Money" subject to pursue the study further, Mr. J. H. Norman has kindly added an appendix to this work, containing an exchange calculus, five papers, and a memorandum on money, with valuable and original tables. These papers I commend to the notice of all thoughtful readers.

EMILY CRUWYS SHARLAND.

82, Sinclair Road,
West Kensington Park, W.

The second part page of treats of the single coin system.

COIN OF THE REALM: WHAT IS IT?*

INTRODUCTION.

What is money?

"JOHN SMITH," said I one day to a certain young friend of mine, "do you know what money is?"

"Yes, Miss Sweet," he replied, laughing, "I rather think I do. It is the gold, and silver, and copper with which we buy things."

"And no doubt you can tell me the names and value of every English coin in present use?" I continued.

John Smith's definition.

"To be sure I can," John answered; and he rattled off the following list glibly enough:—"I'll begin with the money of least value, which is made of copper. A farthing is the smallest copper coin; two farthings make one half-penny; two half-pence go to a penny; twelve copper pence go to one silver shilling."

"Stop a minute," I interrupted, "you are not quite correct, John. We no longer use copper money; our farthings, half-pence, and pence being now made of bronze."

"Oh, are they?" said John, carelessly; "we call them coppers, at any rate. Well, to go on to the silver coins. A threepenny bit, worth three pence, is the smallest; two of them go to a sixpence; two sixpences make a shilling; two shillings go to a florin, commonly called a two-shilling bit; and a half-crown is worth two shillings and sixpence. That's all correct, Miss Sweet, I believe?"

"Quite right, John," I answered. "And now let me hear about the gold coins."

---

* For index to "Coin of the Realm: What is it?" see end of the pamphlet. For contents of Appendix see page 127.

"There are only two kinds of gold coins used in England now," said John; "the sovereign, or pound, which is worth twenty shillings, and the half-sovereign worth ten shillings. Bank notes and cheques are used for large sums of money. A man can carry thousands of pounds at a time in his pocket if he use these."

"That's true enough," I answered, "and there are a great many other kinds of paper money in use besides bank notes and cheques.—But just now we are talking about coins. You are a ready reckoner I know, John; your father tells me that you are a great help to him on busy evenings. Suppose you give me an idea of the value of the different coins you named, by telling me some of the things that could be bought with them at your father's shop."

On the value of coins.

John Smith gives their exchange value.

"All right," said John. "Let me see; I want to bring in a farthing first, don't I? Oh, well! you can get a farthing reel of cotton, or a farthing row of pins. Then potatoes are ½d. a pound just now, or 10d. a score. A sixpenny and a threepenny bit—9d. in all—will get you 6 lbs. of flour. One shilling is the price of a ¼ lb. of the best shag tobacco. A two-shilling piece will buy 1 lb. of tea, though our half-crown article is better. A half-sovereign was the price of my last new trousers; whilst a whole sovereign, or £1, would, *I believe*, buy a coat for father."

"Well done, John," said I, laughing. "You have been quick about it, and you have reckoned it all capitally, I must say. But what more can you tell me about money?"

"What more?" repeated John. "What more do you want? There's nothing more to tell."

"Nothing more to tell, John?" cried I, turning up my eyes, and throwing up my hands. "I am afraid you must be very ignorant to say so!"

"John's face turned very red, for he was a clever boy, and my last remark wounded his pride greatly. But he was a thoroughly good fellow, and the next minute he looked into my face with a roguish smile.

Miss Sweet is asked to define money.

"Ah, Miss Sweet," said he, "you are at your old tricks again, *I* know! That's always your way of going on when you want to tell me something jolly and interesting. Come! let's hear what you've got to tell about money, now that I've had my say."

"It would take a longer time to tell than I can stand here talking, John," I answered; "but if you will drink tea with me next Saturday evening, we will sit over the fire afterwards, and have a talk about the history of money. If you find that you would like to hear more about it, why, you must come to tea again, that's all."

So that was how young John Smith came to know so much about money. Many a cosy tea and chat did we two have together that winter, until John knew as much about the subject as I could tell him.

This leads to a series of conversations.

In the following chapters I hope to give my readers those particulars concerning money which proved of so much interest to John Smith.

Chapter I.

I SUPPOSE everybody values money; but if you could get each of your friends to tell you truly *why* they like to possess pounds, shillings, and pence, you would be quite surprised to discover what a variety of reasons people would be able to give for doing so. Children, I am glad to say, generally value money for its true worth, and that is, *for what it will get.* I do not mean to say that you young people are to be depended upon to spend your money always in the best and wisest way; on the contrary, a present of money often burns a hole in a girl's or boy's pocket—you cannot be happy until you have spent it. For this reason it is a very good thing that you are not likely to possess much money until you have learnt to keep it for real wants, and not to spend it simply because you have it. Yet you *do* value it, I am sure, for what it will buy rather than for its own sake. It is a very rare thing for either of you to put by your little presents of money just for the pleasure of looking at them. At times poor miserly men and women have thus most sadly misused the money they have earned, depriving themselves of all the comforts of life, and of many of its necessities also, for the sake of keeping their poor little coins in a secret place, and counting them over when no one was by. Could anything be more pitiable than this?

On the value of money.

To appreciate the real value of money, you must go back

Exchange or barter.

with me many hundreds of years, and try to imagine how our forefathers lived before money had been invented. How do you suppose men managed to buy and sell in those days, when they had no money to part with, and their neighbours also had none to offer them? They used to *exchange things that they did not want, for things that they did want.* Suppose a man had a flock of sheep, but no corn, he would give a sheep, or part of one, for so many measures of corn. This way of exchanging goods was called *barter* or *truck* (from the French, *troc*), and I suspect that men tried to overreach their neighbours, even in those early times, by asking them to accept worthless things in return for valuable ones, because the word *truck* is now a common expression of contempt in Devonshire: "I don't want any of your *truck!*" a Devonshire man will say if he is offered anything that he considers *rubbishy.*

The difficulty of establishing a fair system of exchange.

But the worst of this sort of trading was the difficulty of establishing a proper ratio of exchange—that is, to determine what number of articles of one description should be considered equivalent to a certain number of articles of another description.

Suppose, for instance, that your mother wanted 2 lbs. of flour, 1 lb. of treacle, and half-a-dozen eggs, and that she had nothing to offer for these things but a pair of new boots: don't you think it would be difficult to arrange matters to her satisfaction? The new boots, perhaps, might be worth 10s., whilst 2 lbs. of flour would cost 3d.; 1 lb. of treacle, 2½d.; and half-a-dozen eggs, 6¼d. Well; your mother would either have to carry home a lot of other things she was not in immediate want of, or else she would lose the value of 9s. 0¼d. by parting with her boots.

But in the early times of which I am writing there were no shops or stores. These exchanges had to be made between private persons, and were even more difficult to arrange fairly. If Mrs. Jones were to go to Mr. Brown, just after he had killed a sheep, and were to say, "I am in want of a joint of meat large enough for a family of seven, and can offer you in exchange for it my best bonnet;" most likely Mr. Brown would reply, "I am sorry I cannot oblige you, Mrs. Jones, but, as I am a bachelor, your best bonnet would be of no use to me!" You will readily understand that this plan did not answer in olden times any better than it would do so now. People often had not suitable things of the same value to offer in exchange for what they wanted, and house-keeping must have been far more difficult to manage in the days when there was little or no money in circulation than it is now.

Furs

Hunting is one of the earliest forms of industrial employment of which we have any trace, and furs or skins were certainly circulated as money by many ancient nations. I daresay you will be surprised at my classing hunting amongst the industries, but I do so because in ancient times men hunted and killed wild animals for the sake of providing food and clothing for themselves and their families, and not for idle pleasure. The flesh of the beasts they killed was their food, and the skins were their clothing by night and by day. Men who were clever at hunting, however, very soon laid in a much larger supply of skins than they could possibly require for themselves and their own families; therefore they parted with them for other things of which they were in need, and in time skins became the regular medium of exchange amongst the hunting tribes. In some parts of the world they are used thus still.

Cattle.

When men became more civilised, and took to cultivating land, and keeping flocks and herds of sheep and cattle, a man's live stock became his money. It will interest many of you to know that the word *fee* is derived from the Anglo-Saxon word *feoh*, which meant either money or cattle; and another fact worth mentioning to you is, that the kine used for exchange purposes, being counted by the head, were named *capitale* (a word derived from the Latin word *caput*, head) and from it our English terms *capital*, *chattel*, and *cattle* had their origin.

Origin of *fee*, *capital*, *chattle* and *cattle*.

I daresay it was convenient enough in the days when there were no shops, to possess money which walked about upon its own legs, and could be easily driven from one piece of pasture land to another; but a cow or a sheep would be rather a cumbersome piece of money in these days, would it not? Just imagine the confusion and commotion that would take place in a town of any size on market day, if all the country folk brought their sheep, or cattle, or pigs into the town with them, and left them at the shops in exchange for the articles of food and clothing that they required! It is bad enough sometimes even now when cattle are driven through the streets of a town to and from the market place; but then, as soon as market is over, they are driven out of the town again—not left behind to be accommodated in some tradesman's backyard or garden.

Ornaments.

The love of finery has shown itself in all ages, though there have always been, and still are, varieties of opinions as to whether the things worn are ornamental or disfiguring to the wearers. For instance, those who imagine that they look lovely in war paint and feathers, with rings through their noses, and tobacco pipes stuck through their ears, appear to us to have rather peculiar ideas on the subject of becoming ornaments, do they not?

Leather money.

At an early stage in the history of money, we find that men and women took to adorning themselves with the things which they were in the habit of exchanging for the necessaries of life. I will tell you some of the odd things which from time to time have been used for this double purpose by the different nations of the world:—Black and white polished shells, made into beads; cowries, (the shells best known as black-a-moors' teeth); whales' teeth; ivory tusks; yellow amber; leather money*; and metal coins.

Coins.

Eastern women adorn their head-dresses to this day with small silver coins, and in India the natives often melt down

---

* Classical writings lead one to suspect that the earliest currency used at Rome, Lacedæmon, and Carthage was formed of leather. Leather money is also said to have been circulated in Russia as late as the reign of Peter the Great, whilst English tradesmen's token-money was probably made of stamped leather at one period. [Since writing these chapters, I have received the following interesting account of a modern leather medal from a young co-operator, in his description of how the Queen's Jubilee was kept at Barnsley, in Yorkshire:—"The cordwainers exhibited a novelty often heard of but seldom seen—a leather medal. I had the pleasure of seeing one of them the day before they were worn. On one side were these words:—'Barnsley Cordwainers' Society, established 1747. In commemoration of Her Majesty's Jubilee, June 21st, 1887.' The medal was circular, the words being stamped round a gilded crown."

The following newspaper cutting has also been contributed by another young co-operator:—

Curious Money.—The battle of Poictiers took place on the 19th of September, 1356, in which King John of France was made prisoner, and many of the French nobility lost their lives. The captive monarch, though respectfully treated, was brought to England to grace the triumph of the conqueror. The peace, in 1360, put an end to his captivity, but to obtain his liberty he made over many of the most valuable provinces of his kingdom to the King of England, and agreed to pay a ransom of three millions of gold crowns, which reduced him to the necessity of paying for the necessaries of his household in leather money, in the middle of which there was a little nail of silver.

their silver money, form it into bracelets or bangles, and wear these upon their wrists or ankles, thus becoming a kind of walking savings bank. But, as their money gains no interest when treated thus, I do not advise any of you to adopt either of these plans.

Suppose English women took to trimming their bonnets and caps with silver money, and used these ornamental coins whenever they required to buy anything: how untidy they would soon be! They would be returning from their shopping expeditions with a coin or two missing from their bonnets, or perhaps with only one earring on. I do not think we should like that style of thing at all in old England!

Corn has been used as a medium of exchange for many centuries past, and is still so employed in some parts of Europe. In Norway it is even deposited in banks, and lent and borrowed. A good many other vegetable productions have been used from time to time for exchange purposes, such as maize, olive oil, cacao nuts and beans, and tobacco. In the beginning of the 17th century tobacco was ordered to be received in the Virginia plantations instead of money, at the rate of 3s. per lb. What do you think was the use made of this permission by the settlers in Virginia? They actually bought *wives* for themselves at the rate of from 100 lbs. to 150 lbs. of tobacco per wife! I only hope that you all think your mothers are worth more than £15 or £22. 10s. apiece!

Corn.

Other vegetable productions.

Tobacco.

And now let us turn our attention to the origin of metal money, though I must not let my pen run on too long about the earlier coinage of our own and other nations, for it would be quite impossible to give you a complete history of coins in these short chapters. But I strongly advise those of you who are within reach of a museum containing a collection of coins, to go and have a good look at them, not *once*, but many times, and to read about them as well. Some holiday time you might do this, and, I think, you would be rewarded for your pains.

The origin of metal money.

Metal money is of very ancient origin. You must not imagine that at the time when furs, or cattle, or corn, or ornaments were being used as mediums of exchange, there were no coins in circulation. They were certainly in use then, but until the metallic mines had been worked for many centuries it would have been impossible to provide whole nations with an unlimited supply of metal for coinage; besides which, every fresh invention takes a long time making its way in the world. Had Mrs. Brown been living in the days when coins were scarce in England, she would have thankfully exchanged away her fire irons, her spare bed, her best tea things—yes, and even her *party frock!*—if by so doing she could have kept the few precious little coins she had managed to get hold of. But now-a-days if Mrs. Brown wishes to be thought respectable amongst her neighbours, she will spend her last shilling before she will part with so much as a pair of sugar tongs in order to supply the family needs. Mrs. Brown is quite right, mind you, and the people who lived generations before her were quite right too. They all showed themselves willing to give up their old habits of exchange and barter when a new and better medium of exchange was provided for them. This is what is called *moving with the times*, and it is only unselfish people who are willing to resign cherished customs and manners of living for the sake of bettering those who will come after them.

Invented about 900 B.C.

It has been pretty certainly proved that metal coins were invented about 900 B.C., and that silver money was in use a century later. The earliest specimens of silver coins are found stamped on one side only, the reason for which is supposed to be as follows: Seals were used at a very early date by persons in authority, and it is thought that some ruler of the land made the impression of his seal upon each coin to certify that it was of true weight.

Ancient coins stamped with seals.

Different kinds of metal used.

All these metals—gold, silver, copper, tin, lead, and iron, were used as money in every age of which we have any historical account; but they were not manufactured into coins and stamped from the very first, though the art of hammering metals into various shapes was early invented.

Primitive forms of metal money.

Rough lumps.

Most of the metals were first circulated in rough lumps, whilst the primitive form of gold money seems to have been gold dust. All of them were bought and sold by weight against other commodities; so many grains of gold dust, for instance, for a skin, a cow, or a measure of corn.

Gold dust.

Bars or spikes.

As soon as metals began to be moulded, iron, copper, and brass appear to have been made into bars or spikes. The size of these bars can be guessed at pretty nearly, for we are told that six of them were as many as a man could grasp in one hand. They were made as nearly of one weight as possible, and parted with by the *tale* or piece.

Is it not lucky that we have no such clumsy pieces of money at the present day? Even *one* bar of iron stowed away in one's pocket would be very uncomfortable, besides which, I don't believe the ancients had any pockets. Perhaps they strapped a bundle of these bars on to their backs when they went to visit a neighbour for the purpose of buying anything of him.

Then, there was ring-money: in some countries men took to melting their gold-dust or silver ore, and working it into thick wire; this they twisted into spiral rings, and probably wore until they were obliged to exchange them away for other things. You see, different nations adopted different fashions even in those early ages: in some countries it was the fashion to wear shell-money, in others silver coins, and we have certain proof that gold and silver ring-money was worn in many countries of the world at different periods of history. For my part, I should not like to wear rings one day, and to have to part with them the next, and I do not suppose that you would approve of this plan of buying food and clothing, either. Ring-money

I have already told you that iron bars were circulated as money in ancient times; Julius Cæsar also mentioned in his writings that he found the ancient Britons using iron rings of a certain weight for money. But, although we have it on good authority that these iron bars and rings were in circulation formerly, not a single specimen of either has ever been discovered. Can you guess the reason for this? It is because iron rusts very rapidly, which makes it a most unsuitable material for coinage. Every bar or ring of iron belonging to those early times must have been eaten away with rust many centuries ago, so that it would be useless for antiquarians to dig and delve in the hope of finding any. I believe specimens of every other kind of metal money have been found and preserved. Iron is so exceedingly cheap, also, that a penny would be properly represented by a pound weight of it! Iron.

Lead has oftened been coined, but it is so soft that any impression stamped upon it would very soon get worn away. At one time leaden bullets were circulated in America as small change, at the rate of a farthing a bullet; and in Burmah lead is accepted by weight for small payments. Lead.

How odd you would think it, if, when you laid down a penny and asked for a halfpenny worth of sweets, a couple of bullets were handed back to you for your change! Or, worse again, to give half-a-crown in payment for two shillings' worth of tea and then to have the store manager weighing you out sixpenny-worth of lead, and expecting you to carry it away instead of a sixpenny bit!

Tin. Tin was, no doubt, the first metal used for British coinage, for there were tin mines in Cornwall at a very early date. Tin is both lighter in weight and higher in price than iron, lead, or copper; but it is so soft that it is liable both to bend and to break.

Picture the following scene: Tom Channing has had a present of a tin shilling. How bright and large it is! He is in school now, but at twelve o'clock he means to go off and spend his treasure. What will it get? A real *blood alley* for one thing, and perhaps a pocket knife with one blade; anything left can be spent at the tuck shop. Whilst Tom is thinking of all this, he is supposed to be learning a lesson. His eyes are upon the book in front of him, but his thoughts are far away from it, and his left hand is in his left trousers pocket, turning the money about, and squeezing one-half towards the other with his hot and sticky fingers. How easily it bends! Tom shows the doubled-up coin to his neighbour, holding it under the desk. "What are you doing, Channing?" thunders the master; "you shall bring me that pretty thing the very next time I catch you looking at it!" and Tom feels that he has only just escaped losing his shilling. By the time school is over, the coin has been bent and unbent a good many times, so Tom then proceeds to straighten it out before going off to spend it. Snap goes the tin shilling in two! Poor Tom need not trouble himself as to what it will buy, for no shopman will accept his broken bits of tin.

Copper. Copper takes a good impression, and keeps its colour well; but it has one great drawback, namely, its excessive cheapness. If a penny contained a real pennyworth of copper, it would weigh nearly 1¾oz. troy, that is, about six times the weight of our present bronze penny. This would be almost as bad as the leaden and iron money. During the last century copper money was very much used in Sweden, and we are told that merchants used to take *wheelbarrows* with them when they went to receive payment for their merchandise!

A good deal of nickel is now made use of in the manufacture of foreign coins, but I believe it is always mixed with some other metal. In Belgium, the United States, and Germany many of the coins are made from a mixture of one part nickel to three parts copper. Nickel.

Brass—a mixture of copper and carbonate of zinc—was used for coinage by the Romans; and pewter has often been coined. The finest pewter is, I believe, a compound of tin, antimony, and copper, the last two being used in very small proportions; but common pewter is merely a mixture of tin and lead. Brass and pewter.

When first platinum mines were discovered in the Ural mountains, an attempt was made by the Russian Government to adopt this metal for coinage; but platinum is very much harder than gold, and the expense of working it is therefore much greater, besides which, it is only found in a few localities. In less than 20 years the few coins that had been circulated were called in, and the idea of using platinum for coinage was given up. Owing, however, to its hardness and durability, platinum is most invaluable in the manufacture of chemical apparatus. Platinum.

And now I must wind up my account of the metals which have been found unsuitable for coinage, by telling you of the famous gun-money which was coined by order of James II., and issued in Ireland. He ordered his officers to collect any old metal that they could lay hands on, and the money which was struck after this collection had been made was said to have been composed of old guns, broken bells, waste copper, brass, pewter, and old kitchen pots and pans. If we leave the old guns and broken bells out of our list, we shall have just such a collection of odds and ends as might be picked out of a nineteenth century scavenger's cart! James II. also tried to get pewter crown-pieces accepted for the value of silver ones. I am afraid he must have had a bad conscience as far as his money matters were concerned, and he was not the only sovereign who has played tricks with the coinage of his kingdom when hard driven for cash. James II.'s gun money. James II.'s pewter crown-pieces.

Chapter II.

Metals in use now.

I have told you all that is necessary for you to know at present concerning the metals which have been found unsuitable for coinage; for the future, therefore, I shall direct your attention to those metals and mixtures of metals which are actually in use at the present day. (When a superior metal is mixed with an inferior one, it is usual to say that there is so much *alloy* in the coin. Gold and silver are *alloyed* with copper before they are sufficiently hard to coin well.)

Alloy.

Success of our present system of coinage due to certain points.

In the first place, you should understand what are the principal points to which we owe the success of our present system of coinage. I will suppose that you are a young man living in a country village, and that you are going to London for a long day's shopping. Your neighbours, as well as your own family, have asked you to do all sorts of commissions for them, so you are anxious to avoid carrying with you anything that will take up much room, for you know well enough what a medley of odd-shaped parcels you will have accumulated by the time you come to the end of your day's shopping—clothes, groceries, meat, stationery, all kinds of things will have to be conveyed about somehow. Well, how would you like to have your money? In what shape, I mean. *Not* in the form of iron bars, or lumps of lead, or big copper pieces, I am sure! Your list of commissions come to over £4, besides which you must have enough money with you to pay for your journey and some food. A £5 note will hardly do, because of your railway ticket to begin with. Suppose you carry three sovereigns, two half-sovereigns, and ten shillings' worth of silver in your purse, hidden away in the depths of the inner breast-pocket of your Sunday coat; the other ten shillings, in the form of small silver and a few coppers, being stowed away in vest and trousers pockets, where you can easily get at them. One necessary point, then, is that money should be *portab e;* that a few coins should represent a sufficiently large sum of money, and that these few coins should be neither too large nor too heavy.

Portability.

Divisibility.

You get to the station by driving six miles in a spring-cart, and at once go to take your ticket, asking for a "Second-class return." "Twelve and fourpence," says the man at the hole, and you hand him a sovereign from your purse. How awkward it would be for you if the ticket issuer were unable to give you change! But no such fear; you get your change clapped down in front of you immediately—three half-crowns and two pennies—which are easily counted as you sweep them into your hand, and move on to make room for the person behind you. Off you go, with a light heart and a heavy purse, but not so heavy as to interfere with your comfort in any way. Arrived at Paddington, you set out to walk, and hail the first 'bus which is going in your direction. Twopence is the fare, very easily picked out and paid.

Then shopping commences, and you go from shop to shop paying various odd sums for the different articles you have to buy: 3s. at one place, a florin and a shilling; 2s. 9d. at another —one of your half-crowns and a threepenny piece; £1 2s. 4d. at the grocer's—a sovereign, two shillings, and four pennies; so you go on. There is no difficulty in paying the exact amounts required, for, if you cannot make it up from your own money in hand, the shopkeepers can readily supply you with change. Any odd sums can be quickly made up, and our English coins are so easily recognised that you need lose no unnecessary time in examining the change that is handed to you. A penny and a half-crown, for instance, are so different in colour that no one could mistake the one for the other; and the same may be said of a halfpenny and a shilling. Then a florin, or two shilling piece, and a half-crown, though both silver coins, differ greatly in appearance; the half-crown is the larger of the two, and the stamps impressed upon it are not at all like those with which a florin is imprinted. A sovereign and a shilling, it is true, are near of a size, the shilling being rather the larger of the two; but only just feel the difference in weight between them! The sovereign is so much the heavier of the two coins that you could tell which was which in the dark, and the same proportional difference in weight exists between a half sovereign and a sixpenny bit. Even our little silver threepenny bit has now no rival, though a few years ago, when fourpenny pieces (called *groats*) were still issued, it was necessary to look closely at the smallest silver coins in one's purse.

I hope I have succeeded in proving three points in favour

of our present system of coinage: first, that it is portable; secondly, that it can be readily divided into odd or even sums; thirdly, that all the coins now in circulation can be easily and immediately recognised by old or young, rich or poor.

Indestructibility.

Another point to be considered in the choice of a material for money is, that it should be *indestructible.*

Furs not indestructible.

No doubt the North American Indians still carry on a brisk trade with furs, exchanging them for other things which they require. But if a fire should ever break out in one of their villages and burn up their stock of skins, the loss would be as disastrous for them as the breaking of a bank would be for more civilised folk. Besides this possible misfortune, there is the certainty that in the course of time furs will wear out; no one would care to accept a fur which had worn into bald patches in exchange for anything new.

Nor cattle.

Then, again, as to cattle. In the days when they were used for exchange purposes, the time must have frequently arrived when a man had to kill and eat his money rather than run the risk of its dying of old age.

Our coins, however, are much more indestructible than furs or cattle; they wear out very slowly, and if the stamps imprinted on them do get rubbed, or the metal so much worn away as to make the coins too light for circulation, they can be melted down and re-coined with very little loss of metal.

Intrinsic value.

And not only do our coins stand a good deal of wear and tear, but they are also made of substances that are valuable in themselves, which is another advantage for them to possess, since they are the chosen medium of exchange for all other rare and valuable things. Those of you who live in large cities or towns have probably often looked into a goldsmith's shop window. What a fine display of beautiful and glittering objects are to be seen there, are there not? particularly at night, when the unshuttered windows, protected with iron bars, invite passers-by to look into the shop, which is one blaze of light. Comparatively few people are rich enough to indulge in the use of such massive gold plate and jewellery as one sees in a goldsmith's window; but pass on to a silversmith's shop—the ornaments, jewellery, and plate displayed to view in his window are quite as beautiful in their way as the gold ones, and not anything like so costly. There are three reasons for this: first,

Gold more valuable than silver.

that it costs a great deal more to produce gold than to produce silver; secondly, that there is much more silver in the world than there is gold; and, thirdly, that gold is about twice as heavy as silver.

Both gold and silver are easily restored, if they get tarnished, and they do not either of them rust, like iron.

And now, recall to your minds the difficulty there was in olden days of exchanging different articles fairly, because of their unequal values. A fur would have been quite spoilt had it been cut up into small pieces to represent the value of pence or halfpence; and, as to a cow, I only hope that many nations did not adopt the barbarous plan which some savage tribes have been known to practise—namely, that of catching a cow, cutting a good-sized piece of flesh out of its living carcase, and then driving it back into the prairie or woods again! This was actually the method which some savage people adopted for supplying their larders with prime beef. But those who were hardly cold-blooded enough to practise such live butchery could not be always slaying their beasts whenever they wanted a pennyworth of milk, or a half-quartern loaf; nor would their neighbours be in constant need of beef, mutton or pork.

Metal easily divided and subdivided.

The metals used for coinage get over this difficulty nicely for us; they are so equal in quality and weight that a large lump of gold or silver can be easily sub-divided into many smaller lumps of equal weight and size, so that each coin will contain as nearly as possible the same number of grains of gold or silver, and will possess the same value. This is another very desirable quality in the material used for money; indeed, the only unsatisfactory point to be mentioned with regard to our present system of coinage is, that gold and silver vary much in their value from time to time, and whenever a change takes place in the value of either metal, somebody has to suffer for it.

Drawback, that the value of metal is fluctuating.

Explanation of technical terms.

Hitherto I have avoided as much as possible using words which you would not easily understand, but the time has arrived when I must explain to you the meanings of several terms which are used in reference to money only.

Currency.

The word currency is applied to all kinds of money which may be freely circulated. You have heard or read of the *current* of a river or stream: the word current means *flowing onward.*

If you take a shilling out of your pocket, and buy something with it at the confectioner's, he may immediately go and spend that same shilling at the draper's, or the grocer's, or wherever he likes. The next person into whose hands it falls may be just starting on a journey; perhaps he pockets your shilling with other silver coins, and when he arrives at his destination, spends it. In the course of a few hours the shilling you possessed so lately may have reached some place two hundred miles or more from the town in which you live, and there is no saying how much further it may not have to travel before it is worn out. In this manner the currency of a kingdom flows on like a river; our coins—known by the name of "current coin"—pass from one person to another, no one knowing through how many hands a coin may not have already passed when it reaches them, nor when it will cease to circulate. Under the term "the currency" are included our British gold, silver, and bronze coins; also a certain amount of paper money, but only such as may be freely circulated. There are many kinds of paper money which can only be presented once for payment, or exchanged for current coin once; such money cannot be considered current money. But a Bank of England note, which, having been issued crisp and clean-looking, passes from hand to hand, from pocket to pocket, until it has become greasy, soft, and soiled, may certainly be said to belong to our currency,

Legal tender.

"Legal tender" is another term used in speaking of money. It is applied to any substance which the laws of the country in which you live allow you to offer in payment for goods. Now, there are two kinds of metal money: (1) Standard money: (2) Token money. The first is called "unlimited legal tender," because it may be coined by permission of the state in unlimited quantities, and freely circulated through the kingdom. A gold sovereign is our British standard coin; our English government allow the issue of an unlimited number of sovereigns from the mint, and any amount of them may be used at a time. Suppose your father went to the head master of your school, and said, "Here are ten sovereigns, due to you for my son's first term at school." Perhaps the master might reply, "I would much rather receive a cheque for £10 from you, if it is all the same to you." But then your father would have a perfect right to say, "I cannot make it convenient to pay you by cheque," and the master would be bound to accept the ten sovereigns.

Standard money.

Token money.

Suppose, however, that your father offered to pay your master the ten pounds in silver. Ah! that would be quite another matter; our silver coins are only token money, not standard money, and they are legal tender only up to a certain amount. Forty shillings is the largest sum in silver that a person is strictly bound by law to accept, and twelve pence only in coppers (as we still call our bronze coins) are legal tender. Of course people often oblige each other by accepting more than forty shillings' worth of silver, or a shilling's worth of coppers; but it is unusual to carry about large amounts of silver or copper—indeed, it would be uselessly loading one's purse or pocket to do so when there is so much representative money in circulation. I have just made use of another term which requires explanation—"representative money." A sovereign represents twenty shillings in silver, does it not? and a half-sovereign ten shillings; besides which there are silver coins representing twelve, six, or three pennies. A coin which represents several coins of an inferior metal, is called "representative coin." These representative coins are more convenient to use than a very large number of less valuable ones; if there were no such things as sovereigns or half-sovereigns in England, wealthy people would have to take about their money in wheelbarrows sometimes, as the Swedish merchants of whom I told you did a hundred years ago, unless they adopted paper money,

Representative money.

Mono-metallists and bi-metallists.

For many years past there has been a great difference of opinion in the minds of learned men as to whether a nation should adopt one standard metal, either gold or silver, for coinage of unlimited legal tender, or whether coins both of gold and silver should be allowed to circulate freely and in unlimited quantities in the same country. Those who are in favour of a single standard are called "mono-metallists," whilst those who approve of a double standard go by the name of "bi-metallists." When you are grown up I daresay you will each of you be able to decide for yourselves which plan you think would work best. I hope some of you will then get up the subject so well, and give it such careful consideration, that you may become authorities on your side of the question, and may use your knowledge for the good of your fellow-men. But I am not competent to be your guide in the matter, nor do I think it necessary that you should trouble your heads about it until you are older and have gained experience. In these papers, therefore, I shall only tell you about the different kinds of money which are in use at the present day.

Paper money.

There are countries in the world—we have one very near to us, Scotland—where people prefer to use paper notes rather than gold; but when this is the case, it is of the utmost importance that those who wish to turn their notes into gold shall be able to do so. For this purpose gold is lodged in vaults, and notes are issued in the place of the gold coin. This plan has one advantage, which is, that the gold coins do not get worn out so quickly; but then, on the other hand, the notes get so dreadfully dirty at times, that they may even endanger the lives of the persons who handle them.

Intrinsic value of coins,

One thing, however, is certain: of whatever substance standard money may be composed, it must be possible (in the long run) to exchange it for something whose cost value is almost equal to the sum which the standard substance represents. Just think of the difference in value between one of our gold sovereigns and a bank-note. The former contains a trifle more than 113 grains of fine gold; 1 grain of gold is worth about $2\frac{1}{8}$d., therefore you will find, if you take the trouble to work out the sum for yourself, that the *intrinsic* or *real* value of a sovereign is worth as nearly as possible what it represents, viz., 20 shillings, or 240 pence; whilst the intrinsic value of a bank-note, no matter how large the sum may be which it represents, is about one-eighth of a penny!

Intrinsic value of paper money.

If you were to go into a silversmith's shop, and ask to look at some watches; and if, when you had chosen the one you liked best, you were to offer the shopman the first bite out of a beef patty you had just bought, he would either be very much insulted by your behaviour and show fight, or else he would take you for an escaped lunatic! And yet a bite out of a freshly-made beef patty would be worth quite as much as the eighth of a penny, which is the actual value of a bank-note for £10 or £20, and the latter could be as easily torn up or burnt as the mouthful of patty could be swallowed.

Intrinsic value of token coins.

Again: Token coins are not really worth the sums which they are allowed by law to represent. For instance, our British silver shilling does not contain a shilling's worth of silver; it is not worth more than 8d. or 9d. at the present market value of silver, and our bronze penny is only worth about one-fourth of itself. For this reason the token coins of one country are not legal tender in another. Were you to visit France, you would find our English silver and bronze coins of no use to you: but with standard money it is different. Each state guarantees (or *answers for it*) that its gold or silver standard coins contain a certain proportion of fine gold or silver, therefore the actual amount of metal which each coin contains fixes its value; for, as I have already told you, gold and silver lose very little in weight or quantity by being melted down. Our British gold standard sovereign is accepted in every country possessing a money currency, in exchange for national coin of almost equal value, because it is a well-known fact that each sovereign which has not had very much wear, contains its 113 grains of fine gold.

Intrinsic value of standard coins.

And now we come to the finding of the precious metals.

I am sure you will all feel a much greater interest in metal coins, and value them more highly, when you know more of their history. You must not imagine that every man who can well handle a pick or shovel is fit to become a miner. I suspect that many a man has gone to the gold diggings with this mistaken idea, and has been much disappointed at not making his fortune in a very short time. A good miner requires to be highly educated in many sciences. To begin with, he should know something of geology, that is, the science which teaches the nature of the various substances of which the earth is composed. A geologist understands in what description of ground miners may dig with a reasonable chance of finding minerals, for without this knowledge men might spend all their work-a-day lives in looking for that which they might never find.*

On the education of a miner.

Geology.

Mineralogy and chemistry are also very necessary sciences; the first teaches men the nature and value of the different mineral substances found underground, and by a knowledge of chemistry they learn how to separate one metal from another

Mineralogy and chemistry.

---

* I have been told that a celebrated mineralogist of the Strand, London, sells boxes containing two sets of fossils, arranged in separate trays. The fossils in one tray belong to those systems of rock in which gold is *not* to be found, whilst the other lot are such as would be found associated with gold. Those who are about to become gold diggers, and who buy one of these useful collections to take with them, have plenty of time for studying the specimens on their outward voyage.

metal or substance. An ignorant person might throw aside as worthless lump after lump of stony-looking substance, which, if they fell into the hands of skilful miners, would be so treated by them as to yield a considerable quantity of valuable metal. Just as one of you might pick up a diseased oyster—"Bah!" you would exclaim, and throw it away in disgust. But that very oyster might contain a pearl of great value, which a pearl diver would have recognised in a moment.

Machinery, &c.

Then again, for underground mining, a knowledge of machinery and mechanical contrivances is necessary before miners can understand how to unearth a metal when they have discovered where it lies; and even then some of them must be good at mathematics and underground surveying, or they will spend a great deal of their time and labour in vain.

Any one of my boy-readers who has a taste for adventure, and would like to go off some day to the gold or silver diggings, will perhaps be surprised to find what a special training he ought to go in for, before he would be fit to undertake much in that line. Of course, there are always a certain number of labouring miners, who just do as they are told without being able to give an intelligent reason for doing it; but those are not the men to *rise*—they will never become agents of any branch of the work, these being only chosen from amongst the miners who have shown a knowledge of mining, can do the required work themselves, and are fit to direct others.

Mr. Bullion and John Smith take a balloon trip.

In the next chapter you must imagine yourself to be John Smith, aged 16, and that your friend Mr. Bullion has invited you to take a voyage through the air with him in his balloon, to visit one or two of the chief mining districts in the world where the precious metals (as gold and silver are usually called) are brought to light and prepared for use. This is by far the most convenient form of travelling. Mr. Bullion understands the management of his balloon so well that you and he will avoid all the dangers and fatigues of travelling by sea or land; and, besides that, will see by the aid of the telescope which is fixed in the balloon a great deal of what is going on below without being obliged to alight. Very often you will pass over vast tracts of country, and see all you wish to see unobserved even by the busy people below you.

Chapter III.

John Smith: Hurrah! I never expected to find myself up in a balloon; but here we are, far away from old England. We must be getting near America now, aren't we, sir?

"Up in a balloon."

Mr. Bullion: Yes; we shall sleep in Panama to-night if all goes well. I hope you like balloon life as much as you expected to do so?

John Smith: I couldn't have believed it would have been so jolly! To roll oneself up at night in one of your big furs is luxury, and it is great fun cooking one's own meals over a jolly little spirit stove. Then, the country all along has been grand to look down upon from this height; I do not think I ever realised before how beautiful the world is.

Mr. Bullion: I am glad you can appreciate that. You will find also that the study of mining reveals to us many wonders and beauties of creation which lie hidden beneath the earth's surface. And now that we are fast approaching the gold mining districts of California, it is high time to prepare you a little for what we are going to see. Tell me first whether you can remember what our course has been so far.

Route from Land's End to Panama.

John Smith: I think I can do that off pat, for there has not been time to forget it yet. We started from the Land's End, Cornwall, in a southerly direction, and came down at Brest Harbour, on the north-west coast of France. The next day we still travelled southward, keeping the western coast line of France well in sight. We passed the north-west corner of Spain, and, bearing down the western side of Portugal as far as Lisbon, took another rest there. Up we went again the following morning, and skimmed along over the Azores, the Canary and Madeira Islands, until we reached the Cape de Verde group, when you let us down into St. Jago; and now we are scudding along over the Atlantic due west, have crossed the line, and are nearing the Isthmus of Panama. Why, it's the best geography lesson I have ever had in my life, and one that I am not likely to forget in a hurry, either!

Mr. Bullion: You have certainly learnt your lesson well. Perhaps you are as good at geology as you are at geography, and can tell me in what kind of soil gold is found in California?

John Smith's ideas of mining.

John Smith: I know nothing about such things, Mr. Bullion, but I have always supposed that men dug deep down into the earth, and then burrowed about like rabbits until they found some big nuggets of gold, and that the bigger the nugget was, the greater the luck of the man who discovered it.

Mr. Bullion (laughing): I believe a good many people run away with that idea. You, my dear young fellow, would expect if you joined a mining expedition, to work with your mates until you hit upon a nugget of several pounds weight at least, when you would decamp with your treasure, carry it home to old England, and make your fortune by disposing of it at the Mint.

John Smith: That is exactly what I should do, sir, you may depend!

Mr. Bullion: And, pray, how do you think a mining company would flourish, if, after they had gone to the great expense of furnishing all the requisite machinery and appliances for working a mine, the men whom they had engaged to do the required manual labour, or even those who superintended the different departments, were allowed to go off with their treasure whenever either of them came upon a find worth having?

John Smith: That never struck me before, but of course it would not be at all fair. I thought everybody went off to the diggings on his own hook.

Soil in which the precious metals are found.

Mr. Bullion: Sometimes mines are worked by enterprising individuals with sufficient capital to make a good start. In districts also where the metals lie near the surface of the earth, one or two men without capital may combine to work together and make a living out of what they find. But when the ore lies deep down below the earth's surface, and has to be extracted from rock, experience has taught men that it is better to form a company for this purpose, on account of the large amount of capital required, and of the uncertainty as to how long it may be before a mine begins to pay. When you and I have visited a few mines you will understand this a great deal better.

Mining companies.

John Smith: Do tell me, sir, how mining companies are managed. I should like to know something about it before we get there.

Mr. Bullion: Suppose, then, that I had every reason to suspect the existence of gold under any particular plot of ground.

I will tell you what I should do: First, I should pay a visit to the owner of that land, and obtain from him permission to look for gold. I should next try to form a mining company amongst my trusty friends, choosing only men who were as ready to risk their capital in the enterprise as myself; having done which, we should make our terms with the landowner. Probably he would mark out the extent of ground within which he would allow us to carry on our mining operations; we should pay a fair rent for the ground, and also agree to hand over to the landlord a certain proportion of all the metal we took out of his ground, ready prepared for the market.

Rent of ground.

John Smith: But what about the labourers? It would be hard lines indeed if those men, who are the real finders of the metal, could never make a good thing of it.

Mr. Bullion: So it would, John; but that is not the case. Mining is generally managed on fairer principles than almost any other industry which necessitates the employment of a large number of hands. In our own county of Cornwall, where such extensive mining operations have been carried on for a great number of years, the whole system of mining has been brought to such perfection that in many other districts the same rules have been adopted. The gold mines which we shall soon be visiting belong to a British company, whose superintendent or general manager is a great friend of mine; and as the whole of the work is being carried out in Cornish fashion, I cannot do better than explain it to you. There are two kinds of labour required in mining—first, that which consists in sinking shafts, and making underground excavations in search of metals; and secondly, taking the metal out of the ground and preparing it for use. The first kind of work Cornishmen call *tut work* or *dead work*; it necessitates an immense amount of manual labour, therefore men are paid so much per fathom, according to the quantity of work they get through in a day. But when metal is being extracted, the miners are paid so much in wages for every ton of gold, silver, or copper ore they raise. Sometimes in Cornwall they have been allowed, instead of receiving wages, to keep a certain proportion of the ore, and for this reason the extraction of metal is there called *tribute work;* but I do not imagine that this plan would be adopted when gold or silver are being extracted.

Cornish mining rules.

Tut work.

Tribute work.

John Smith: Is a ton of ore always worth the same amount of money?

Mining contracts.

Mr. Bullion: No; some ores yield a greater proportion of grains of fine metal than others, for which reason (as well as for others) the contracts or agreements by which the miners are bound are made only for very short periods of time. Fresh arrangements are generally entered into every few months, which seems to me a very fair state of things. It gives the miners frequent opportunities of agreeing for higher wages whenever a paying piece of work turns up, whilst the company also are at liberty to lower their standard of daily wage when there is a failure for a time in the quantity of metal produced.

John Smith: All that sounds as fair as fair can be. But it must give the managers of the mines a lot of trouble.

Mr. Bullion: I do not think they make a trouble of it. On a given day, when a new contract is to be entered into, the miners gather round the mine office, and the agents call out each piece of work that has to be contracted for from a book in which the portions of work have all been entered. Then the men bid for the work—one will undertake it for so much; another will do it for a little less; until the work or bargain is considered as taken by the lowest bidder, and his name is immediately registered opposite to his piece of work in the setting book.

John Smith: It must be just like an auction turned upside down—each bargain is knocked down to the lowest instead of to the highest bidder.

Mr. Bullion: Yes; and you may be sure that the first few bids are for very much more money than the piece of work is worth. Generally one man is chosen to be spokesman by the mates with whom he is accustomed to work; the contract is made with him, and he and his gang carry it out together. There are certain rules laid down also, a copy of which every miner has to sign; if this were not done, some of the men might throw up their work before a contract was fulfilled, or whenever they were finding less metal than they hoped or expected to find.

John Smith: I suppose there are always certain miners appointed to overlook what the labouring men are doing?

Mining officers.

Mr. Bullion: Oh, dear, yes! The business of a miner is divided into several departments. There are the underground operations, the pit work and machinery, the dressing and surface work, the accounts and financial matters, and, lastly, the general control. For each of these departments there is a superintendent or agent, and, over them all, a general manager, who reports progress to the committee of the mining company from time to time, and gives them his advice. This general manager, as you may well believe, requires a good *head-piece* (as Devonshire folk say), and the agents also are generally chosen from the most intelligent of the miners; so you see it is a great advantage to a labouring miner to gain as much knowledge as he can about all the different branches of mining operations, in order that he may fit himself for one or other of these responsible posts. But it is high time to think about dinner, so let us leave our *mining* for some *cooking operations* now.

(Mr. Bullion and John Smith had an excellent dinner: the former minced some tinned meat, and made and fried a good dish of rissoles; whilst John vigorously plied his egg-whisk, and turned out a very respectable cheese omelet for the second course. Then followed coffee, and Mr. Bullion's pipe.) Dinner in the balloon.

John Smith: Please, sir, are you ready for a talk? I wouldn't ask you until I saw that you had finished your pipe, but I am longing to hear some more about mines.

Mr. Bullion (smiling): You have been very forbearing, John, I must allow. I am ready for anything now, so what is it to be?

John Smith: You asked me about geology, and the kind of soil in which gold is to be found; but I know nothing about such things.

Mr. Bullion: I am so glad you have reminded me of it, for I want to talk to you about those very things before we arrive at the gold mines. I am not going to teach you geology, young man! no, nor mineralogy either; but only so much of these sciences as may help you to understand *where* certain metals are to be found, and in what form.

John Smith: Those are just the very things I am most anxious to understand, so I shall listen to you with all my might.

Mr. Bullion: Very well, then. Geologists tell us on good authority that the earth must once have been a molten mass—that is, a mass of substance made fluid by heat. Imagine it, if you can: a heated fluid mass revolving in space with great rapidity. As it revolved it became gradually cooler, and was at Formation of rock.

length coated with a solid surface, composed principally of the rock crystals named mica, quartz, and felspar. This crystal surface was granite, the oldest solid substance of which the earth is formed. Various gases were thrown out from the heated body of the globe; amongst others, those known by the names of oxygen and hydrogen, which, when combined, form water. You know quite well that if water were kept boiling—that is, at a temperature of 212 degrees—it would all turn to steam; but perhaps you do not know the reason for this, which is that oxygen and hydrogen become separated at that high temperature. For the same reason, therefore, oxygen and hydrogen will not combine at a very high temperature, consequently the earth could not have been surrounded with water until its surface had sufficiently cooled down to allow of the union of these two gases.

John Smith: How very interesting this is! I had no idea that geologists had found out so much.

Mr. Bullion: I felt sure that this part of our subject would interest you. Well, whilst the earth's surface was becoming gradually cooler, the interior of the globe must still have been boiling and seething, just as the inside of a volcanic mountain does at the time of an eruption. There were constant eruptions of mud and gases going on from beneath, breaking through the granite coating in all directions; and, wherever this happened, the action of the water from without, and the mud and gases from within, broke off fragments of the granite, which gradually formed a deposit at the bottom of the ocean. By degrees, one deposit or sediment was formed above the other, in beds or layers, called strata (strata is the plural form of the Latin word *stratum*, a bed or layer); as they cooled and hardened, these strata became rock, and are called by geologists stratified rocks. They are also named aqueous or sedimentary rocks (from the Latin word *aqua*, water), on account of their having been formed by the action of water; whilst those rocks which were formed by the action of fire or heat are called igneous rocks (from the Latin word *ignis*, fire).

Formation of strata.

Igneous and aqueous rocks.

John Smith: As granite rocks were formed before there was any water, they must be igneous rocks, are they not?

Unstratified and stratified ocks.

Mr. Bullion: Yes; granite rocks are igneous, and, as they were not formed in beds or layers, they are called unstratified rocks. To this class also belong all rocks of volcanic origin, such as those formed of lava.

John Smith: Are there a great many different kinds of rock, sir?

Mr. Bullion: There are many kinds of stratified rocks which were formed at different periods in the world's life, but not nearly so many varieties of unstratified rocks. At present it will be sufficient for you to remember the two classes, igneous and aqueous; you will very soon learn to distinguish the one from the other. It is a great temptation to me to run on with this geological talk, and to tell you all about the different systems of rocks and the order in which they were formed; but I really must not do so now, there is so much still to be said about other things before we go a-gold-digging.

John Smith: I must say I should like to learn geology.

Mr. Bullion: I will certainly teach you all I know about it some day, I hope. But for the present I must content myself with giving you those particulars which will be a help to you when we reach California. Recollect, then, that granite is the oldest kind of rock; all other rocks were gradually built up on this foundation, most of them having been produced by the wear and tear of that class of rock which immediately preceded them.

John Smith: When you say "most of them," I suppose you mean that the igneous rocks were not formed in that manner?

Limestone.

Mr. Bullion: There are aqueous as well as igneous rocks, which were not formed merely of sedimentary deposits. Limestone, for instance, which was formed by some chemical process. You see, earthquakes and volcanic eruptions were constantly taking place at all periods of the earth's history. At times they must have been very violent, for we owe our mountains to these internal convulsions of nature.

Origin of mountains.

John Smith: Was that the origin of mountains? Well, I never knew that before!

Mr. Bullion: Yes; mountains were upheaved by the action of internal heat, and high ground was often sunk beneath the seas by the same wonderful influence; whilst the various gases which forced their way through the different strata at such times, combined with newly-created substances, caused all sorts of variations in the natures and textures of these stratified rocks.

Systems sometimes missing.

John Smith: Surely it must be very difficult to distinguish one class of rock from another?

Mr. Bullion: It requires careful study, certainly, especially as in many districts some of the systems will be found missing.

John Smith: How can that be if they were formed one after the other in proper order?

Mr. Bullion: For the simple reason that the various volcanic disturbances which were constantly taking place, combined with the action of floods and storms, altered the surface of the earth continually. What was dry land during one period might be covered with water during the next. Dry land, you know, would have no sediment deposited on it—that only took place under water; therefore dry land might miss over a system, and then sink low enough to be covered with a layer of the next deposit.

John Smith: The world certainly has been subject to strange "ups-and-downs" in its life! Do you think that those changes still take place?

Land rising.

Mr. Bullion: Undoubtedly they do, but in a more gradual and less violent manner. There is a large tract of land situated on the northern shores of the Baltic Sea, which has been for many years, and still is, rising at the rate of four feet in a century; while, on the other hand, a great portion of the coast of Greenland has been subsiding during the last four hundred years, and the whole continent of South America is supposed to be sinking.

Land subsiding.

John Smith: But surely, sir, that gradual sinking and rising is not due to earthquakes and eruptions.

Mr. Bullion: Do not you know, John, the difference between fiercely boiling water and water that is just beginning to simmer? There is every reason to believe that, although the internal disturbances of the earth are far less frequent and violent than they used to be, yet they are still taking place and causing changes in elevation.

John Smith: But all those alterations that took place long ago must have made it even more difficult to distinguish one system of rocks from another.

Order of strata always the same.

Mr. Bullion: Not at all, for this reason. The *order* in which these systems were originally deposited has never been disturbed. Suppose you and I were digging deeply into a mine, and observing the different strata as we came upon them. If one system of strata were missed over, it would be an older deposit than that through which we had just penetrated, and the strata we should next come to would be older still. This rule always holds good, and is a very safe one to go by: you will never find a later deposit underneath an earlier one. And this same rule, also, is most useful to miners; for, as I have already told you, there are some strata in which they know that it is of no use whatever to look for metals.

John Smith: I well understand now. But how could so much have been found out in the first place, when all the lower systems of strata must have been covered by the last?

Mr. Bullion: That, also, was brought about by those wonderful volcanic disturbances. When mountains of granite or of some early stratified rock were upheaved through various systems of later deposits, the edges of these later strata were forced up on each side of the mountain and exposed to view. Water, also, often lays bare different strata of rock; you know how the cliffs on the sea coast get worn away and altered by the dashing of the waves upon them, do you not?

Volcanic eruptions and water make this known.

John Smith: Yes, to be sure, I do. I shall notice all those sort of things much more for the future.

Mr. Bullion: As we shall be chiefly concerned with the contents of the oldest stratified rocks, I must say a little more about them. I told you that granite was composed of mica, quartz, and felspar, therefore you will be able to tell me of what the next system was composed.

Granite.

John Smith: Surely it must have been of worn away granite, sir?

Mr. Bullion: Yes; these fragments of mica, quartz, and felspar, being deposited upon a highly heated surface, became crystallized by the combined effects of the heat, mud, and gases which penetrated them. These rocks are sometimes called metamorphic rocks because they underwent this metamorphosis or change; and some geologists call them gneiss and mica schist rocks. The next system deposited was less crystallised and more stratified.

Metamorphic rocks.

John Smith: If every system has three or four names, like

the first, I shall have enough to do to remember them! Let me see; the earliest stratified rocks are called aqueous, metamorphic, and gneiss and mica schist!

Quartz.

Mr. Bullion (laughing): You will get as much puzzled by these various words as a good old friend of mine does—a Devonshire man. He says that there are a great many *stratagems* to be met with underneath the surface soil. But I am not going to burden you with any more systems at present; I only want you to remember that to this class of stratified rocks belong those commonly spoken of as quartz rocks. When we get to the diggings you will hear a good deal about quartz, for gold, silver, tin, and copper are all found embedded in the various kinds of rock-crystal to which this term is applied.

Finding of metals.

John Smith: I suppose the miners have to dig down deeply before they come upon the metal, haven't they, sir?

Mr. Bullion: The depth varies considerably, but, as you may imagine, working in such hard, rocky ground requires a great amount of manual labour, and the workings of a mine are often continued to a very great depth. I will give you an idea of the manner in which metallic or mineral ore may be unearthed. A party of miners, whilst breaking up rocky ground, perhaps come upon a fissure or large crack. As they proceed to open it and follow its track, they find that it extends in a downward-slanting direction ever so deep into the ground. This fissure may be filled either with sparry and stony substances, with here and there bright spangles of the metal they are in search of; or else it may contain earthy or non-metallic mineral ore—a softer composition than metal, and one in which you would not expect to find treasure. With renewed energy the miners work on, and at length they are rewarded for their pains by coming upon irregular masses or bunches of metallic ore, sometimes of immense size and value. These masses of ore may possibly occur at intervals throughout the whole of the fissure. These fissures are called veins, and veins that contain metal are styled lodes, to distinguish them from those fissures or veins which are filled with non-metallic minerals.

Veins and odes.

John Smith: How jolly it must be to come upon a bunch of gold!

Mr. Bullion (laughing): Very jolly indeed when you do; but unfortunately gold is more frequently found in small crystals or grains accompanying other metals, such as silver, copper, lead, or tin. Again, although gold is frequently found in quartz veins, it is discovered in greater abundance in what are called fragmentary deposits—that is, in the sands of rivers and in other alluvial soils.

Gold found in fragmentary deposits.

John Smith: I do not know what alluvial soil is.

Mr. Bullion: The word alluvial is derived from the Latin word *alluvio*, a flood or inundation; alluvial soil, therefore, means a deposit made up of loose gravel, sand, and mud. It is found chiefly in low ground, and is supposed to have been carried there by a stream, or else by floods. Very often gold is found in this kind of soil, situated in the neighbourhood of a group of rocks of early origin, and it is thought that the alluvial deposit was at one period washed off those neighbouring rocks by heavy rains or floods.

Alluvial soil.

John Smith: It seems a very likely thing to have happened. I suppose the gold is all mixed up with the soil, isn't it?

Mr. Bullion: The gold found in alluvial beds, although always in a metallic state, is not quite pure or native, but generally combined with silver, copper, and small quantities of other metals, including iron. The grains of metal generally form a layer underneath the soil. They sink through it, owing to their greater specific gravity.

Gold not always native.

John Smith: Oh, Mr. Bullion, I am so glad you have used that expression, "specific gravity," for I have often met with it in books, and have never been able to find out what it meant.

Specific gravity.

Mr. Bullion: I can soon explain it to you. But you must allow me a few minutes' grace, for I really think I have earned another pipe, don't you?

John Smith (laughing): I should rather think you had, sir; so I'll fill your pipe for you, and light it, too!

Chapter IV.

As soon as Mr. Bullion's pipe was drawing comfortably, he began as follows:

Mr. Bullion: To specify the weight of any one substance, you must compare it with another. All solid substances are compared in weight with an equal bulk of water, and this ingenious operation is called taking the *specific gravity* of a solid substance.

John Smith: But how ever can they find out the weight of the water, sir?

Mr. Bullion: In this way. Let me suppose that you have a small cube of gold, and that you wish to find out its specific gravity. You bring it to me, and I lend you a very delicately adjusted balance, with an open wire-work scale in which to place your gold cube. (I hope you would take care of my beautiful little scales, if I were ever soft-hearted enough to lend them to you, my boy!)

John Smith (eagerly): Of course I should, sir!

Mr. Bullion: I daresay you would but it is only a case of supposing now, as my scales are reposing safely in my drawer at home. Well, I next send you off to the nearest chemist's for a bottle of distilled water, and we warm this to a temperature of about 60°: we can easily test it by placing a thermometer in it, you know. Now comes the weighing process. First weigh the cube very exactly, and make a note of its weight. Then immerse the wire-work scale, gold cube and all, in the distilled water; balance the gold very carefully under water, and you will find it will weigh a good deal less than it did out of the water. Subtract the lighter weight from the heavier one, and divide the first or heavier weight by the difference: the result will be the specific gravity of your gold cube.

John Smith: Thank you so much, Mr. Bullion; but I must confess I do not see how the thing works.

Mr. Bullion: In this manner: when your gold cube is put into the water, it takes the place, does it not, of a body of water exactly equal in bulk to itself?

John Smith: Yes, I suppose it must do so.

Mr. Bullion: Very well, then, the weight lost by the immersion in water of your gold cube is the weight of a quantity of water equal in bulk to the solid cube which has taken its place. Therefore you can compare the weight of your cube of gold with that of an equal volume of water; and when you read that the specific gravity of gold is 19, and of silver 10½, you know that gold is 19 times and silver 10½ times as heavy as water.

John Smith: Thank you, sir; I see it much better now. But what is the use of finding out the specific gravity of metals when they are bought and sold according to their real weight?

Mr. Bullion: You must know as well as I do that there are tricks in every trade; it is highly desirable to be able to distinguish easily between a precious stone, or a metal, of great value, and those cheap imitations of them with which persons have so often been taken in. By knowing the specific gravity of these substances a jeweller would most likely be able to detect at once the difference between a precious stone and a piece of well-cut coloured glass, for instance; or between fine gold and a good imitation of it.

John Smith (rubbing his hands together gleefully): As soon as we get home again I shall be able to try all sorts of jolly experiments in this way.

Mr. Bullion: If you do so, you must have the patience to learn to weigh all solid substances with the most minute exactness, for finding out the specific gravity of a solid is a very delicate operation. The *shape* of the substance you want to weigh makes all the difference, even. A small, compact, solid—like a cube or a well-formed crystal—will be found to possess a higher specific gravity than the same substance in a larger less compact form. For this reason it is usual to give both the highest and lowest specific gravity of any particular species.

John Smith: I remember having met with the two numbers in some of my books. But it will be very interesting for me to try some experiments at home, sir, won't it?

Mr. Bullion: I believe it will be just the sort of study you will delight in, John. But see! we are fast approaching our destination. Yonder distant haze is the north-east coast line of South America. I must finish what I have to say about the metals as quickly as possible.

John Smith: I feel quite off my head at the thought of our being only an hour's journey or thereabouts from America. But go on, please, sir, I want to learn all I can before we get there.

Mr. Bullion: It will not take me half an hour to finish telling you about those metals of which our British coins are composed. After that, our whole thoughts and attention shall be given to the country below us.

John Smith: That will be jolly; and, meanwhile, attending to what you are saying will make the time pass quickly.

Gold the only metal always found in a metallic state

Mr. Bullion: First, I must explain to you that metals are taken from the earth in two different conditions; they are found either in a native, that is, metallic state, or else so blended with other minerals as to be deprived for the time of their distinctive metallic character. Gold is the only metal that is always found in a metallic state; silver and copper are sometimes found native; tin and zinc never so.

John Smith: What ever are they like, then, when discovered?

Metals hidden in mineral or earthy ore.

Mr. Bullion: They are often so unlike themselves that only a practised eye is aware of their being hidden away in the earthy or mineral ore which contains them. You must make no mistake as to the meaning of the word "native," however. Gold is very often found alloyed with silver and other metals, or it is embedded in quartz and other rocky substances, which have to be crushed before the metal can be extracted. At other times, also, gold is quite hidden in earthy ore, throughout which it may be scattered in minute particles. But, in all these conditions, gold is easily separated from other metals and minerals by the use of chemicals.

John Smith: I am greatly puzzled, sir. If gold is found hidden in the midst of other things, how can it be properly called native?

Mr. Bullion: I can explain this to you by reminding you of that delicious cake we made the other day. You will remember that I attended to the dry ingredients, whilst you looked after the wet ones. First, I stirred into the flour some baking powder, sugar, ground spice, and powdered almonds; whilst you beat the eggs, together with some milk and warmed butter. Before your mixture had been added to mine, the dry ingredients were just themselves—the flour was still flour; the sugar, sugar;

and so on; although I should have required some knowledge of chemistry to have been able to separate any one ingredient from the rest. But as soon as you had poured your wet mixture upon my dry one—I vigorously stirring them together the while with my wooden spoon—the nature of the dry ingredients began to be affected by the acid contained in the baking powder; and, by the time the cake had been well baked, the character of some of its original ingredients had been considerably altered. To apply this to the ores. Gold, when alloyed with other metals, or hidden in earthy soil, does not lose its individual character any more than flour does when mixed with other dry ingredients. But silver, copper, tin or zinc are often blended with sulphur, antimony, arsenic, and many other mineral substances, which act upon these metals chemically so as to deprive them of their metallic character, as much as the eggs, the baking powder, and the heat of the oven changed the conditions of some of the ingredients of which our cake was composed.

John Smith: That is as plain as possible now, thank you, sir. But does gold never get mixed up with sulphur or anything of that kind?

Gold and tin unaffected by water or air.

Mr. Bullion: Gold is an indestructible metal, and neither sulphur nor any other mineral substance deprives it of its metallic nature, as they do other metals. Then, again, most of the metals gradually decompose, or become eaten away with rust if exposed to air or moisture; but it is not so with gold or tin. Gold is unaffected by the influence of either element, and the rust of tin does not wear the latter metal away. When gold or tin are found in river beds, or in any alluvial deposit, they are unaccompanied by other metals, which seems to be most reasonably accounted for by what I have just told you.

John Smith: You mean that the other metals were probably there when the soil was first washed off the rocks, but that they have gradually disappeared since, owing to the dampness of the soil?

Mr. Bullion: That is it. Change of climate does not suit every constitution. The metals had been resting in a high and dry situation, carefully protected from air and moisture, for many a long year. When, therefore, they were violently swept by floods of water into the valley beneath them, and deposited in a damp situation, only the strong ones survived such treatment. It wore out the constitutions of the weaker metals.

Countries in which gold and silver are found.

But now I am going to put a question to *you*, John. Can you tell me in what countries gold, silver, copper, and tin are found?

John Smith: Gold and silver are found in North and South America. Gold is also found in Australia; but I am not so sure about silver.

Mr. Bullion: Yes; silver is also found in Australia.

John Smith: And I know there are African gold mines, because people talk of Guinea gold. As to copper and tin, you can get plenty of them in our own old England. That is about all I can remember about metals.

Mr. Bullion: Then I can show you a list of the countries in which gold and silver are produced, which will enlarge your mind considerably. Just read that (and he handed a paper to John).

John Smith (reading aloud): "Gold and silver producing countries of the world, taken from the report of the director of the Mint, U.S.A., 1885: United States, Russia, Australasia, Mexico, Germany, Austria-Hungary, Sweden, Italy, Turkey, Argentine Republic, Colombia, Bolivia, Chili, Japan, Peru, and Great Britain." That is a goodly list; but you don't mean to say that gold is found in our own United Kingdom now, sir?

Mr. Bullion: It is, indeed; but not in sufficient quantities to repay the expense of working it. Finish reading your list and then we will talk about it. Those countries whose names you have already read produce both gold and silver.

John Smith: Then here are the names of the countries where only gold is produced (he reads): "Brazil, Africa, British Columbia, and Venezuela;" and "Norway, Spain, and France" produce silver only. I did not know that a quarter of those countries produced metal.

Mr. Bullion: In some few of the countries you named, the gold and silver are found in small quantities accompanying less valuable metals, such as lead, copper, or tin. For instance, grains of gold are found by the Cornish miners in the tin streams, and are carefully preserved by them in quills. A good deal of gold was formerly found in various parts of Wales, and some fine specimens were produced there. I am told that even now there are some rich gold mines known to exist in Wales, but the gold they contain occurs in the shape of nuggets, and the miners so easily make away with these, that the landowners cannot afford to work the mines in consequence, and they are closed.

John Smith: What a pity that this cannot be prevented! I'd have them all searched before they left work, wouldn't you, sir?

Mr. Bullion: It seems odd that the difficulty cannot be overcome. But it is wonderful what ingenious tricks men will be up to for the sake of stealing the precious metals. At one place gold was found mixed with a very fine, black sand, and the miners used to blow the sand off the gold in their impatience to get at the latter. An old man took advantage of this habit of theirs: he pretended that he was too lame to toil at the mines, but was earning what he could by selling the black sand for emery powder. So this old rascal requested the miners to blow the sand into a tin tray with which he provided them, and he used to come round of an evening to fetch his sand and carry it off to his hut. When safely at home, he managed with the aid of quicksilver to extract double as much gold from these black sands as was obtained from them by the hardest-working man.

Miners' tricks.

John Smith: The old wretch! I only hope that he was caught at last.

Mr. Bullion: That I cannot tell you. Another trick, practised by some Indians at the silver mines of Pasco, in Peru, was as follows: A good deal of silver was found in a dark, powdery kind of ore; so the workmen used to take off their clothes, moisten their bodies all over with water, and then roll in the powdery ore, which, of course, stuck to their skins. They then dressed themselves and went on with their work; but on their return home of an evening, they used to wash the silver dust off, and afterwards sell it.

John Smith: Well, I never heard of such a thing! But how uncomfortable they must have been, and hot too, with that coat of dust about them whilst they were working.

Mr. Bullion: I do not suppose they disliked it as much as you and I should. But their trick was at length discovered, and they were all obliged afterwards to strip before leaving work.

John Smith: Serve them right, too!

Copper mines.

Mr. Bullion: There are plenty of copper mines in England, and a good deal of copper is also obtained from other European countries, as well as from Asia, Africa, Australia, and the two Americas. Now and then, copper is found native, and in very large masses. One piece, found in Canada, measured fifteen feet in circumference.

John Smith: Fifteen feet! Why, it must have required a team of horses to raise it, I should think!

Mr. Bullion: The greater quantity of copper, however, is found in all kinds of ores, one of the commonest, copper pyrites, being a combination of copper and iron, and a large portion of sulphur.

John Smith: I cannot yet grasp the idea of these metals being found in a non-metallic state.

Mr. Bullion: Well, you shall have every opportunity of becoming familiar with the idea before we bring our balloon trip to an end.

John Smith: It is very jolly indeed of you, Mr. Bullion, to take me about like this; it will be something to remember all my life.

Mr. Bullion: We must stop talking now, for we are bearing down towards Panama rapidly, and I want you to observe the country as we approach the shore. Tin, as you know, is chiefly produced in Cornwall, but it is found also in other parts of Europe, and in Asia, Malacca, Banca, and Australia. As I told you before, tin is never found native; it occurs in the oldest rocks, spread about in crystals through their mass, or in veins, and is then called mine tin; but when found in alluvial deposits it is called stream tin.

Tin mines.

Tin never found native.

John Smith: Oh, Mr. Bullion! I do believe I can see a lot of people down yonder!

Mr. Bullion: We shall startle those good people in another quarter of an hour by descending in their midst; so let us enjoy ourselves while we can.

Chapter V.

Route from Panama to California.

Several days have elapsed since the last recorded conversation took place between Mr. Bullion and John Smith. After spending a night at Panama they ascended from the western side of the isthmus; and as soon as the balloon had risen sufficiently high, steered out over the Pacific Ocean. Their route lay in a north-westerly direction, past the western coasts of Costa Rica, Nicaragua, Salvador, Guatemala, Mexico, and the lower part of California, until at length they came in sight of the big city of San Francisco, with its beautiful bay, and its grand background of hill country. Mr. Bullion had decided that they should pass a couple of nights here, in order that they might devote one whole day to sight-seeing; so they steered inland, and, having been observed by some of the inhabitants a short while before, descended into the midst of a considerable crowd just in front of the arched entrance of the Palace Hotel. This hotel is said to be the largest in the world, and certainly John was very much impressed with its central glass-covered court, and the big galleries running round it, one above the other, to which they could ascend at all hours of the day by means of a lift.

Palace Hotel, San Francisco.

Mr. Verdigris at the mining district.

On the second morning after their arrival, Mr. Bullion and John started at a very early hour for the mining district to which they were bound; they reached their destination in the course of the afternoon, and were warmly and heartily received by Mr. Verdigris, the general manager. Both he and the men working under him had been watching for many days with no small amount of curiosity for the arrival of the balloon; as soon, therefore, as she hove in sight, a signal was given, and the whole party of miners turned out to see them alight.

Mr. Bullion and John Smith's quarters.

Mr. Bullion and John found themselves placed in a delightfully independent position. They were the guests of Mr. Verdigris by day, and at night slept at a little shanty close to the mine-office. Moreover, they were to be free of the mines whenever the manager was too busy to accompany them on their rounds.

It would be impossible for me to describe at full length all that our two travellers saw during their visit to Mr. Verdigris;

I will therefore only repeat the conversation that took place between Mr. Bullion and John Smith after they had retired to their own shanty, the night before they leave California.

Mr. Bullion: Well, John, I hope you have been interested in all that you have seen during our stay?

John Smith: It has been all so new and interesting, sir, that I am quite afraid of forgetting some of it before I have had time to write it down.

Mr. Bullion: Do you feel wide awake enough to give me a description of gold mining so far as you can remember it, before turning in to-night? If so, come along: you shall make a pot of coffee whilst I smoke my last pipe.

John Smith: That will be jolly, for I don't feel a bit like going to sleep yet. (As soon as they were settled, the following conversation took place):—

Description of gold and silver mining in quartz rocks.

John Smith: Let me see: first comes digging down into the ground and sinking the shafts. My word! what hard work it is, breaking up that rocky ground. The men need to be paid well for it, I am sure!

Mr. Bullion: I thought Mr. Verdigris exercised good judgment in taking us first down into the valley, and showing us the entrance to the adit level. You saw the use of it, didn't you?

Sinking shafts.

John Smith: Yes, quite well. The miners first dig into the rocky ground, and sink a shaft; then they go into the neighbouring valley, and tunnel into the side of the hill till they meet the hole of the shaft, and there they cut through the mineral vein as low down as possible. This tunnel is called an adit level; it serves two purposes, viz.—(1) for the drainage off of a good deal of water, and (2) for the removal of the ore.

Adit level.

Mr. Bullion: I think you told me that even in the adit level the pumps are obliged to be kept at work?

John Smith: Yes, the steam pumps are constantly at it, because the shafts are in some places sunk ever so much below the level of the adit; but there, you see, it saves a great deal of labour if the water has not to be pumped up to the surface of the high ground. I wish you had gone down into the mine with me, Mr. Bullion.

Mr. Bullion: I have been down into a mine more than once, John, and I confess I am not anxious to repeat the performance.

But I am very glad you went down; it must have given you a better idea of it than all the telling could have done.

John Smith: It was great fun. You know, besides the proper adit level, there are short galleries leading from the big shaft into the hill at all sorts of different levels. These passages cut across the mineral lode, and by their means the lode can be worked ever so múch more quickly than if only one set of men dug down to it from above. I went into several of the galleries, and found men hard at work in each of them; all that they dig down is sent up the shaft in buckets, and it is wonderful how easily they know which lumps of earthy or sparry-looking stuff are likely to contain ore, and which may be thrown away with the rubbish.

Mr. Bullion: I have been told that the miners judge a good deal by the *heft* or weight of each lump.

Dressing floors.

John Smith: Yes, so the men said; and by the look of it too, sometimes. Quite close to the mouth of the shaft are the dressing floors, where the lumps containing ore are knocked to pieces with hammers, and separated more carefully from the rubbish before being sent on to the crushing mills.

Mr. Bullion: I did not visit those mills, but I suppose the ore is there prepared for the stamping which you and I saw?

Crushing, stamping, and grinding mills.

John Smith: Yes, they have huge cylindrical rollers of cast-iron, moving in opposite directions, which crush the ore into smaller pieces than they can be knocked into by hand. These small fragments are passed on to the stamping mills to be crushed even smaller, and sometimes they have still to be sent to a grinding mill and reduced to powder before the metal can be thoroughly separated from the ore.

Mr. Bullion: What immense force those stamping machines bring to bear upon the ore, do they not?

John Smith: They do smash it up, and no mistake! A man told me that the pestles which were doing the stamping weigh between three and four hundred pounds each. Those we saw were made of iron, but sometimes wooden pestles with iron heads are used. They are set in motion either by steam or water power; I suppose by whichever of the two can be most easily worked at each particular mine.

Mr. Bullion: Do you think you understood the process that the powdered ore was undergoing in the water?

The treatment of powdered ores.

John Smith: I didn't take it in the first time; but when you and Mr. Verdigris were gone, I went back and got a fellow to explain the whole dodge to me. Underneath the iron pestles which smash the ore there is a big wooden trough, which has openings fitted with perforated sheet-iron strainers. A stream of water is kept flowing through the trough, which carries the ore down through the strainers, and over an inclined table Upon this table, which is kept moving by means of chains attached to the machinery, the heavier and richer pieces of ore collect, whilst the lighter particles are washed away into reservoirs.

Mr. Bullion: I expect a good many small particles of metal get washed away during the process.

Use of reservoirs.

John Smith: Yes, sir; but that is the beauty of letting the stream run into reservoirs. The particles containing metal sink to the bottom of the tanks, owing to their greater weight; and after separating themselves in this manner from the lighter earthy ore, they are easily secured and made use of.

Mr. Bullion: So far you have had no difficulty in remembering your mining experiences.

John Smith: That comes of your allowing me to give them to you "hot from the book," as I might say. Going over it to-night will refresh my memory famously. Do you know where I have been to-day, sir?

Mr. Bullion: I have not a notion; but I did not feel any anxiety on your account, having seen you collar an excellent luncheon for yourself from the breakfast table this morning.

Gold washing.

John Smith: Ah, yes; you see, I require keeping up whilst I am going in for such hard study. One of the clerks told me that he should have to visit a place some miles off to-day, where gold diggings were being carried on in a river bed. He asked me if I should like to go with him, and I jumped at the offer, as I wanted to see what gold washing was like.

Mr. Bullion: That was capital; I have never seen the cradles worked myself, although I have often read descriptions of the process.

John Smith: Well, then, I believe I can explain it all to you in first-rate style. Of course, you know as well as I do that the gold taken from the gravelly soil of river beds is found either in the shape of dust or particles, or else in nuggets—mostly small ones, though very big lumps have been found from time to time. To separate the gold particles from the earthy matter, a machine called a cradle is used. *To rock the cradle* is a more serious undertaking where gold is concerned than if a baby were in it, for it takes four men to manage each cradle properly; all the same, I'd rather rock gold than babies! Cradle rocking.

Mr. Bullion (laughing): I daresay you would, and I am sure the babies would rather you should do so!

John Smith: Don't you believe that, sir! but, at all events, the contents of a Californian cradle would suit me better than the domestic article. The gold washer's cradle is a great wooden trough, six or seven feet long, with two rockers underneath it, just like a baby's. Some of these cradles rest on the ground, whilst others are swung; but in either case one end has to be lower than the other, so as to let the water run off. The four men at a cradle are employed in this manner: One digs the sand, the second shovels it on to a grating or sieve at the higher end of the cradle, a third does the rocking, and a fourth keeps up the supply of water and attends to the proper washing of the sand.

Mr. Bullion: I have seen pictures of cradles, and they all had bars at the bottom. I suppose they are put there for some purpose?

John Smith: Yes, I forgot them just now. The wooden bars which are fitted into the bottom of each cradle help to catch the heavier particles, and to prevent their being washed overboard.

Mr. Bullion: In some countries—Hungary, for instance—the auriferous (or golden) sands are washed upon inclined planks. The Bohemians use a plank with twenty-four grooves cut in its surface; they place the sand in the first, or top groove, hold the plank in an inclined position, and pour water over it. The gold, being heavy, collects with a little sand towards the bottom groove; it is then placed in a flat bowl, and when stirred in water with a peculiar motion of the hand, the sand entirely separates from the metal. Gold washing in Hungary and Bohemia.

John Smith: That is very much like what they do in Brazil. The clerk told me that the negroes do the gold-washing there, and use wooden bowls instead of cradles. They wash the sand over and over again in their big wooden bowls, and gradually Brazil.

stow away the gold dust which it contains in leather bags, which they wear fastened in front of them. I believe the cradles are mostly used in Australia and California.

Sulphurets.

Mr. Bullion: Then there are some ores called sulphurets, because they contain a good deal of sulphur. The sulphurets of silver, arsenic, and iron, although often very poor in metal, may yet contain a small proportion of gold which, with careful treatment, can be extracted with profit. Sometimes the gold is separated from them in this manner: The ores are first roasted, to free them from the sulphur, ; then they are melted into what are called mattes, which are again roasted, and next fused (or melted) with lead. By this plan an auriferous lead is obtained, which can be refined by a process called cupellation. When ores are very rich in gold they are melted directly with the lead, without being roasted.

John Smith: I know nothing about cupellation.

Mr. Bullion: I will give you a full description of it in its proper place. But there is another and better method of separating gold from its ores, called amalgamation, which is practised wherever quicksilver is obtainable. I suppose you did not see anything of it yesterday?

Amalgamation.

John Smith: No; but the clerk had visited some districts quite lately where it is done, so he took the trouble to explain the process to me. A lot of small lumps of quartz are placed in a circular stone trough, and several pounds of mercury are poured upon them. Then a heavy circular stone is set going, which grinds the quartz to powder, whilst a stream of water is kept trickling through the trough, and flows over a particular spot, carrying with it the finer ground earthy particles. Four or five goatskin bags, each containing quicksilver, are hung one below the other beneath the falling stream, so that the water and earthy particles are caught in the top bag, and whatever is fine enough to be carried through it passes down into the bags below. Gold has a great affinity for quicksilver or mercury; it readily gets mixed—or amalgamated as it is called—with it. By the time the stream and its contents have trickled through these four or five bags, most of the gold has become amalgamated with the mercury contained either in the trough or in one or other of the bags.

Mr. Bullion: That is certainly a very clever way of collecting the gold.

John Smith: When the mill has been working for several hours, all the quicksilver is collected and put into a narrow linen bag, and the uncombined mercury is squeezed out of the bag, leaving the amalgam of gold behind.

Mr. Bullion: You have quite turned the tables upon me John, by becoming my instructor. I never before heard of the process which you have just described so well.

John Smith: The clerk says it is only one of many ways of separating gold from other ores, and that various kinds of apparatus are employed for this purpose. He told me that in 1853, when there was such a rush for the gold-diggings, a Mr. Burdon of New York, invented a very clever machine, now well known as "Burdon's gold ore pulverizer and amalgamator." But, would you like me to finish my story by telling you how the gold is got out of the amalgam, sir?

Burdon's gold ore pulverizer and amalgamator.

Mr. Bullion: Pray do; I shall like to hear that.

John Smith: The combined gold and quicksilver, commonly known as the "amalgam," is placed upon a piece of iron strongly heated and resting on a brick which is standing in water. The whole is covered with a cup, called a "cupola," which forms a water joint at its bottom edge and keeps out the air, whilst the neck of the cupola dips into a vessel of water. The heat of the iron plate drives the mercury out, and it becomes condensed in the water, leaving a spongy mass of gold upon the iron plate.

Separating the gold from the amalgam.

Mr. Bullion: I quite understand. And the condensed mercury need not be wasted, for it can be collected for further use.

John Smith: Yes; so the clerk said. I wanted very much to know how the gold is made up ready for use after being separated from the amalgam, but unfortunately he could not tell me that.

Mr. Bullion: Well, I am glad to say I can give you that information. A crucible—that is, a pot made of plumbago (black lead) is first heated in a furnace; then the gold is put into it, with some dried borax, and the heat is kept up until the gold is melted, when the coarse impurities, called slag, rise to the surface and are skimmed off. The metal is poured into ingot moulds which have been warmed and greased, and when cold the ingots are ready to be sent to the assay office or mint. An ingot, I should tell you, is a block of metal very much like

Gold made up into ingots

a brick in shape. But no more talking to-night, if you please; it is getting very late, and to-morrow we set forth upon our travels again.

John Smith: Just tell me before I go, please, sir, what we are to see next. I shall not sleep a wink if you don't tell me that!

Mr. Bullion (laughing): I will answer for your not lying awake when once you lay your head upon your pillow; but I will satisfy your curiosity. We shall start to-morrow morning on a balloon trip to New York, accompanied by Mr. Verdigris, who intends to visit with us the Assay Office, and get leave for us to be let into all the mysteries of parting and refining gold and silver bullion.

Proposed trip to New York.

John Smith: How delightful! But I do not yet know anything about the separation of silver from its various ores.

Mr. Bullion: Mr. Verdigris thought of that; but he says he will explain it fully to you during our journey. You must recollect we shall have plenty of time for talk, for we have to make our way right across the United States, from extreme west to extreme east, and shall probably be many days doing so, even if the weather is favourable. Now go to bed at once, or you will never be ready to start at seven o'clock to-morrow morning.

Chapter VI.

The balloon starts.

THE next morning proved very fine, and a large party of miners, with their wives and little ones, had collected long before seven o'clock to see the balloon go up. She ascended in fine style, and, having risen steadily to the required height, sailed majestically off in an eastward direction, followed by the cheers of the assembled party. Mr. Verdigris felt by no means comfortable when he first found himself suspended in mid-air, but both John and Mr. Bullion seemed so perfectly at home in the latter's aerial carriage that by degrees his nervousness wore off, and, after he and Mr. Bullion had enjoyed a smoke together, he was quite ready to have a chat with John Smith about the treatment of silver ores.

Mr. Verdigris: What do you know about silver ores, John? Just give me an idea, that I may know where to begin.

John Smith: Only this: that silver is rarely discovered in a native or pure condition, and is often hidden in a non-metallic state in its different ores.

Silver ores.

Mr. Verdigris: That is quite true. There are a great many different mineral ores from which silver may be extracted, but the principal silver ores properly so-called are: Native silver, vitreous silver or silver glance, black silver, red silver, and horn silver. Besides these, there are sulphides of lead and copper, from which small proportions of silver are obtained, and the two ways in which silver is extracted from its various ores are—(1) smelting, and (2) amalgamation.

John Smith: I am never sure that I understand what is meant by smelting, although I know the process has something to do with furnaces.

Smelting.

Mr. Verdigris: To smelt ores is to extract the metal from them by means of heat. Smelting is called the dry method, whilst amalgamation is known as the wet method of treating ores. The former is practised chiefly on the argentiferous (or silvery) sulphides of lead; the ore is first roasted and reduced to powder so as to expel the sulphur, after which it is ready for refining and cupellation.

John Smith: Gold is treated very much like that sometimes; but I have yet to learn the meaning of cupellation.

Amalgamation.

Mr. Verdigris: You shall see the process with your own eyes when we get to New York. Amalgamation is a very complicated process as far as silver is concerned; the ores best suited to this treatment are native silver, and vitreous silver. First, the ores have to be selected, so as to form a proper mixture as to the silver and sulphur they contain. It has been found that this process succeeds best where about seventy-five ounces of silver are produced to the ton of ore, and regard has also to be paid to the quantity of sulphide present, which it is the business of the assayer to find out beforehand. The sulphur is got rid of by adding to the mixture of raw ore ten per cent. of common salt, and in the furnace operations which follow, the sulphur is oxidised by the salt, and the acid thus formed, uniting with the base of the salt, forms sulphate of soda; whilst the hydro-chloric acid thus set free combines with the silver in the ore that was not in a metallic state, and forms chloride of silver.

Mr. Bullion: All that is rather a tough nut for John to crack.

Mr. Verdigris: Try how much you can remember before I go further; I will answer for it, you will soon master the particulars.

(Accordingly John did his best to repeat what had just been related to him, and with very little prompting from Mr. Verdigris, succeeded most satisfactorily.)

Mr. Verdigris (turning to Mr. Bullion): John knows more about it than you gave him credit for, eh?

John Smith: I used a word that I did not understand—oxidise.

To oxidise.

Mr. Verdigris: A metal is oxidised when it becomes encrusted with a kind of rust or film, oxide being a rust which is formed by the action of a gas called oxygen upon metal. And now I think you will easily take in all that I can tell you about the process of amalgamation, especially as you understand the principle of it already. After the ores have been submitted to the furnace, you must imagine that we have to deal with a mixed ore made up of sulphate of soda, chloride of silver, and other metallic and earthy ingredients. This ore goes through various mechanical operations with riddles, mills, and sieves, until it is reduced to a very fine powder, and fit to be submitted to the action of mercury.

Further treatment of silver.

John Smith: I had no idea that the finding and preparing of silver was such a business.

Mr. Verdigris: It does seem a lot of trouble, but machinery saves a good deal of labour now-a-days. To form the amalgam, a number of barrels are each charged with certain known proportions of sifted calcined ore, mercury, metallic iron, and water. The barrels are made to revolve by machinery upon their own axes for sixteen or eighteen hours, during which time the chloride of silver becomes decomposed by the action of the iron, and produces chloride of iron and metallic silver. The silver combines with the mercury and forms an amalgam, whilst the sulphate of silver, the chloride of iron, and other salts, are dissolved in the water. The combined mercury and silver is then filtered, by which process the surplus metal is separated, and a compound remains consisting of six parts of mercury and one of silver. This amalgam is subjected to the action of heat, by which means the mercury is sublimed, that is, extracted by heat, and the silver remains.

John Smith: What a very elaborate business, to be sure! But it is most interesting to be told all these particulars; thank you so much, Mr. Verdigris, for explaining everything so clearly.

Some more cookery.

Mr. Bullion: And now, John, it is high time you and I set about shewing Mr. Verdigris what skilful cooks we have become since we set forth on our travels together. We are going to operate on some lamb chops and tinned tomatoes directly, so light up the stove, there's a good fellow. (Mr. Verdigris was much astonished at the tasty luncheon provided for him by Mr. Bullion and John; the former fried some breaded lamb chops, whilst John made as good a preparation of tomato sauce as anyone could wish to partake of. There were boiled potatoes also; and bread and cheese, biscuits, and butter to finish up with.)

Mr. Verdigris: You have given me such a luncheon as I never expected to enjoy in a balloon; in fact, I brought plenty of tobacco with me in case I found that we were short of victuals.

Mr. Bullion: I cannot promise you fresh meat at every meal, but I hope you will discover that we do not go in for fasting up here.

John Smith: No, that we don't; I grew quite fat on my outward voyage, what with good living and having no chance of running it down.

Mr. Verdigris: I have so little more to say that I think we may as well give ourselves up to the enjoyment of scenery this afternoon, and postpone the rest of our "silver" talk until to-morrow morning.

Mr Bullion: A capital suggestion; the morning is always the best time for head-work. But, if you will take my advice, John, you will make notes of Mr. Verdigris' morning lecture in the course of the afternoon.

John Smith: All right, sir, so I will. (The remainder of the day was spent by our travellers in rest, enjoyment, and in observing much that was going on below them. The next morning when they had breakfasted, and the two elder gentlemen had smoked their first pipes, Mr. Verdigris began as follows):—

Pattinson's process of extracting silver from lead.

Mr. Verdigris: Did you ever hear of the Pattinson process of extracting silver from lead?

John Smith: No, I do not think I ever heard of it, though I have often been told that a good deal of silver is generally found in the lead ore.

Mr. Verdigris: Then I will give you a description of the process, so called because it was invented and patented by the late Mr. Pattinson, of Newcastle-on-Tyne. It is one of the simplest and best plans that has ever been discovered. Imagine nine cast-iron pots, each pot being about 6 ft. in diameter, and having a fire underneath it. In the middle, or fifth pot, is placed a quantity of lead containining about 10 ozs. of silver to the ton, and called "original lead." Pure lead becomes solid at a higher temperature than lead with silver in it; therefore, the lead and silver, when quite melted, are allowed to cool slowly; the fluid metal is kept stirred, and as small portions of pure lead become crystallised, they sink to the bottom of the pot, and are ladled into the first pot on the right. The ladle used for this purpose has holes in it, so that the fluid metal runs through it, and only the solid bits of lead remain in it. The metal which remains liquid contains silver, and is removed into the first pot on the left. With both kinds of metal this process is repeated, one becoming poorer and the other richer every time, until the lead in the pot on the extreme right has hardly any silver left in it, whilst the pot on the extreme left contains about 300 ounces of silver to the ton. This last metal, called "lead riches," is cast into bars about 2 ins. square.

John Smith: How I should like to see it done!

Mr. Bullion: I daresay you will be able to do so when we get back to England. I have read that nearly 600,000 ounces of silver are in this way separated from British lead every year, and, what is more, the quality of the lead is greatly improved by the process.

Cupellation.

Mr. Verdigris: All that is true enough. But now, Mr. Bullion, I think you must allow me to explain to John the process of cupellation, otherwise I cannot tell him how those bars of argentiferous lead that I have just been talking about are finished off.

Mr. Bullion: By all means; you will do it a greal deal better than I could.

Mr. Verdigris (politely): That is not at all likely.

John Smith: By hearing about cupellation beforehand, I shall take it in all the quicker if I am lucky enough to see the thing done when we get to New York.

Mr. Verdigris: Certainly you will, so I will do my best to make you understand it. The object of cupellation is the first thing you must grasp. Copper, tin, and other inferior metals readily oxidise, or absorb oxygen gas, when melted with lead, whilst gold and silver have only a very slight affinity for oxygen. The principle of cupellation, therefore, is to melt the gold or silver ores with a proper proportion of lead, so that the inferior metals contained in these ores may become oxidised and separated from the precious metals. Do you follow me so far?

John Smith: I believe I do, perfectly.

Mr. Verdigris: Now then—to describe to you the process of cupellation, as it would be applied to the bars of lead riches, of which I was talking just now.

John Smith: The 2 in. square bars, containing a proportion of 300 ounces of silver to the ton?

Mr. Verdigris: Just so. The next thing to be done is to extract the silver from the lead, and this has to be accomplished by means of cupellation, in the following manner: First, the metal has to be melted in a peculiar shaped dish, called a test, or cupel, very much like a meat dish, its framework being made of iron, and being covered with a porous mixture of earth composed of burnt bones and fern ashes. This porous coating sucks up a great deal of the oxidised metal.

John Smith: What a very odd mixture, to be sure; burnt bones and fern ashes!

Mr. Verdigris: The cupel is placed in a furnace, so constructed that the heated air and flame pass over it and up the chimney. This is managed by means of dampers, and a furnace of this description is called a reverberatory furnace. Great care has to be taken to prevent the cupel being cracked by the heat, and when it is sufficiently hot, the lead riches, which have been previously melted in a side furnace, are poured into the cupel. At first, the surface of the metal gets to look as if covered with dross, but very soon that clears off, the surface of the melted lead increases, and a film of melted litharge—that is, oxide of lead—appears, which sinks into the cupel as into a sponge; but when this is full, then a draught of air is directed over the argentiferous lead, and as the cupel is kept constantly filled with lead riches, the litharge collects on the top, floats over the hollow part of the cupel, and is caught in a pot beneath. Directly the last portion of lead is oxidised and removed, the whole surface of the metal in the cupel suddenly brightens up, and looks exceedingly beautiful. If the silver were left to cool, it would take to spirting—that is, a quantity of oxygen gas that becomes dissolved in the fluid would explode; but this is avoided by pouring water upon it or by sprinkling the surface with powdered charcoal.

John Smith: Thank you so much, Mr. Verdigris; it has all been most interesting, and I am sure I understand it.

Eliquation. *Mr. Verdigris:* One other separation of ores I may as well tell you of,—that called "eliquation," being the process by which silver is sometimes extracted from ores containing a good deal of copper. Lead has a greater affinity for silver than for copper; therefore, a certain proportion of lead is melted with the silver and copper alloy. The silver separates from the copper, and forms a new compound with the lead, after which it can be treated by Pattinson's process; whilst the coarse copper from which the silver has been separated is refined. You will learn all about the treatment of copper when you turn your attention to that metal.

John Smith: Which will not be until we return to England, I suppose. But will you kindly tell me another thing; are the gold ingots which are brought to the mint quite ready to be made into money?

Mr. Bullion: No; they are not composed of sufficiently fine gold to be fit for that purpose, John. When we reach New York, you will see what further process they have to go through.

Refining. *Mr. Verdigris:* Both gold and silver are brought to the mints and assay offices containing a considerable amount of alloy, unless they have passed through a private refinery first.

John Smith: Which is supposed to be the best plan,—to take the metals to private refiners first, or to let the government people do the refining business?

Government v. private refiners.

Mr. Verdigris: In America, the greater part of the gold produced is brought straight to the government mints to be refined, for the government do not charge any more for refining base bullion, and parting gold and silver, than the private refiners do, and most of the gold producers prefer dealing with the institutions belonging to the governmental mint service, for the sake of having their fine gold stamped with the official stamp. This stamp, you see, is a guarantee that every gold purchaser would accept for the fineness of the gold he is about to buy.

Gold bullion.

John Smith: Suppose a gold producer does not want to have back his gold when it has been refined, but would rather have it turned into gold coins?

Mr. Verdigris: In that case, he can receive the value of his gold in coins, all except the small sum which is deducted for refining. The government make no charge for converting gold bullion into coin; they will always allow depositors of gold bullion to receive the value of their metal either in stamped and refined bars, or in coin, whichever suits them best.

John Smith: That is very jolly of them. And does nearly all the silver find its way to the government mints also?

Silver bullion.

Mr. Verdigris: No, not anything like so much silver as gold, because depositors of silver can only receive bars of unparted, fine, sterling, or standard silver in return for their silver bullion; the government will not undertake to pay for silver in either gold or silver coin. Silver containing gold—called "Doré Gold"—is purchased at the mints, to be used for refining purposes; and the silver contained in gold deposits is always allowed for at all the government institutions.

Doré gold

John Smith: The depositors cannot complain if they can get paid for the silver contained in their bullion; but it is a curious thing that they may only have silver bars, and not silver coins in return for their deposits.

A few days afterwards the following conversation took place:

John Smith: What a vast extent of country we have passed over during the last few days, to be sure! Why I should think we must have travelled at least 1,000 miles by this time.

Mr Bullion: When we reach New York, which we hope to do this evening, we shall have passed over more than 2,000 miles of country. It is lucky we have been able to let ourselves down into civilised parts to take in provisions, or I fear we should only have been fit for the crows to peck at by this time. But now that our journey is nearly at an end, what do you remember of the route, John?

Route from California to New York.

John Smith: I remember it all, sir, perfectly well; I should never have been such a duffer at geography if I had been allowed to learn it by making balloon trips with you. I will give you our route at once, in a very few words: Salt Lake City (of Mormon fame), and over the Rocky Mountains, to Denver, Colorado. Then across Nebraska State and River Platte to Iowa City; across the Mississippi and Lake Michigan to Detroit. From Detroit we went northward, so as to visit Toronto and the Canadian lakes. Never shall I forget those great tideless oceans! Mr Verdigris says that Great Britain could be put down into Lake Superior, and that even then there would be a margin enough round it for heavy seas to rise in a gale. And that reminds me—you never heard about the silver island, did you? It was told us by an old fellow at the hotel at Toronto the evening that you were not very well, and did not leave your room. I wish we had heard of it before passing over Lake Superior, for we should certainly have looked out for it.

Silver Island.

Mr. Bullion: I was much puzzled by overhearing some chance words about a "Silver Island," when you and Mr. Verdigris were talking together last night, and I meant to have asked you what it was all about.

John Smith: Let me tell you now, sir. You know there are not many islands in Lake Superior, and they are all near the shores, so that there is a vast space of open water, and, being fresh, the seas that arise there are tremendous. There is, of course, no tide, but in summer time the water falls a good deal, rising again in the autumn and spring. One of the small islands in this lake was a bright, silvery-looking rock whose reef could be traced, shining through the clear water, to the mainland. I do not know when its silvery appearance first attracted attention, but at all events about twenty years ago a Canadian company, without much capital, took possession of the silver island and determined to work it. They made a dam round the island at low water, but year after year the rising water and heavy autumnal seas broke it away and flooded it ; in fact, they could only work for a short time in each year, with heavy expenses for repairs. Then the company lost heart, and just at that time a smart Yankee appeared at Toronto, who had evidently visited the island before, for he made a bid for it to the Canadian company, which seemed so good that they closed with his offer, stipulating only to be paid in cash. The Yankee asked for a week, and at the end of that time he had organised a small American company, who paid down a good round sum to the Canadian company for the island. There were seven men only, I believe, and our Yankee friend was, of course, one of them.

Mr. Bullion (laughing): Well done, Mr. Yankee! Those sharp Americans always know where to lay their hands on men with money, and ready for a good "spec."

John Smith: And a jolly good "spec." it was, I can tell you. They set to work, made an outer and inner dam, each much more substantial than the Canadian one, and the result of the first six months was that, after all the heavy expenses, including buying 1,000 acres of ground on the mainland, where the reef touched, they divided 20 per cent. on their capital!

Mr Bullion: What a splendid success! I should not think the Canadian company liked it, though.

John Smith: No ; they were very sore to think that so good a thing had been snapped up by the Yankees. But "let those laugh who win." The hotel-keeper was able to tell us that the silver island has by no means come up to its first brilliant expectations; indeed, I fear it has proved a disappointing failure.

Mr. Verdigris: Look yonder, John: those houses nestling in the hills are part of New York; we shall be there in no time now.

John Smith: We have passed over a goodly stretch of country since the morning, haven't we? Across Lake Ontario and the Alleghany Mountains. It is so delightful to be independent of mountains, lakes, rivers, and seas, as we are in this jolly old balloon.

Arrival at New York.

In a short time the travellers arrived under Mr. Verdigris' directions, right over a small pleasure ground situated in the very heart of the city, and close to the hotel in which Mr. Verdigris had engaged rooms for them. As usual, by the time they came down a large number of people had assembled to see them alight, and they were escorted to Madison-square by a crowd of admirers, some of whom insisted on carrying the balloon.

Fifth Avenue Hotel and its surroundings.

Fifth Avenue Hotel, where Mr. Verdigris had taken rooms for himself and his friends, stands on the western side of Madison-square. It has a white marble front, and it is quite the handsomest of the many fine hotels situated in that part of the city. After the travellers had dined and rested, they turned out to have a look at their surroundings. Madison-square is close to the union of the two most celebrated streets in New York City—Fifth-avenue, with its beautiful brown-stone mansions; and Broadway, a splendid street, five miles in length, full of fine shops, restaurants, hotels, and great business houses. Brilliant electric lights added much to the effectiveness of the scene, and the streets were crowded with people and vehicles long after our three friends had returned to their hotel and retired to rest.

Chapter VII.

Mr. Tizzy's invitation.

Mr. Verdigris: We must find our way to the Assay Office this morning, John, before we go anywhere else, for I have had a very kind note from Mr. Tizzy, the superintendent of the Assay Office, inviting you to spend the morning with him, and to lunch with him, after seeing all that is to be seen.

John Smith: How very kind of him; but are not you and Mr. Bullion coming too, sir?

Mr. Verdigris: I have other business which must be attended to; so, as Mr. Bullion has already been let into the secrets of the assaying process, he proposes accompanying me to another part of the city as soon as I have introduced you to my friend, Mr. Tizzy.

John Smith: I hope Mr. Tizzy will let me see everything.

Mr. Verdigris: You will find him a delightful companion, and will probably get much more out of him by having him all to yourself, than you would if I were there to discuss the money market with him. Come along, both of you, as soon as you are ready. My friend is an early bird, and we must not keep him waiting.

The Assay Office and its surroundings.

(Very soon after breakfast Mr. Bullion and John were ready to start, and Mr. Verdigris led them down Broadway-street until they reached the corner of Wall-street.)

Mr. Verdigris: Here we are. Just observe what a collection of great business houses are brought together at this corner. That white marble building is the United States Treasury, with the Assay Office alongside of it. Opposite is the Drexel building and the Stock Exchange is close at hand.

Mr. Bullion: The Treasury is very fine; a flight of steps always gives an imposing air to a building.

Mr. Verdigris (pointing to a monument): That is Washington's statue; it stands on the very spot on which he was inaugurated first President of the United States. But see, here comes Mr. Tizzy. The top of the morning to you, sir; allow me to introduce you to Mr. Bullion and Mr. John Smith.

Mr. Tizzy.

Mr. Tizzy: Glad to see you, gentlemen, and very much at your service.

Mr. Verdigris (laughing): It is lucky you say so, Tizzy, for I have desired John to pump you quite dry before he allows you to leave the office to-day. This young friend of Mr. Bullion's has come all the way from England in a balloon for the sole purpose of studying mines and precious metals.

Mr. Tizzy: Dear me, you don't say so! Then you must be in earnest about your studies, and no mistake. Well, I shall be proud to show you my department.

Mr. Verdigris: We will not detain you now, but I hope you can come back with John, and dine with us this evening.

Mr. Tizzy: Thanks; I shall have much pleasure (and linking his arm within John's he drew him into his own private room).

Mr. Tizzy: We are going to test some gold ingots this morning, so you will be able to see the whole process. Ask as many questions as you like; to have an intelligent fellow like you looking on, who wants to know all about it, will make our morning's work more interesting than usual.

John Smith: That is a very kind way of putting it, sir. I am glad you do not mind answering questions, for I shall be sure to think of lots that I want to ask.

The duties of an assayer.

Mr. Tizzy: Fire away, then! I only hope you will not manage to ask me anything I cannot answer. But first tell me, do you fully understand the duties of an assayer?

John Smith: I believe you have to test the ores, and I suppose that is done just as a chemist analyses anything.

Mr. Tizzy: Not so. In a chemical analysis it is the business of a chemist to find out every separate ingredient contained in a compound mixture, and the relative proportions of each. But an assayer need not do that; his business is merely to find out how much precious metal the sample of bullion brought to him contains.

John Smith: I see. And is all the gold and silver you receive here made into money?

Various uses of gold and silver.

Mr. Tizzy: Oh, dear, no! We accommodate everybody who has anything to do with the precious metals—miners, bankers, jewellers, and all sorts. Anyone who brings us bullion—that is, unmelted gold or silver—to the value of 100 dollars or more, can leave it with us and receive payment for it. For gold we give either gold coin or fine bars; for silver we do not give coin, but fine or standard silver bars. These gold and silver bars have their weight and fineness stamped on them, and the gold bars have also their value stamped upon them.

John Smith: I should have thought that people would always rather have had money for their bullion than bars.

Mr. Tizzy: That depends on what they are going to use the metal for. Now that jewellers and gold and silver workers can get bars of the precious metals, a vast number of standard coins are saved from destruction every year; and this is a very good thing, for you must remember the newest and best coins had to be selected for melting down, whilst the worn coins remained in circulation until some unfortunate persons were told that their money was of light weight and could not be accepted.

Light coins.

John Smith: What did they do, poor things, when they could not pass their coins?

Mr. Tizzy: The only thing they could do was to take them

to one of the mints, or to a money dealer, and sell them for as much as they would fetch; but they had to do so at a loss. Now, come with me and take a lesson in assaying.

* * * * *

The next morning John related his experiences to Mr. Bullion in the following manner:—

Mr. Bullion: Well, John, and what sort of a day did you have yesterday? Did it come up to your expectations?"

John Smith: I never had such an out-and-out delightful day before. Mr. Tizzy was as jolly as could be, and I saw everything.

Mr. Bullion: That is right, then. Mr. Verdigris is obliged to leave us to our own devices this morning; so suppose you begin at the very beginning, and tell me all that you saw and heard described yesterday.

John Smith: That is just what I have been wanting to do before I forget any of it, though I do not think there is much fear of that—it is so much easier to recollect when one has seen the real thing.

Mr. Bullion: To be sure it is; that conclusion holds good for other kinds of knowledge besides balloon trips and geography lessons.

John Smith: Well, first I was shown some lumps of gold and silver bullion which had lately been sold by a depositor to the Assay Office, and Mr. Tizzy told me that the gold bullion was going to be assayed, parted, and refined that very day, so I was in luck's way, wasn't I?

Mr. Bullion: You were, indeed.

Gold and silver bullion melted.

John Smith: The bullion has always to be melted down before anything can be done with it. The gold bullion was melted in a crucible, and poured into iron moulds; when cold, the bars of metal were turned out, and some small cuttings taken from them for assay samples. The silver bullion has to be melted also, but instead of being cast into bars it is carefully stirred whilst fluid, and a small quantity of it is dipped up and granulated by being dropped into cold water. Silver is treated thus, because it is apt to segregate—that is, to get separated from its alloys in little lumps whilst cooling, in which case it would be very difficult to get a fair sample of the whole melt. But the granulations taken from the stirred fluid are very fair samples of the rest of the contents of the crucible, Mr. Tizzy said.

Mr. Bullion: So I should imagine.

Gold samples tested.

John Smith: After I had seen the gold bullion melted and cast into bars, small samples were cut from these bars—little bits of metal weighing only about half a gramme each—that is, 7½ grains; in fact, everything seemed to be done on a miniature scale; the furnace used was only 2½ ft. high, and the samples went through the process of cupellation in it. The *principle* was the same as that described by Mr. Verdigris, when he was telling me about the treatment of silver ores, but the things used were rather different. There was a curious-looking clay box, called a muffle, in which were placed the little cupels or cups, containing the assay samples. This muffle had its top and three of its sides perforated, whilst the fourth side was left open altogether, to allow of the cupels being put into it. The holes in the top and sides of the muffle, I learnt afterwards, were to let the heated air pass freely over the cupels.

Cupellation of gold samples.

Mr. Bullion: Did you happen to hear what the cupels were made of?

Cupels.

John Smith: Yes, and even *how* they were made. Sometimes phosphate of lime, which is really bone ash, is used, but those cupels I saw were made of calcined cores of ox-horn. The powdered ashes are mixed with just enough water to moisten them, and pressed tightly into steel moulds; then each cupel is shaped, by a polished steel rammer being hammered violently into the hollow of the mould until the moistened ashes have become a solid, hard substance. The cupels when made are put aside for several weeks to dry.

Mr. Bullion: Now that you know what the cupels are made of, you can better understand their becoming porous when heated, can you not?

John Smith: Ever so much better; I thought they were made of solid metal before. The little assay samples were placed each in its own cupel, with a certain proportion of silver.

Mr. Bullion: And what was the silver for?

John Smith: There must be more silver than gold in the melt, to separate well the gold particles, otherwise the gold prevents the copper and other alloys from dissolving in the sulphuric acid which is afterwards used. When the cupellation business was completed, and the cupels had been cooled, there was a small button of metal in the middle of each cupel. These little buttons had to go through the further process of parting and refining.

Gold buttons refined.

Mr. Bullion: Did you see the fine gold produced from those little metal buttons?

John Smith: I did, indeed. Each button went through the following treatment:—First, it was hammered out flat into a ribbon, thin enough to coil round one's finger; then it was *annealed*—that is, made red-hot and cooled, which softened it, for the hammering makes the metal too hard. When cold, it was coiled up and called a "cornet." This cornet was boiled two or three times in sulphuric acid, the acid being poured off after each boiling, and replaced with a fresh lot; this is done to rid the gold of the silver it contains, for silver dissolves in the acid, and gold does not. The cornet was next washed twice in distilled water, to free it from the acid, after which it was once more made red-hot, then cooled and very carefully weighed, to determine the fineness of the gold. Having weighed the assay sample at the beginning, you see, they were able to find out how much of that sample was alloy.

Mr. Bullion: You certainly saw a very great deal in a wonderfully short space of time.

John Smith: And all the times between, whilst we were waiting for the metals to melt or cool, Mr. Tizzy was talking away about all sorts of interesting things. He told me that a chemist named Baumé invented a very clever instrument called an "Areometer," for finding out the specific gravity of liquids. With the aid of this instrument, and by making very careful calculations, they can determine as nearly as possible the proportions of the different metals contained in an alloy, and by being able to do this, they also know how much metal of any particular kind they must add to a melt to bring about the required results.

Baumé's Areometer, for discovering the specific gravity of liquids.

Mr. Bullion: I suppose Mr. Tizzy did a little sight-seeing with you after luncheon?

John Smith: Not until we had spent a long time in the melting and refining department of the Assay Office. We lunched

Twenty-third Street.

at a very grand restaurant in Twenty-third-street,—that street which crosses Fifth-avenue at right angles just where Broadway intersects them both diagonally.

Mr. Bullion: I know; a very wide street, not far from Madison-square.

Separation of gold and silver.

John Smith: That's it, sir. After lunch we went back to the Assay Office, and then Mr. Tizzy took me into the refining department and explained the whole process to me, from beginning to end. The gold and silver deposits are both melted down and granulated for the purpose of separation; the deposits being so combined that the gold granulatious shall have over two parts of silver and copper to one of gold, taking care that there shall be not more than 8 per cent. of copper in the mixture; whilst the silver granulations are all right if there is not more than 14 per cent. of copper alloy in them.

Amount of alloy allowed.

Mr. Bullion: Did you see it all done?

John Smith: No, there would not have been time to see everything. We went straight to the separating room, and there Mr. Tizzy told me how the gold and silver granulations had been prepared. In this room there are four huge cast-iron kettles set in two furnaces, each kettle being made to hold 168 gallons. Two of them are generally kept for gold, and two for silver granulations, and the sulphuric acid is added to the granulations from time to time from a reservoir on the floor above, into which it has been forced by air pressure from a receiving cylinder into the basement. I will tell you what happens to the gold granulations first.

Treatment of gold granulations.

Mr. Bullion: I think you must have a good head on your shoulders to be able to stand so much cramming without getting *mixed*, like the metals, in your descriptions!

John Smith: As I said before, it all comes of my having actually seen these things with my own eyes, and having had the different apparatus explained to me. After the gold granulations have been boiled for four or five hours, a pitcher or two of stuff called "waste acid" is carefully poured into each kettle to help settle any floating gold. Mr. Tizzy timed our visit to the separating room so that we arrived at the end of the five hours' boiling, and saw the waste acid poured into the kettles; then we took a tram whilst the gold was settling, and went down Broadway to the end of all things, and when there we visited the emigrants' landing station, and the park and rotunda where the emigrants are able to put up and get their money changed on their way through New York.

Visit to the emigrants' landing-station.

Mr. Bullion: And did you get back in good time? for it is a long way down to the landing-station.

John Smith: We were not back in time for the whole process, but Mr. Tizzy made it all clear to me. When the solution had been left cooling for an hour it was siphoned into the silver-reducing vats on the floor below, and by-and-bye you shall hear what became of it. The gold left in the kettles had fresh acid added to it, after which it was transferred to a sixty-gallon kettle by means of cast-iron scoops made like colanders, and was boiled again in two successive charges of acid. By this time nearly all the silver must have been boiled out of the gold; so the weak solutions of silver were siphoned off, and the gold was well washed, first by being decanted into a lead-lined wooden vat, and then filtered through wooden tubs having false bottoms with many holes in them, and covered with filtering paper and sheeting. All this treatment was repeated twice, a fresh kettle being used each time; and when the contents of the third kettle had been washed and filtered, it yielded gold which when it had been melted, fluxed, and cast into bars was from 997 to 998½ per mil fine. A coating of bone ash on the surface of the melted metal was used to absorb the base metal oxides and the flux.

Gold bars 997 to 998½ per mil fine.

Mr. Bullion: They do, indeed, manage to produce very fine gold; it is weighed by the carat, I presume, and 997 to 998½ carats of pure gold would mean from 1½ to 3 carats only of alloy in a thousand.

John Smith: A carat being twelve grains, you know; the amount of alloy left in the gold is hardly worth mentioning. I did not know what the *flux* was until I had asked Mr. Tizzy; he explained to me that it is something added to the metal to make it melt more readily; in this instance the gold was fluxed with borax and nitrate of soda. They have brought their refining process to great perfection, have they not, sir?

Flux.

Mr. Bullion: They have, indeed!

John Smith: Let me finish off the silver now. I must take up my story at the point where the contents of the four big kettles had been boiled for four or five hours, some waste acid

Treatment of silver granulations.

added to them, and the solutions allowed to cool for an hour. The solutions, which contained dissolved silver and baser metals, were siphoned from the two kettles, which contained the gold granulations, into the silver reducing vats on the floor below.

Mr. Bullion: I followed you as far as that.

John Smith: The solutions from the two kettles in which the silver granulations had been boiled were also siphoned into these same vats.

Mr. Bullion: What are the silver-reducing vats like?

John Smith: There are four of them, two being used on each alternate day. They are each 14 ft. long, by 6 ft. wide, but only 2½ ft. deep, so as to allow of their contents being easily handled from the outside. From day to day the water and weak solution, in which the gold has been washed and filtered, runs into a leaden vat, from which it is siphoned into one of two tanks which stand on a high platform on the floor below—that is, in the same room with the silver-reducing vats. The solution is allowed to stand all night, so as to settle any gold that might be left in it, and is then run into the silver-reducing vats.

Mr. Bullion: It seems to me that the silver-reducing vats are made to hold a ha'porth of all sorts!

John Smith (laughing): That is quite true, sir. When the silver in the big kettles is washed and filtered, the weak sulphate of copper, which is the result of the filtering, runs into these same silver-reducing vats. Just think what a mixture it is! Strong solutions of silver from the silver granulations, weak ditto from the gold granulations, and sulphate of copper and weak solutions of all sorts of baser metals! Water is often added to the mixture to reduce its strength, and finally the contents of the vats are boiled for four or five hours by means of steam. The silver gradually gets deposited on the copper plates placed at the bottom and on the sides of the vats, part of the copper having gradually replaced the silver in the solution. The next morning this copper solution is siphoned into two large concentrating tanks, which stand on platforms on a still lower level than the silver-reducing vats; and the silver, after being scraped from the copper plates, is transferred to filters and washed free from sulphate of copper. When melted, fluxed, and cast into bars, this silver is found to be from 999 to 999½ per mil fine; even finer than the gold, you see! Silver bars 999 to 999½ per mil fine.

(That same day, when Mr. Bullion and Mr. Verdigris were smoking their after-luncheon pipes, the following conversation took place).

John Smith: I am so sorry to be saying good-bye to you to-morrow, Mr. Verdigris; I cannot thank you enough for all your great kindness; but, please, come and see me when you visit England, and you will find a warm welcome ready for you at my father's house. Goodbye to Mr. Verdigris.

Mr. Verdigris: Thank you, John; I shall probably take you at your word, for it is quite my present intention to go over to Europe next year, if all be well.

Mr. Bullion: Then be sure to let us know when you are coming, for I shall invite you, and John also, to accompany me in my balloon on a visit to some of our tin and copper mines.

Mr. Verdigris: I shall be delighted to do so, for I have had no experience of either tin or copper mining, and I do not consider my education complete as far as coinage is concerned until I have done so.

John Smith: I can understand your wanting to know all about copper, sir; but what has tin to do with it? We haven't any tin-money, though we do speak of our "tin" sometimes! Tin used in coinage.

Mr. Verdigris: Although we have no tin coins, we have plenty of bronze ones. Our pence, half-pence, and farthings are made of a compound metal, composed of ninety-five parts of copper to four of tin and one of zinc. Bronze for coinage.

John Smith: How stupid of me never to have asked of what bronze was made!

Mr. Verdigris: Then again: both the gold and silver of which our coins are made are alloyed with copper. The gold employed in the manufacture of sovereigns and half-sovereigns contains eleven-twelfths of gold to one-twelfth of copper; whilst silver money contains silver and copper, mixed in the proportions of 925 parts of silver to 75 parts of copper. Coins made of pure gold or silver would be too soft to retain long any impression stamped upon them, and would soon get worn out of shape; but the right quantity of copper alloy when mixed Gold for coinage. Silver for coinage.

with either of these metals give it just the necessary hardness and durability required for the purpose.

The following account of a new process of separating gold from its ores by amalgamation appeared in the "Times" last September; it is so interesting that I have obtained the kind permission of the editor of the "Times" to republish the article in full, word for word, as it was given:—

The Hydrogen-Amalgam Process.

"The difficulty, or rather the impossibility, of obtaining by mercurial amalgamation anything like the full yield of gold from what are known as refractory ores has long been recognised, and has led to the application of various remedies from time to time. The difficulty arises from the circumstance that in some ores the gold is variously associated with sulphur, iron oxide, arsenic, antimony, or zinc; and the presence of any of these ingredients destroys the 'quickness' of the mercury and so renders it sluggish and incapable of seizing and retaining the atoms of gold. The most recent invention in connection with the present subject is the hydrogen-amalgam process, which has been invented by Mr. B. C. Molloy, M.P., the working of which on a practical scale we recently witnessed at the laboratory of Messrs. Johnson and Sons, of Cross-street, Finsbury, assayers to the Bank of England. The principle involved is the well-known one that when gold is brought into absolute and maintained contact with clean or 'quick' mercury, the gold is absorbed by and retained in the mercury, from which it is afterwards retorted. In cases where refractory ores have to be dealt with, they cause the mercury to 'sicken'—that is, to become coated with an oxide, which lies like a sheet of paper on the surface of the body of the mercury, preventing contact between the particles of gold and the clean portion of the mercury. This sick mercury also powders away, or, as it is termed, 'flours;' so that the floured fluid metal is carried away and lost, leaving fresh surfaces to be attacked by the injurious ingredients in the ore. The result

Inventor of hydrogen-amalgam process.

Refractory ores cause mercury to sicken.

is, therefore, that not only is the gold not captured, but mercury is lost or carried away in the refuse or tailings. With some of the less refractory ores the loss of mercury is from 2lbs. to 6lbs. per ton of ore treated, while in some other cases the loss is much greater. Owing to this difficulty in the treatment of auriferous ores, it has been estimated that an average of 40 per cent. of the gold contained in the ores treated is annually lost. The object of the hydrogen-amalgam process is to save this enormous loss of gold and mercury, and, according to authoritative reports, this object is completely and successfully attained. The method pursued is, first, to maintain the 'quickness' of the mercury, no matter how deleterious the character of the ore; and secondly, to insure a continual contact between each separate particle of the pulverised ore and the 'quick' mercury. The apparatus for accomplishing this consists of a shallow pan about 1in. in depth and 41½in. in diameter, which contains mercury about ½in. in depth. In the centre of this pan is a porous jar, so placed and fixed that the mercury cannot enter or move it. Within this jar is a cylinder of lead and a solution of sulphate of soda. This lead cylinder, which constitutes the anode, is connected with the positive pole of a small dynamo machine, while the mercury is connected with the negative pole of the same dynamo. When the current passes, oxygen is evolved from the surface of the lead anode, while hydrogen is evolved from the surface of the mercury. This action, which is apparent to the eye, is of course due to the decomposition of the electrolyte formed by the solution of sulphate of soda. The mercury combines with a portion of the hydrogen, and so forms a hydrogen-amalgam, while the excess of hydrogen so formed passes away. Now, while the mercury is thus charged with hydrogen, it cannot oxidise, because of the presence of an excess of hydrogen. Thus, no matter what the character of the ore, the mercury under these conditions is always quick, and greedily attacks and absorbs the gold into itself.

Loss of gold

How to maintain the "quickness" of the mercury.

"So far the ingenious but simple method of maintaining the mercury in a quick condition. We now have to describe the equally ingenious and simple means whereby the pulverised gold ore is brought into absolute and maintained contact with the quick mercury. Floating upon the surface of the mercury is a

How to bring the powdered ore into continual contact with the mercury.

disc 40in. in diameter, which dimension leaves a narrow outside channel all round the edge of the pan where the mercury is uncovered. The centre of the disc has a circular hole in it, so as to clear the porous jar by about 2in. This central opening in the disc has a rim about 2in. high which forms a hopper. The disc as it floats on the mercury is slowly revolved by simple mechanism. The pulverised ore as it leaves the stamps or other crusher, flows into the hopper accompanied by a stream of water, and is then by centrifugal action carried under the revolving disc and rolled round in the mercury in ever-increasing circles, until it reaches the periphery of the disc, and consequently the outward channel between the edge of the disc and that of the pan. Here, freed from the pressure of the disc, the pulverised ore floats up and over the edge of the pan, and passes away, leaving behind it in the mercury every atom of gold it previously contained. This perfect extraction is due to the rolling action, which separates each particle of the ore and rolls it for some ten seconds in the bright, quick mercury, which wrests every atom of gold from it. The whole machine weighs only about 5 cwt., and its working capacity is 10 tons per day. It will be seen that the conditions which here obtain are the most perfect for the purpose of amalgamation. Owing to the perfection of contact no floating gold can escape, and in the presence of hydrogen no sickening of the mercury can take place. Hence, every particle of the gold is secured, unless mechanically encased in an atom of ore. The process has long since passed the experimental stage, but the Hydrogen-Amalgam Company, who are working the patents, were careful not to publish any particulars of the invention until it had assumed a practical form, and could be deemed a commercial as well as a scientific success. Machines are at work in the United States of America (where they have been tested and favourably reported on by Professor P. de Pierre Ricketts), the Transvaal, and Mexico, while some are now on their way to India, Australia, and New Zealand. It is stated that the increased quantity of gold extracted by this process has never been less than 10 per cent., and that in most cases a much larger percentage is reached. In short, this method of applying electricity, with the intervention of a porous wall or cell, has overcome all the difficulties previously encountered, while the

Machines at work in different countries.

Increased quantity of gold extracted.

whole cost of treatment by this process is said to amount to only about threepence per ton for both electrical and mechanical force, and for labour." From the *Times*, September 9th, 1887. Small cost of treatment by this process.

Chapter VIII.

Mr. Bullion and John Smith have just returned to England. They are pursuing their way steadily through certain streets in the great city of London, on foot, and with a decided air of business. A visit to the Mint.

Mr. Bullion: Well, John, your education is nearly complete so far as the history of metal money is concerned. At this moment we are on our way to the place where I propose that you shall take some finishing lessons.

John Smith: Which means that we are going to pay a visit to the Mint, does it not, sir? The Tower of London is close at hand, and I know that the Royal Mint is not far from it.

Mr. Bullion: You have made a good guess. Mr. Consol has promised to be there, and to shew us over the premises. There he is, standing at the entrance-gates looking for us. Mr. Consol.

Mr. Consol: Good morning, Bullion; you are pretty true to time. So this is the young man who wants to be let into all our secrets, is it? Well, sir (giving him his hand), you shall see all that is to be seen, only you must not try to pocket any of our money! Come this way. (He led them into the reception room, where they entered their names in the visitors' book.)

Mr. Consol: We are going to take things in their right order, so our first visit will be to the melting department. These blocks looking like bricks are called ingots. Just take this one into your hand. (John's hand involuntarily dropped with the weight of the ingot.) Ah! I thought you would be taken by surprise! Each of those ingots weighs 200 ounces, and is worth £800. Every ingot has to be tested by the assayer, and according to his report the melter adds either gold or alloy to bring the metal to its standard fineness,—twenty-two The melting department. Weight of gold ingots.

parts of fine gold to two parts of alloy. In this crucible the metal is melted, and then cast into bars like these you see, about 10 lbs. each in weight, and measuring twenty-one inches long, one and a half inches broad, and three-eighths of an inch thick.

Gold bars.

Silver bars.

John Smith: And is this what our silver coins are made of? (pointing to some rather dull-looking bars of metal.)

Mr. Consol: Yes; they do not look a very promising colour yet, do they? that dulness is the result of oxidation, or the coating of the alloy with oxide; but it is easily removed with acid, as you will see by-and-bye. The processes of manufacturing gold, silver, and bronze coins are so nearly the same, that if we follow up the history of these gold bars, you will know quite enough about coining.

John Smith: Is it quite certain that those bars have the right quantity of fine gold in them?

Mr. Consol: The assayer has to test every set of bars before they are allowed to be sent on to the coining department. But come with me and see what becomes of our gold bars.

They followed Mr. Consol into another large room.

Gold bars rolled and annealed.

Mr. Consol: These pairs of rolls are worked by steam. Just notice what an uncomfortable squeeze they can give! Each bar undergoes six or more pinches, which reduce it in thickness whilst its breadth is increased. After the pinches, the bars are enclosed in copper tubes, and put into the annealing furnace, where they are subjected to a dull red heat for twenty minutes.

Mr. Bullion: John looks as if he wanted to ask a question.

John Smith: I know that to *anneal* metal is to soften it by making it red-hot; but I should like to know why that is done to these metal bars.

Fillets brought to right thickness and weighed.

Mr. Consol: Those pinches between the heavy rolls make the bars too hard to receive a good impression from the dies with which the coins are stamped; so the metal is annealed in the manner I have just described. Here are some bars that have come from the annealing furnace, and must now go through the pinching process again until they are reduced to a thickness corresponding to that of the coins to be made. When the fillets (as these strips of metal are called) have been rolled and gauged until thought to be the right thickness, they are passed on to the tryer. Just observe what he is doing: he is cutting blanks from each fillet and weighing them.

John Smith: Is the weight of each blank obliged to be quite exact?

Mr. Consol: Should it vary so much as $\frac{2}{7}$ths of a grain, it is rejected, and sent back to the melting-room. We will now pass on to the cutting-room.

Cutting room.

Mr. Bullion: I hope you are taking it all in, John?

John Smith: Yes; I am making notes in my pocket-book of the weights Mr. Consol gives me, so that I may not forget them by-and-bye.

Making blanks.

Mr. Consol: Here we come to another stage in the proceedings. The fillets of metal are passed under these machines, and the blanks which are to become coins are punched out of them.

John Smith: What a lot of scraps of metal are left! I suppose they are not wasted?

Marking machines.

Mr. Consol: No; the value is in the fine grains of gold those scraps contain, so the scissel (as it is called) goes back to the melter. And now these blanks are further prepared for receiving their impression in a marking machine, which presses the edge of each piece inward.

John Smith: How fast they are done! The pieces flow from the machine like a stream of water.

Blanks annealed and washed.

Mr. Consol: The blanks have become hard again by all the rolling and punching the metal has undergone, so now they are once more sent to be annealed, otherwise they would not receive a clear impression. After this the gold blanks are put into hot dilute of sulphuric acid for a few minutes, to remove any oxide of copper from their surfaces. Then they are carefully washed and dried and are ready to be stamped. The beautiful bloom on the face of a new sovereign is due to this removal of the superficial copper.

Treatment of silver blanks.

John Smith: And what has been done to these silver blanks? They do look beautifully new, just like frosted silver.

Mr. Consol: You saw how dark and dull the silver looks at first? Well these blanks have been dipped in the acid and then dried in hot sawdust.

John Smith: I could not have believed it would have made such a difference to the look of them.

Press room.

Mr. Consol: This room which we have now entered is the press-room. In the lower part of the presses are dies, with movable steel collars surrounding them. Each blank drops into one of the steel collars, round the inside of which the milling is cut, and this is transferred to the edge of the coin at the same time that the two impressions are stamped upon its back and face from the two dies.

Stamping the coins.

Mr. Bullion: Look at the little ridges round the edge of a gold or silver coin, John, and you will know what Mr. Consol means by the milling.

John Smith: I see. Each blank is laid upon a die in the press, and the other die, which is fixed in the upper part of the machine, comes down upon it. That's very clever,—to stamp both sides of the coin and its edge with one heavy blow.

Mr. Consol: The machinery is very perfect, is it not? These boys have only to fill the tubes with blanks and the machinery connected with the press places each coin in the steel collar, stamps it, and removes it from the press. About ninety coins can be stamped per minute in each press, and as there are fourteen presses which can be kept going at one time, we make money here rather faster than most people can earn it, do we not?

John Smith: I should just think you do! Is there ever anything wrong about the coins made in these presses, sir?

Weighing the coins.

Mr. Consol: Occasionally, but not often. Now, come along and see the coins weighed. Twenty-three coins per minute is the rate at which the operation can be performed, and their exact weight is ascertained to within one hundredth part of a grain.

John Smith: A sovereign contains about 113 grains on issuing from the Mint, doesn't it, sir?

Mr. Consol: Yes; but you must remember that though the value of each soverrign depends on the weight of fine gold in it, there is also a certain amount of alloy in each coin, so that its full weight is, as nearly as possible 123¼ or 123·274 grains. It is not possible to be quite exact, so there is a limit, or *remedy* as it is called. No sovereign is allowed to be issued weighing more than 123·474 grains or less than 123·074 grains. The coins which come within this remedy are passed on to be issued, whilst the heavier and the lighter ones are sent back to the melting room.

John Smith: Altogether a good deal of the day's work seems to find its way back to the melting room.

Mr. Consol: Yes; but it would not do to be careless about our current coin. These little weighing machines were invented by a Mr. Cotton, formerly a director of the Bank of England, and are most wonderfully and perfectly constructed. You see, we have no less than 30 of them standing upon the tables in this room. The pieces of money are fed into a hopper at the top of each machine, a quantity at a time, so that one man can attend to several machines at once. The machinery pushes out the pieces, one at a time, from the bottom of the heap in the hopper; they rest for a moment on one pan of a pair of scales, and then fall over.

Inventor of weighing machine.

John Smith: Look, Mr. Bullion! Isn't it curious to see them coming; they are falling into different compartments!

Mr. Consol: That is the cleverest part of the dodge. That large heap of the coins which are falling off in the centre, consists of sovereigns of true weight, or within the remedy; those which drop to the right are over weight, whilst those to the left are under weight, and must all go back to the melting room.

John Smith: It is one of the most splendid machines I ever saw! But what a lot of weighing and fuss each coin goes through.

Mr. Consol: Even now these coins of true weight are not quite safe from the melting room. Come and take a look at another kind of machine. Several coins at a time are being shown off upon a cloth belt—first one side of them, and then the other. If any imperfection is detected upon either face of a coin, it is picked out, and back it goes to be melted down with the other rejected coins.

Imperfections picked out.

John Smith: It is lucky that so many of the coins come out all right, otherwise a lot of time and trouble would be wasted every day. But what becomes of the coins which are all right?

Mr. Consol: They are tied up in bags containing so many pounds' weight each. Then some of the contents of each bag are taken out, just as they come, and weighed and tested by certain officers of the Mint; and finally one piece of money from each bag is sealed up in a packet and put away in the *Pyx chest*, there to remain until the next "trial of the Pyx" comes on. Do you know anything about this "trial of the Pyx"?

Perfect coins.

Trial of the Pyx.

John Smith: I think I remember that the money in the Pyx chest is examined every now and then by a jury of the Goldsmiths' Company, to see that it is of the right standard and of true weight.

Mr. Consol: Yes; this takes place every year at the Goldsmiths' Hall. And now I think I have come to the end of all I have to show you.

John Smith: I am greatly obliged to you, sir, for all the trouble you have taken.

Mr. Bullion: Thank you very much, Consol. We have taken up a great deal of your time; but I am sure John has appreciated your kindness, and will make a good use of what he has seen.

British money coined at Melbourne and Sydney.

(N.B. I have thought it best to assume that gold as well as silver and copper coins were being coined at our British Mint. Sovereigns and half-sovereigns are also coined at Melbourne and Sydney. When this is the case, a very minute "M" or "S" will be found engraved under the impression of our Queen's head, just at the edge of the neck, or under the shield on the reverse side. The coins issued from our Mint are not thus lettered.—E. C. S.)

SECOND SERIES.

Chapter I.

You must now imagine that three months have elapsed since the last chapter of the first series was written. During that time John Smith has been working steadily at school; but he has not been forgotten by his friend, Mr. Bullion. To his great delight he has been invited to spend part of his Christmas holidays at a charming country house about three miles from Manchester, with Mr. and Mrs. Bullion, their daughter Alice aged seventeen, and their son William, aged fourteen years. I shall begin this chapter with an account of a conversation that took place between Mr. Bullion and John Smith on the evening of his arrival at Ingotsville.

John Smith's visit to Ingotsville.

Mr. Bullion's family.

Mr. Bullion: Whilst you are staying with us, John, shall you be inclined to pursue your coinage studies with me?

John Smith: I should like it awfully, sir. I have forgotten nothing yet, and you promised to show me, some day, how to make use of what you taught me.

Mr. Bullion: I believe I did make that promise, and I shall be quite ready to fulfil it as soon as I have explained to you a few more terms which are used expressly in speaking of money, Let me see; you already know something about the systems of exchange which were in use before metal money became the recognised medium of exchange in nearly all civilised countries; also, why metal is superior to all other substances for this purpose?

John Smith: Yes; and besides that I know how the metals are taken out of the earth and converted into money.

Mr. Bullion: Then comes the question,—What use can you make of this knowledge?

John Smith: And that's what I cannot answer, for I do not yet know what is to come of all your teaching.

Proposed practical lessons on the value and use of money.

Mr. Bullion: To-morrow, then, you shall begin a new and practical course of study, which I think you will enjoy sharing with Alice and Will, who are just now much interested in the same subject. I shall send you young people to do all our shopping for us, and you will have to give me an account of what you have spent each time by the help of the new system I am going to teach you.

John Smith: It sounds as if this new study was going to be a jolly one; but I have always been told that money was a very dry subject to take up.

Mr. Bullion: Probably you would find it dry if you had to sit down and read some of the books which have been written about it; but I don't think the subject need be an uninteresting one by any means if mastered in a practical manner. I believe you are fond of arithmetic, and so are my children; therefore you will not mind having to do some decimal multiplication and division, I hope?

John Smith: Not a bit; I like anything in that line. But have you time to-night, sir, to teach me the meanings of the new terms you were speaking of just now? If you have, I shall be ready to start fair with the others to-morrow.

Mr. Bullion: I shall be only too glad to have a talk with you now. You understand the difference between standard and token money, do you not? (Readers are recommended to refresh their memories on these points by turning back to Chapter II. First series.)

John Smith: Quite well, I believe.

Unit of value.

Mr. Bullion: Very well; then you are prepared to face the new facts I am going to give you. Three terms are employed in speaking of a nation's currency, which, although they need not mean the same thing, are closely related to one another. They are (1) coin; (2) unit of value; (3) money of account. The word *coin* needs no explanation, as you understand it already. The *unit of value* is a certain weight of standard metal, but it is not always made up into a standard coin. Sometimes it is too large or too small a quantity to be made into a convenient-sized coin; and when this is the case it is only necessary that current coins should be multiples or sub-multiples of the unit of value.

John Smith: I am afraid I don't quite take in all that yet, sir.

Mr. Bullion: Suppose there were no gold coins in England, but that silver was our standard metal. I do not think we should care to have one-pound pieces coined in silver—they would be so large and heavy; and yet our standard unit of value might be one pound all the same, and we might reckon half-a-crown to be an eighth part of it, a florin a tenth part, a shilling a twentieth part—and so on.

John Smith: I quite understand now, thank you.

Money of account.

Mr. Bullion: Then, as to the *moneys of account*, or numbers by which we express value, they need not be composed of either standard or current coin. Imagine a silver crown, or five-shilling piece, to be the money of account in England. For convenience sake it might never be coined, and yet we might express the value of things by saying that they were worth so many crowns or fractions of a crown. Our money of account would be a fourth part of the standard unit of value, supposing the latter to be one pound.

British sovereign.

John Smith; A sovereign really is our standard unit of value, I know; but what is our money of account, please, sir?

Mr. Bullion: In England it most conveniently happens that the principal coin, a gold sovereign, is both the unit of value and also the money of account for all large sums. Small sums are still spoken of as so many shillings, although a shilling is now only a token, instead of being, as in former time, the English money of account.

* * * * * * *

Shopping in Manchester.

At breakfast time the next morning, John Smith heard, to his great delight, that Will Bullion was going to drive him and Alice into Manchester, where they were to put up the pony and carriage for some hours, make various purchases, and lunch together at a coffee house. Mr. Bullion invited the young people to come to him in his study at eleven o'clock, so that he might give them their first lesson in "Norman's Single Grain System" before they started on their shopping expedition. As soon, then, as they were seated at his study table, with paper and pen before each of them, Mr. Bullion began, as follows:—

Norman's single grain system.

Denominational expression for a grain of gold in a gold standard country.

Mr. Bullion: The first thing we have to do is to find the denominational expression in British money of a single grain of gold. How many of these grains does a sovereign contain on its first issue from the Mint?

Will: 113·0016 grains, father.

Mr. Bullion: Then how are you going to set about discovering the demominational expression of a grain of gold?

They all shook their heads as Mr. Bullion looked from one to the other.

Alice: You must tell us, father, for we cannot be expected to guess this sort of thing, you know.

Mr. Bullion: There are 240 pence in a sovereign, are there not? Then if you will divide those 240 pence by the weight, namely, by 113·0016 grains of gold, which a British sovereign contains, you will get at the denominational expression in pence of a single grain of gold.

John Smith: What a duffer I must have been not to have thought of that when you asked how it was to be done, sir! (And before the others had finished their calculations he added): A grain of gold is worth 2·123863 pence, that is, as nearly as possible $2\frac{1}{8}$d.

Mr. Bullion: That is quite right. Well, now, I want you to make yourselves at home with this "single grain system" by keeping a faithful account of all that you spend when you go shopping for us, and by stating the price of each purchase that you make in grains and decimal parts of grains.

Will: That will require a good deal of consideration and totting up at first, father.

Alice: But what fun it will be! Don't you think so, John?

John Smith: I should rather think I did! It will be a great joke, and we must see which of us can be quickest at reckoning the number of grains each thing costs.

Mr. Bullion: As this way of reckoning money will require some practice, you had better work out for yourselves *the weight in grains of fine gold* of every British standard and token coin; you will have time to do this before you start.

Will: But, father, surely we must find out the number of grains of silver in each silver coin, and of copper in each copper coin?

Mr. Bullion: Not so, Will. Our silver and copper, or, rather, *bronze,* coins are only tokens; their value does not depend on the quantity of silver or copper they contain, but on their being legal tender for some fractional part of our standard coin, the gold sovereign. A shilling, for instance, represents the twentieth part of a sovereign, therefore its exchange value is the twentieth part of 113·0016 grains of gold. Here is a new pocket-book for each one of you in which all future reckonings are to be made.

Alice: You are a dear, delightful old father to have thought of everything like this.

Mr. Bullion: Remember, I am not to be expected to examine the contents of your pocket-books; but to-morrow morning I shall hope to find three fairly written-out accounts of to-day's shopping laid upon my table.

John Smith: Are we to give the price of each thing we buy in grains of gold only, sir?

Mr. Bullion: I think you must give both the price in money of each article, and also the number of grains of gold it is worth. Each of you shall have some commissions to do; your mother will provide you with your list of errands, Alice, whilst I make out a couple of papers for John and Will.

Before starting for their drive, the three young people made the following calculations, and entered them in their respective pocket-books:—

Denominational Expressions of British Coins, with their Real and Representative Weights in Fine Gold.

Denominational expressions of all the British coins with their real and representative weights in fine gold.

Standards.					
£1	contains	113·0016,	or about	113	grains.
10s	„	56·5008,	„	$56\frac{1}{2}$	„
Tokens.					
5s. 0d.	is worth	28·2504,	„	$28\frac{1}{4}$	„
2s. 6d.	„	14·1252,	„	$14\frac{1}{8}$	„
2s. 0d.	„	11·30016,	„	$11\frac{3}{10}$	„
1s. 0d.	„	5·65008,	„	$5\frac{13}{20}$	„
6d.	„	2·82504,	„	$2\frac{4}{5}$	„
3d.	„	1·41252,	„	$1\frac{1}{2}$	„
2d.	„	·94168,	or nearly	$\frac{9}{10}$	„
1d.	„	·4708,	„	$\frac{1}{2}$	„
$\frac{1}{2}$d.	„	·2354,	„	$\frac{1}{4}$	„
$\frac{1}{4}$d.	„	·1177,	or rather more than $\frac{1}{8}$ of a grain.		

Mr. Bullion: One thing more I wish you to bear in mind in

Conditions of standard metal money.

connection with standard metal money. It is this: If a metal is to become the monetary standard of a country, it must be received in unlimited quantities at the mint (or institution which answers to it), fitted for currency, and appointed unlimited legal tender.

John Smith: But I thought that was always the case?

Mr. Bullion: In some countries, both gold and silver are appointed unlimited legal tender, but they are not now both received in unlimited quantities at any mint. Those countries cannot properly be said to possess a *dual standard* or *bi-metallic currency*, for their international trade (that is, their trade with foreign countries) is conducted on the dearer metal only, therefore the dearer metal is their standard metal.

John Smith: I long for to-morrow, that we may begin our shopping!

Mr. Bullion: I told you that all your calculations will have to be made by means of a new system, but I must also tell you that this system is not my own.

John Smith: Then whose can it be?

Great Pyramid of Egypt.

Mr. Bullion: I shall answer your question with another Did you ever hear of the Great Pyramid of Egypt?

John Smith: Well, yes, I believe I have; but I can't say that I know anything about it.

Mr. Bullion: Then I must tell you a few particulars about this Great Pyramid before I can answer your question. It is a wonderful piece of masonry; the oldest and most wonderful that has ever been discovered. It has a square base, each side of which measures over 760 feet. The four sides, sloping inwards and upwards, meet at a point 486 feet above the base of the pyramid. Several years ago, Professor Piazzi Smyth (the Astronomer Royal for Scotland), Major Tracey, R.A., and other learned men found out some very interesting facts connected with this wonderful building and the plan of its erection. One of their discoveries was as follows: Inside the pyramid, there are two small chambers, approached by long passages; and certain measurements contained in one of these little rooms—the one named the "Queen's Chamber"—are the key to the standard of measure, according to which every part of the pyramid was planned and built. Many of these discovered measurements are found to agree with scientific facts which were

Professor Piazzi Smyth and Major Tracey, R.A.

Queen's Chamber standard of measure.

unknown to us until three or four thousand years after the building of the pyramid, such as the number of days in a solar year, and the distance of the sun from the earth.

John Smith: I certainly never heard about these things before, but I cannot think what the Great Pyramid of Egypt can have to do with the new system that you are going to teach us.

Mr. Bullion (laughing): I thought I should puzzle you by wandering so far from our subject; but now I will tell you in what respects these two seemingly different branches of study agree. Just as scientific men were led through the passages of the Great Pyramid until they reached the Queen's Chamber, wherein they found a standard of measure revealed to them by the hand of the architect who planned the building; so have you and I wandered together through one passage in the history of money to another, until at length, in this jubilee year of our gracious Queen's reign, a new standard of monetary measure has been revealed to us by the hand of a friend of mine, Mr. J. H. Norman. This standard of measure is a unit of weight, *a grain of precious metal*, and it is the key to the true value of every standard coin in the world.

Norman's single grain standard of measure.

John Smith: How very interesting! And will the grain of metal have anything to do with our shopping expeditions, sir?

Mr. Bullion: It will have everything to do with them, my boy, for I am going to try to make you, and Alice, and Will work out for yourselves by practical experience "Norman's Single Grain System."

Chapter II.

The three young people started in high spirits. They drove into Manchester at a brisk pace, and after putting up the pony, proceeded to consult their different lists of commissions.

Visit to Manchester.

John Smith: Ladies first! so, Miss Bullion, you must decide where our shopping is to begin.

Alice: Mother wants a whole lot of things at the ironmonger's, which I may as well get here (pointing to a shop close by); but you needn't come with me, for I daresay I shall be some time choosing all the things.

Will: We wouldn't miss seeing you do it on any account, Allie. Besides, I am sure you won't know how many grains of gold to give for each article without our help.

Alice Bullion at the iron-monger's.

Alice: Don't be so foolish, Will; we are not going to reckon by grains until we get home. (So saying, she walked into the shop and addressed herself to the first shopman she encountered). I want to look at some moderate-sized saucepans.

Shopman: Enamel-lined, miss?

Alice (trying to talk as much like her mother as possible). No; tin-lined will suit my purpose. (Having selected three she asked the prices of them.)

Shopman: This one is 1s. 8d., and the two smaller sizes 1s. 3d. and 1s. 2d.

Will (taking up the largest saucepan): How many grains of gold did he say this was worth?

Shopman: That size is 1s. 8d.

Will: Yes, I know. And how many grains of gold is that, Allie?

Alice (trying in vain not to smile): Hush, Will! (and she turned her back upon him). I will take these three saucepans, and I want a steamer that will fit the largest of them.

John Smith (in a low voice): That biggest saucepan is worth about $9\frac{1}{2}$ grains.

This time Alice could not help laughing, but she resolutely turned a deaf ear upon the two boys, and went steadily through her list of wants, interrupted first on one side of her and then on the other by such remarks as, "The water-can comes to 12·71268 grains;" "The pepper-pot at 1·8833 grains;" "Oh! I say; I haven't time to reckon if you go so fast!"

At length the bill was paid, and the goods ordered to be sent round to be put into the pony carriage. As soon as they had left the shop, Alice turned with a merry laugh to the two boys. "You really are behaving shamefully, you two!" she said. "I cannot have you going on like that in the shops."

The Tailor.

"We are only doing as we were bid," Will answered, and I shall tell father when we get home that you were a naughty, disobedient girl, who wouldn't reckon by grains as he expressly told you to do. But here is the tailor's; I have to pay a bill for father."

"Then I shall go on to the grocer's," said Alice, "and get over a little of my shopping in peace." When the boys rejoined Alice, they were laughing at some fresh joke. "I asked Mr. Hodder how many grains of gold my new coat and waistcoat were worth," said Will, "and he evidently thought I had taken leave of my senses."

The Grocer.

"You will really get us into trouble if you go on like this," remonstrated Alice; "do promise not to humbug in the shops, Will." "I shall make no rash promises, he replied. "But, I say, Allie: it is high time we went to the coffee-house and had some food; I am getting perfectly ravenous."

The boys behaved tolerably well over their luncheon, for John, being the visitor, was too polite to carry on a joke when he saw that Alice was really worried by it, and he managed to keep Will a little in check. Once a waiter looked astonished at Will gravely remarking, as the former set down a dish of cheese-cakes before them, "These cheese-cakes are worth as nearly as possible a grain of gold apiece!"

Coffee-house luncheon.

At length the day's shopping came to an end, and the young folks drove home, highly delighted with the outing they had had. Mr. Bullion was on the look-out for them. "Well, young people," he cried, as they drove up to the door: "and what sort of a day have you had?"

Home again.

"Awfully jolly, sir!" John answered.

"Only Allie turned prudish, and wanted to spoil our sport," Will added.

"Oh, no! Will," John exclaimed; whilst Alice retorted quite good-temperedly, "and a good thing that I *did* turn prudish, Master Will, when you began to question the shopmen as to the number of grains a thing was worth!"

"That was carrying your fun too far, my boy," Mr. Bullion said; "you never know when to stop. I only hope you were not rude to anyone?"

"Oh, no, father," Alice rejoined, quickly; "Will soon shut up. We have had a delightful day, and after tea we are going to sit in the schoolroom and write our papers for you." So saying, she ran into the house.

The next morning Mr. Bullion was duly informed that he would find three papers waiting for him in the study, and he promised to look them through, and be ready to talk them over by eleven o'clock. Alice and John were both in their places before the clock had finished striking the hour, and Will rushed in a few minutes afterwards; they were all anxious to hear the result of their calculations.

Mr. Bullion: I am very much pleased with your papers; they are very well done on the whole. Alice and John have made every item out correctly, whilst Will has only given one wrong figure.

Will: What, I? I thought mine was sure to be right; I did it so carefully.

Mr. Bullion: You shall each read your papers aloud; and when your turn comes, Will, I daresay the mistake will soon be explained. Alice, you are the eldest, so you shall open the proceedings.

Alice (with heightened colour): I declare you make me quite nervous, father! I am "not accustomed to public speaking," gentlemen, so you must excuse all mistakes. Well, I will first read you my list of ironmongery; I think it is a wonder I got that right, though, for the boys were bothering me every minute in that shop.

Will: I am sure we helped you ever so much. You would probably never have found out the value of your water-can, or your biggest saucepan either, if we hadn't reckoned it for you on the spot.

Mr. Bullion (rapping the table): Now, then, to business. Come, Alice!

List of ironmongery.

Alice (reading her paper): This is what I bought at Tapps:—

	Price. s.	d.		Grains of Fine Gold.
One water-can	2	3	or	12·7126
One saucepan	1	8	„	9·4168
One ditto...	1	3	„	7·0626
One ditto...	1	2	„	6·5917
One steamer	1	5	„	8·0042
One frying-pan	1	4	„	7·5334
One zinc washup	1	6	„	8·4751
One pepper-box	0	4	„	1·8833
One bucket	1	2	„	6·5917
One stewpan	3	3	„	18·3627
One pastry-board	3	6	„	19·7752
One dozen patty-pans	1	0	„	5·6500
Total... ...	19	10	„	112·0593

Mr. Bullion: That was a goodly list to work out, Alice; but it is all perfectly correct.

Alice: My grocer's bill is not nearly so long—only four items—and yet it comes to more altogether. List of grocery.

	Price. £	s.	d.		Grains of Fine Gold.
6lbs. coffee, at 1s. 8d. per lb. ...	0	10	0	or	56·5008
3lbs. tea, at 2s. 6d. per lb.	0	7	6	,,	42·3756
6lbs. lump sugar, at 3½d. per lb. ...	0	1	9	,,	9·8876
6lbs. Demerara sugar, at 2½d. per lb.	0	1	3	,,	7·0626
Total... ...	£1	0	6	,,	115·8266

Mr. Bullion: You have worked out your accounts very well indeed, Alice, and I have only one improvement to suggest. In stating the price of each separate article, in grains of fine gold, you are quite right to give the number of grains and fractions of grains in decimals to four or five places; but, after you have added the items together, you will be more correct if you give the total result in decimals of two or three places only. By-and-bye you can prove this for yourself by dividing 238 pence (the number of pence your ironmonger's bill comes to) by 2·123863 pence—that is, the denominational expression of one grain; you will then discover that the fourth decimal figure should be nine instead of three. John already realises this, I see; for his totals are given in decimals to three places only. Now, John, let us hear what you have made of your day's shopping.

John Smith: I first went to Robinson's, to pay for your new hall barometer, sir. That came to £3, or 339·004 grains of fine gold. Then followed our lunch at the coffee-house. We had as much beef from a hot joint as we wanted, with potatoes and bread, for sixpence each. Miss Bullion's glass of milk came to twopence; whilst Will and I each polished off a couple of bottles of ginger beer, at twopence a bottle. Our cheese-cakes—eight of them—were not at all equally shared, for Miss Bullion only ate one, whilst I managed three of them very comfortably, and Will had four. Barometer. Bill at coffee-house.

Mr. Bullion: Well done, Will! If you are the youngest of the party, you do your best to make up for it.

Will (laughing): I could have eaten four more of those cheese-cakes—only I didn't.

Mr. Bullion: Lucky for you to-day that you didn't I should say! Let us hear the items, and the total amount of your lunch bill, John.

John Smith (reading from his paper):—

	Price. s.	d.		Grains of Fine Gold.
Three of beef, &c., at 6d... ...	1	6	or	8·4751
One cheese-cake	0	2	„	·9416
Three ditto	0	6	„	2·8250
Four ditto	0	8	„	3·7667
One glass of milk...	0	2	„	·9416
Four bottles of ginger-beer, at 2d.	0	8	„	3·7667
Total... ...	3	8	„	20·716

Pony's feed, &c.

I also paid one shilling for the pony's feed of corn—that was 5·650 grains of fine gold; and the ostler's tip came to sixpence, or 2·825 fine grains.

Will: And now my turn has come. I am longing to know what is wrong.

Mr. Bullion: Let me see. Your mistake occurs in the second item of your tailor's bill, where you have stated the price in grains of fine gold of my seventeen-shilling vest to be 96·0513 grains. How did you arrive at that?

Will: I looked at my table, and there I saw that 10s. is worth 56·5008 grains; 5s. is worth 28·2504 grains; and 2s. is worth 11·3001 grains. These three amounts added together come to 96·0513 grains. Where's the mistake, father?

Will's manner of reckoning corrected.

Mr. Bullion: So that is the way you obtained your results, is it? Well now, I will tell you how *I* should set about finding the value of seventeen shillings. First, I should reduce my seventeen shillings to pence, and then I should divide my pence by 2·123863d.—that is, by the denominational expression of one grain of fine gold. This would produce 96·0542 grains—a more correct result than yours You were quite right, however, not to carry your calculations beyond three places in decimals, for your items were all large ones; and when that is the case the fewer decimal fractions you employ the more correct you will be, unless you choose to add greatly to your labour by working out the denominational expression of one grain of gold to at least nine or ten places in decimals; 2·123863d. you must remember, is only an *approximate* value of one grain of gold.

Will: Your way is certainly less roundabout than mine, and I quite see my mistake now.

Mr. Bullion: Then give us all your particulars, please, for you have only made that one mistake.

Will: Mr. Hodder's bill is the biggest of the lot, but I think Allie's account with Tapp was more troublesome to work out. This is what I paid:

Tailor's bill.

	Price. £	s.	d.		Grains of Fine Gold.
One frock coat (father's "Sunday go-to-meeting" one)	4	4	0	or	474·606
One vest (yours, father)	0	17	0	„	96·054
One overcoat (mine)	2	5	0	„	254·253
One pair of trousers (mine)	0	18	0	„	101·701
One coat & vest (the ones I have on now)	1	0	0	„	113·001
Total... ...	£9	4	0	„	1039·615

Hat and coal bills.

Mr. Bullion: Yes; your bill came to a good deal altogether.

Will: Then there was my new bowler—that was 6s. 6d., or 36·725 grains; and Mr. Clarke's coal bill came to two guineas, or 237·303 grains. But father, I don't yet see the *good* of our reckoning in grains of gold, like this.

Use of single grain system.

Mr. Bullion: I will try to make that clear to you, Will. Were I sure you would never be called upon to handle or think about any metal money except that which is circulated in Great Britain, I should still wish you to master this "Single grain system," because by it you will acquire a knowledge of the true value of every coin of the realm. I have already told you that the value of our silver and bronze token coins is much less than it passes for, and depends entirely on the number of grains of standard metal they represent; but there are very few people who recognise this important fact. I trust that from henceforth you three young people will never lose sight of this truth—namely, that silver and bronze coins are only tokens of gold in this land. I want you also, from this day forth, to think of *price* as a definite weight of fine metal, that metal which is the standard in the country where the price is quoted. You cannot get the article priced unless you can command this metal, or one of its tokens which has equivalent value with the metal. There is another great reason, however, for my wishing you to get into the habit of thinking that every coin you handle contains a certain number of grains of gold, or represents so many grains or fractions of a grain of fine gold. We are not going to stop at British coins; I want you all to be able to tell me by the end of this week the value in England of the moneys of account of every other country I may choose to name; and also the value in foreign countries of our own standard money of account.

(There was a general outcry at this proposal.)

Value in English money of moneys of account in foreign countries.

Alice: My dear father! You are giving us a dreadfully short time in which to get all that into our heads. Why, I don't suppose that either one of us knows the value of ten foreign coins yet!

Mr. Bullion: I did not say that I should expect you to know the names and values of all the foreign moneys of account *by heart*, now, did I, Alice?

Alice: No; but I thought we should be obliged to do so.

Mr. Bullion: You shall each be provided with a copy of Mr. Norman's Money Table, which gives all the particulars you can possibly want, and then I shall expect you to make good use of it.

Will: *Do* let us begin this morning, father.

Mr. Bullion: I cannot possibly do that, Will, for I have to go into Manchester almost immediately. But to-morrow morning at eleven o'clock I shall be ready to give another lesson in the use of "Norman's Single Grain System."

Value and price.

I have just ten minutes to spare you yet, I see (looking at his watch), so I will put a question to you all. Can either of you tell me the difference between the meanings of the two words "Value" and "Price"?

Will's definition.

Will: "Price" is what is given for a thing, and "value" is what it is worth.

Mr. Bullion: Come, Alice, I hope you can give me a rather better definition than that!

Alice's definition.

Alice: You have already told us that "price" means a definite weight of standard metal, father; and as to "value," why, I suppose the value of any article we buy is shown by the amount of standard metal we have to give for it?

Mr. Bullion: You are right as to "price," but I cannot say that your definition of "value" is much better than Will's, my dear. Now then, John, let us hear what *you* have to say about it.

John Smith: I confess to feeling very shakey on the subject, sir, but I should define "value" thus: it is the relation of a commodity, article, or utility possessed by one individual, to the need of another person.

John's definition.

Will: You're too grand for me, John. I can't understand you.

John Smith: I'll try to make myself plainer. If I were travelling in a desert, and had run short of victuals, I should be ready to give my gold watch (if I possessed one) to the first traveller I met with who was able to supply my need; whereas the *price* of the goods, if bought in a shop, would be something very small compared to the price of a gold watch.

Mr. Bullion: Your definition is good as far as it goes. But I want to have no mistake in your minds as to the distinction between "Value" and "Price." Barter, as you know, preceded the use of a standard of value and a means of payment. Under a system of barter there was no such term as price. There are two descriptions of value, viz., *cost value*, and *exchange value*.

Mr. Bullion's definition.

Cost value is the sum of value-giving factors expended upon anything. These value-giving factors are labour, land and water (where rent is paid), shelter, machinery, interest on capital, and any other factors costing anything, which have helped to make the commodity or service exposed for sale or exchange.

Cost value.

Exchange value is that for which anything can be exchanged.

Exchange value.

Barter and price illustrated.

Let us suppose that I adopt the barter system, and exchange Manchester shirtings for Indian wheat (I choose these two commodities for my examples, because you will have more to do with them hereafter). The amount of wheat that a Calcutta merchant would offer me for, say, 1,000 pieces of Manchester shirtings, would depend on the amount of labour and other value-giving factors which he knew to have been expended on the production of the wheat and the preparation of it for sale, compared with the amount of labour and other value-giving factors which had been expended on the manufacture of the shirtings.

Alice: I see that as plainly as can be, now.

Mr. Bullion: But suppose I determine to adopt the monetary system, and to sell my Manchester shirtings in India—now comes in *price*. It depends on the market price of shirtings in India at the time of the sale, whether I receive in exchange for my shirtings a weight of Indian standard metal (represented you must remember by standard Indian money) equivalent to the cost value of the shirtings.

Will: Are cost value and exchange value the same thing, father?

Mr. Bullion: By no means. Sometimes a commodity that is fashionable or in great request will fetch a far higher exchange-value than it would if its cost value alone were calculated: whereas the disclosures (for instance) made lately in connection with the sweating system, show us only too plainly that many working men and women are at present receiving starvation remuneration in return for a vast expenditure of labour and other value-giving factors. The exchange value of their work is far below its cost value.

John Smith: I suppose the exchange value of everything is regulated by the price it can fetch?

Supply and demand.

Mr. Bullion: That is a question of what political economists call "supply and demand"—the greater the demand the greater must be the supply. Under a monetary system the greater the demand for any particular commodity, the more likely that its exchange value will be a *price* or *weight of standard metal* equivalent to its cost value. But when you have studied political economy you will find that the conditions of barter or exchange are not supposed to have been in the slightest degree altered by the later introduction of the monetary system. It is stated that prices may rise and fall owing to certain causes which affect the precious metals, but that the terms upon which goods are exchanged are governed by the principles of barter.

Monetary system does not affect principles of barter.

Chapter III.

Mr. Bullion had no cause to complain of any lack of interest on the part of his pupils in "Norman's Single Grain System." Several times during the day he overheard Alice and the boys talking of it, and at eleven o'clock the next morning the three young people were waiting for him, with their books and pencils, all in a hurry to begin.

Mr. Bullion: Come, now, I call this punctuality. Although

my school is small, it is very select, and my scholars show no signs of falling off as yet.

Will: If all school work was like this, father, we should not bumbug our masters nearly so much.

Mr. Bullion: You're a nice sort of fellow—to talk as if masters must be humbugged unless they can make all your work pleasant and interesting for you! I call upon you, in consequence, to answer the first question: How did you find out what the denominational expression of a grain of fine gold is in England, where gold is the only standard metal used for money?

Will: I have not forgotten how to do that yet. There are 240 pence in one sovereign, and there are 113·0016 grains of fine gold in a sovereign on its issue from the Mint; 240 divided by 113·0016 gives 2·123863 pence, and that is the denominational expression, as near as we need reckon it, of one grain of fine gold in the currency of the United Kingdom.

Mr. Bullion: You have really driven that into your head, I see. Now, tell me, Alice, what use you have so far made of this discovery.

Alice: After we had been shopping we divided each sum of money we spent by the denominational expression in pence of a grain of fine gold, and that gave us the price in grains of fine gold of each thing we had bought.

Denominational expression of a grain of silver in India.

Mr. Bullion: So far, so good. The hardest question falls to John Smith's lot. In some countries—India, for silver—silver is the standard metal, not gold. How would you find out the denominational expression of a grain of fine silver in India, John? Take your time to think out the problem.

(John Smith walked about the room for a few minutes, with his hands in his trousers pockets, and then returned to his seat.)

John Smith: If only I knew how many grains of fine silver there are in a rupee, I could do it, sir.

Mr. Bullion (smiling): There are 165 grains of fine silver in a rupee on its issue from the mint. Come, Alice and Will, set your brains to work; John is on the right track.

(In a very few minutes John was ready.)

John Smith: There are 192 pies in one rupee, and 165 grains of fine silver. So I divided 192 by 165, and find that 1·16363 pies is the denominational expression of a grain of fine silver in India.

Mr. Bullion: Well done, John; that is perfectly right.

Alice: I do think you must be very clever, John; for I was not a bit the better off for knowing how many grains of silver a rupee contained.

Will: I could have done it quite easily if I had only known how many pies a rupee is worth.

Price of a grain of silver in a gold standard country.

Mr. Bullion: But that "if" made all the difference, Will. John has been studying the money question for some time now, and I expect you will find that he knows a good many things that you don't. The next problem, however, I think will stump even our young friend. How can you find out the gold price of one grain of fine silver in a country like England, where gold is the standard metal?

John Smith (after some minutes' thought): I cannot make head or tail of that problem, sir.

Mr. Bullion: It was not to be expected that you could, so I will explain it without further loss of time. The first thing to be discovered is the latest gold price of silver in London which can be found out by referring to the daily papers. I saw this morning, under the heading "London Stock Exchange. "Bar silver, 44d."

Alice: How very strange, to buy silver by the pound!

Mr. Bullion: Silver is always quoted as being worth so much *per ounce.* Yesterday, therefore, it was worth 44d. per ounce. Bar silver is always reckoned to contain 444 grains of fine silver in every ounce weight of metal, the other 36 grains being alloy. And this is the way to solve the new problem: Divide the 44d. by 444, and that will give you ·099099 pence, which is the gold price of one grain of fine silver in England just now.

John Smith (after making a rapid calculation in his note book): 165 grains multiplied by ·099099 make 16·3513 pence, so that was the price of an Indian rupee in England yesterday, about $16\frac{3}{10}$d.

Mr. Bullion: Just so; you have a capital head for making practical use of any fresh information you pick up, John. Formerly silver was worth 60d. per ounce in England, so you see it has declined greatly in price.

Alice: Let me guess what comes next, father. Isn't it, how to find out the price of a grain of fine gold in a silver-standard country?

Price of a grain of gold in a silver standard country.

Mr. Bullion: That is it, Alice. And what else can you guess?

Alice: That to do so we must first know the market price of gold in that country.

Mr. Bullion: Capital, girl! To-day India shall be our silver standard, and England our gold standard country; but, when you understand these problems perfectly, I shall set you to work out some exchanges between less well-known countries. Gold is reckoned by the *tola* in India, a tola being 180 grains of fine gold. Let us suppose the market price of gold in India to-day to be 22 rupees, 14 annas, 3 pies per tola; how many pies is that?

Will: (grumbling): It is these stupid old outlandish coins that stump me.

John Smith: 12 pies 1 anna, 16 annas 1 rupee, Will.

(With this help Alice and Will were not far behind John with their figures when he gave out as follows:)

John Smith: 4,395 pies, sir.

Mr. Bullion: Right. Then what comes next?

Will (speaking in a great hurry): Divide it by 180.

Mr. Bullion: Quite correct, Will. Divide the 4,395 pies, the price of a tola or 180 grains of fine gold, by 180, so as to find out the price of one grain. Let Will do this sum, John, you are too quick for him and Alice.

Will (after a short reckoning): 24·4166 pies is the Indian silver price of a grain of fine gold.

Mr. Bullion: Right again, Will. By this time I am sure you can easily find out the price of a British sovereign in India.

Price of a British sovereign in India.

Alice: By multiplying 113·0016 grains of fine gold, the number contained in a sovereign, by 24·4166 pies, the price of one grain, is it not, father?

Mr. Bullion: Yes, to be sure. Who will have done that first, Alice, or Will? (To Will's great delight, he finished his sum before his sister).

Will (reading out his figures with a loud voice): A British sovereign is worth 14 rupees, 5 annas, 11 pies to-day in India.

Oh, this is famous! give us some shopping to do for you over in India, do, father.

Mr. Bullion: Two more problems, and only two, remain, which I want you to master before you will be quite fit to undertake my foreign affairs for me. These two problems are (1) How to find out the proportion established between gold and silver in a gold standard country; and (2) How to find out the proportion established between silver and gold in a silver standard country.

Will: Are we obliged to learn this before we can go on to the interesting part? I do not see what use it will be to us.

Proportion established between gold and silver in a gold standard country.

Mr. Bullion: Have a little more patience, Will, and I think you will find out that this is a useful thing to know. Let us first take—How to find out the proportion between gold and silver in our own country. Divide the gold price of silver by the denominational expression of one grain of fine gold; do you follow me?

John Smith (jotting down some figures rapidly): Yes, sir. Divide 44d., which is to-day the gold price of one ounce of silver, by 2·123863d., the denominational expression of a grain of fine gold. That comes to 20·71 grains of fine gold.

Will: How can that be? You divide a larger number of pence by a smaller number of pence, and then call the result *grains!* That won't do, Master John.

John Smith (laughing): Won't it do, my young friend? Let us see: 2·123863d. represents one grain, doesn't it?

Will: Yes; that is the denominational expression of one grain of fine gold.

John Smith: Then, if 2·123863 goes into 44d. 20·71 times, 20·71 grains of fine gold is the price of an ounce of silver. Aha, Master Will, I have you there!

Will: So you have; but you shan't catch me again in a hurry.

Mr. Bullion: Now that John has decided that knotty point, let me finish my problem. You must recollect that an ounce of silver contains 444 grains of silver. Therefore, if 444 grains of fine silver can be bought for 20·71 grains of fine gold, how are you going to discover the proportion established between gold and silver in this country?

(John and Alice began speaking at the same moment; so

John immediately held his tongue, and allowed Alice to answer her father's question.)

Alice: Divide 444 by 20·71, and that will give the proportion.

Mr. Bullion: Alice is quite right; she ran neck and neck with John this time.

John Smith (who has meanwhile made the calculation): 21·43 parts of silver go to one grain of gold in England just now.

Will: Does that mean that a grain of gold is worth nearly 21½ grains of silver?

Mr. Bullion: Yes. And can either of you see how to apply this knowledge of the proportion established between gold and silver?

Alice (very hesitatingly): I suppose if a merchant came over to England from India, bringing a whole lot of silver with him, he could find out how much gold it was likely to fetch by dividing the number of grains of fine silver his money contained by 21·43.

Mr. Bullion: You are quite right, Alice; I am pleased to find you are taking to this subject so well. Having found out in this manner how much gold his silver was fully worth, the merchant would next find out what percentage he would have to pay for effecting the exchange—it would be something very small—and then he would know what price he could get for his silver.

Will: I now see the good of learning this, though I am longing to go shopping in foreign countries.

Mr. Bullion: Well, we will get over the last problem now, and to-morrow morning you shall go to India and do various commissions for me.

Proportion established between silver and gold in a silver standard country.

John Smith (eagerly): Do give me a few minutes, sir, so that I may try to work out the proportion established between silver and gold in a silver standard country: I think I can do it.

Mr. Bullion (smiling): Well; go ahead, then.

Will: I am sure *I* couldn't do it! (So he amused himself by drawing pigs with his eyes shut, whilst Alice knitted her brows and tried in vain to follow John's example. After ten minutes' hard work John looked up triumphantly.)

John Smith: I believe I have it all right, sir; I like working out these jolly sums.

Mr. Bullion: Let us hear what you make of it.

John Smith: The price of 180 grains of fine gold is 4,395 pies—this I divided by 1·16363 pies, the denominational expression of a grain of fine silver, and it came to 3,775 grains of silver.

Will: 3,775 grains of silver the price of 180 grains of gold!

John Smith: Just so. Then I divided the 3,775 by the 180 grains, and find that the proportion established between silver and gold in India is 20·97 parts of silver to one of gold.

Mr. Bullion: Well done, John! That was a sum requiring a good deal of thought. But we have had a long sitting to-day, and it is high time you all went out. To morrow morning at eleven o'clock I shall be ready to send you all to India on my behalf.

Chapter IV.

Commercial dealings between India and England.

Will: Now, then, ladies and gentlemen, take your seats; the boat is just about to start for H.M.S. "Salamander," and you will be frizzling in Calcutta in another three weeks.

Mr. Bullion: Wait a bit, young man, you are too fast. Please to recollect that I am a Manchester cotton manufacturer, and until you have received a commission from me, you cannot leave Manchester.

John Smith: Besides which, a man-of-war would not be the kind of vessel in which you and your goods would be sent to India, Will. I hope you will give *me* your commission, sir, for I am much steadier than your junior clerk.

Alice: And what am I to do? I will not be left out in the cold!

Mr. Bullion: Dear, dear! I do believe I shall have to let all three of you go together! Yes; that will be my best plan, and I will furnish each one of you with a separate commission.

Will: Shall we have to give the prices of everything in grains of gold or silver?

Mr. Bullion: Most certainly, Will. Do not forget that the *real price* of everything that can be obtained for money, is a certain weight of standard metal, and that all kinds of paper money, and coins other than standard coins, are *signs* of these standard weights. I hope you now remember the difference between standard and token coins?

Will: To be sure I do. A standard coin contains the full weight of standard metal, and a token does not. But I tell you what I do not know, father, and that is, how much a sovereign weighs altogether with its alloy. I only know that it contains 113·0016 grains of fine gold.

John Smith: I can tell you. A sovereign weighs 123·274 grains troy; so that it contains about 10·27 grains of alloy.

Mr. Bullion: And an Indian rupee weighs 180 grains troy —that is, 165 grains of fine silver and 15 grains of alloy. Now, then, Alice, take down what I am going to dictate to you. I will give over to your care 3,000 pieces of Manchester shirtings (packed in 50 bales), at 7s. 11¼d. per piece. The freight, insurance, and all other charges will cost you £53 2s., so you must add that sum to the price of the shirtings. When you get to Calcutta, a well-known firm whose address I will give you will be ready to buy the shirtings of you at 5 rupees per piece, and you will find that you will have to pay 3 per cent. for all Indian charges, which you must remember to deduct from the sum you make by the shirtings. What have you written down, so far?

Alice's commission.

Alice (reading): Three thousand pieces of Manchester shirtings, at 7s. 11¼d. per piece; £53 2s. for expenses at starting. The shirtings are to be sold at Calcutta for 5 rupees per piece, less 3 per cent. for Indian charges.

Mr. Bullion: That is right.

Alice: Then, father, dear, may I ask a question before I begin my sum?

Mr. Bullion: By all means, my dear.

Alice: I want to know what the *expenses* are that you spoke of just now—freight, insurance, Indian charges? And when you were talking of an Indian merchant, yesterday, you said he must find out what percentage he would have to pay before parting with his silver in England.

Mr. Bullion: Your question reminds me that I have never yet talked to you about "metal points;" but it is very necessary that you should understand the meaning of this term before

Metal points.

working out any foreign commissions for me. "Metal points" is a technical term meaning *the limits within which exchanges may vary*, the boundaries of these limits being the cost of sending metal from one country to another, coinage, and other charges. I will just read to you a passage from Mr. Norman's pamphlet on his "Single Grain System," referring to exchanges between England and India, and his remarks apply equally to all other foreign exchanges. He says: "The *Daily News* quotation of the price of silver is not a sufficient guide alone to the rate of exchange which you will find existing with India. You must know whether India is requiring or parting with silver. The knowledge of the par of exchange, and this knowledge combined, would enable you to make a good estimate of the rate that should exist. To ascertain what the metal points are, it is necessary to know the regulations of each mint in the world—that is, the charge for coinage; the time occupied between the presentation of the standard metal and its return in the shape of coins by the mints; the expenses connected with packing and shipping the metal, and the extra length of time requisite for the release of the coin from the mint to which it is sent, over that occupied by the transmission of a bill, payable on demand—these are essential items of information. This information, together with the knowledge of the par value between countries of gold for gold, silver for silver, gold for silver, or silver for gold, is the foundation of the exchanges, and should be understood by everyone."

Alice (dolefully): Well, I did hope that we had learnt enough to be able to do these foreign commissions right off; but now it appears that there is a whole lot more to be learnt!

Mr. Bullion (laughing): You do look melancholy, to be sure! But cheer up, Alice; I am not going to take any of you into the mysteries of "metal points." That is a subject to be studied by those who really make foreign exchanges—whether in metal or commodities—the business of their lives. I will, in all cases, tell each one of you what percentage you are to reckon for expenses; but it was necessary that you should understand the meaning of these charges.

Alice: Thank you, father; that is a great relief to my mind. One more question, please. I suppose we are to reckon a rupee to be worth 1s. 4·35d., as John made it out to be the other day?

Mr. Bullion: No; I wish to put a fancy price upon our rupee to-day, so that when you arrive at the next stage—that of working out these foreign commissions entirely without help, —you may not find half your calculations waiting for you at your fingers' ends.

Will: Oh, father; how very wily of you to make sure of not giving us too much help!

Mr. Bullion: Yes, Master Will. After to-day you must depend entirely on your own wits, for I shall not so much as squeak until your papers are handed in, done or not done. This morning, therefore, we will suppose silver to have risen greatly in price, and everything shall be reckoned at the prices which existed 14 years ago. Imagine a rupee to be worth 22·65d., if you please, Alice; and try to begin your paper whilst I am talking to the others.

Will's commission.

Your turn shall come next, Will, and then you can be doing your paper whilst John and I are having it out. Write down 3,000 pieces of Manchester shirtings, at 7s.11¼d. per piece.

Will: Oh, father, please don't give me the same order as Allie; there will no fun at all in that!

Mr. Bullion: You are too ready to cry out, Will. I am not going to give you the same commission as Alice, but you are both to be entrusted with the sale of the same quantity of shirtings at Calcutta, after which it will be interesting to see which of you will realise the largest profits on your different transactions, for instead of sending me the money, as Alice will have to do, you, Will, are to invest the amount you make by your shirtings in wheat, and then you will have to bring the Indian wheat home to England and sell it for me.

Will (looking delighted): Hooray! that's something like a commission. I shall like doing that, father, very much.

Mr. Bullion: Well; put down £53 2s. at starting for the freight, insurance, &c. of your Manchester shirtings, and then go with Alice to my friends' house of business, and sell the shirtings at five rupees per piece, less 3 per cent. for all Indian charges. So far, you and Alice will be together, and you will be her natural protector, I hope.

Alice (looking up from her paper and laughing): Father, dear, you look quite grave, and talk as if I was really going out of the country, and likely to require a protector.

Mr. Bullion: To be sure I do, otherwise there would be no moral to my tale. When the shirtings are disposed of, Alice will only have to arrange about remitting the money to me through a Calcutta banker, to whom I shall give her a letter of introduction. Hullo, though! We have said nothing about sending home the money, have we, Alice? The expenses of sending the silver to England and selling it in London must be reckoned to cost 1 per cent.

Alice: Well, luckily, I had not arrived as far as sending home my silver yet.

Mr. Bullion: Make a note of that 1 per cent., so that you may not forget it. Well, Will, my boy, the next part of your programme will be, that as soon as you have been paid so many rupees for your Manchester shirtings, you must invest your silver in a cargo of wheat. You may reckon the price of your Indian wheat to be 16·12 rupees per quarter, including freight to England and all charges.

Will (writing busily): Woa, please, father; I haven't quite done. Indian wheat to be bought at 16·12 rupees per quarter, all charges included. You give one rather hard sums, I must say, father.

Mr. Bullion: On your return to England you are to sell the Indian wheat for me at 35s. per quarter (does not the English farmer wish he could command that price for his wheat!); and from the sum you realise by the sale of the wheat, you will have to deduct 2 per cent. for London charges. There's your commission, Will.

Will: And a mighty long one it is! but I mean to tackle it. Mind you give John a stiff lot of it, won't you, father?

Mr. Bullion: If you don't take care, John will soon overtake you, even with a paper much harder and longer than either yours or Alice's. I warn you, John, that I am going to quote all sums of money and prices of commodities in grains of standard metal, which you must turn into pounds, shillings, pence, and rupees, when doing your paper.

John Smith: That ought not to take me any longer than turning the coins named into standard metal.

Mr. Bullion: No; I do not think it will hinder you. Your work for me will not begin until you have arrived in India; so I hope you will keep an eye on my young people, and be ready to lend a helping hand, or, rather, a helping *brain*, when wanted.

John (laughing): All right, sir.

John's commission.

Mr. Bullion: Well, once you are in India, the first thing I wish you to do is to call on my Calcutta banker, and ask him to make known to you some reliable Indian wheat merchant. By the time you get to Calcutta my banker will have heard from me, and will be ready to assist you in this manner, and also to let you draw upon him for the amounts you will require for my commissions. Having been directed to a wheat merchant, you are to give him an order for 2,707·62 quarters of wheat, for which he will charge you 2,600 grains of fine silver per quarter; this charge to include shipping and all other expenses.

John Smith: Will the merchant undertake to send the wheat to England for me, then?

Mr. Bullion: Yes; it will be safely shipped without any more trouble on your part. But the purchase of the wheat will only be the beginning of your work. I will give you the address of a London agent, whom you can employ to sell your wheat for you in the London markets. He is a capital man, and will observe any directions you give him implicitly. As soon as the wheat is bought, you must write to this agent and desire him to receive the wheat, and to sell it for you at 197·572 grains of fine gold per quarter. The proceeds of the sale you must arrange to have sent out to you in three different forms.

John Smith: My London agent will require an angelic disposition if he is to take all this trouble for me.

Mr. Bullion (smiling): Very well, then, we will conclude that such is the case, for these instructions must positively be carried out. (1) One-third of the proceeds of the sale is to be remitted to you through a London banker in the form of gold; it will reach you *less* $\frac{3}{4}$ *per cent.* for carriage and other charges, and you will have to convert the gold into silver. (2) You are to desire your London agent to invest another third part of the wheat-money in silver, and to send that commodity out to you. The charges for shipping, brokerage, packing, and freight will be only $\frac{7}{8}$ of 1 per cent., but on its reaching India you will have to pay for coinage charge $2\frac{1}{8}$ per cent., and other charges $\frac{1}{8}$ of 1 per cent.—$2\frac{1}{4}$ per cent. in all.

Will: My word! isn't father giving you a long sum, John!

John Smith (shaking his head): It sounds an awful lot of it, I must say.

Mr. Bullion: You won't find it too much for your long head when you come to do it, I hope. At all events we have reached the last item. The remaining third part of the proceeds of your wheat sale is to be invested in Manchester shirtings, at 46·8475 grains of fine gold per piece, the price to include freight and all charges to India. When you receive these pieces of Manchester shirtings, be good enough to sell them for me at 825 grains of fine silver per piece, and let me know what profit you make upon the transaction after paying 3 per cent. for all Indian charges. There, John, when you come to write out the problems in order, I do not think they will frighten you much. Now, put away work, all of you; you may have a good go at them this evening before supper time, and recollect, I am willing to give help if required.

Chapter V.

(John Smith and Alice and Will Bullion are waiting to hear the result of their work last night. Their papers were placed upon the study table before breakfast, and they are wandering about the garden listening for the signal agreed upon. At last Mr. Bullion opens the window and whistles, whereupon the three young people scamper into the house and arrive breathless in the study.)

Report on commissions.

Mr. Bullion: You have all done your papers so remarkably well that I have decided on giving you a set of questions to work out, with the help of Mr. Norman's "Tables," before we talk over these Indian commissions. Let them, therefore, form part of your examination papers.

Will: So we haven't made any mistakes this time, father?

Mr. Bullion: Hardly any, Will—just a few slips of the pen. Your work shows that you have, each one of you, grasped the "Single Grain System," I am glad to say.

Alice: It is a comfort to know that we have not done badly, at all events.

John Smith: But what I now want to know, sir, is why you think this way of working out foreign exchanges better than the ordinary method, which is very simple? For instance, 3,000 pieces of shirting at 7s. 11¼d. per piece comes to £1,190 12s. 6d. Freight, &c., to India, £53 2s.—£1,243 14s. 6d. in all. The shirtings are sold at Calcutta for 5 Rs. per piece, a rupee being reckoned worth 22·65d. You reduce £1,243 14s. 6d. to pence, and divide by 22·65d.; the answer is in rupees. Deduct 3 per cent. for Indian charges, and there you are.

Ordinary methods of working out foreign exchanges.

Mr. Bullion: Yes, there you are, no doubt; but there isn't one ordinary person in a hundred to whom the answer, given in rupees instead of in English money, conveys any idea as to whether you gained or lost by the transaction. But when you put it in my way—Manchester shirtings, bought in England for so many grains of fine gold, and sold at Calcutta for so many grains of fine silver, for which you can command so many grains of fine gold—you see at a glance whether you have lost or gained by the transaction, by comparing your two weights of fine gold, which are the real prices of your commodities.

Single grain system. Comparative weights of standard metal seen at a glance.

John Smith: I see that, now.

Mr. Bullion: The same rule applies to all countries where there is a standard currency—America, China, Germany—no matter with which of them you wish to effect a monetary exchange, or to deal commercially. The "Single Grain System" shows you at once the comparative weights of standard metal to be paid or received. One more application of the "Single Grain System" I wish to make clear to you before handing you Mr. Norman's "Tables" and giving you your examination questions.

John Smith: Is it about the quotations of foreign exchanges in the daily papers, sir? For I have been longing to understand those quotations.

Mr. Bullion: Then, I am glad to say that is the very matter I wish to explain to you. Under the heading, "American Markets," you will find in most daily newspapers *three quotations*, dated from New York, namely: (1) Exchange on London (sixty days' sight); (2) Exchange on Berlin; (3) Exchange on Paris (sixty days). Here is my morning paper. Let us take

Foreign exchanges.

the first quotation: "Exchange on London at sixty days' sight, 4·86¾." This message was telegraphed from New York yesterday, to let business people know what was the rate of exchange between the United States, America, and England on that day. What is the money of account in America?

Exchange on London.

John Smith: I suppose it is a dollar.

Mr. Bullion: Yes; a gold dollar of 100 cents, as you will find by referring to Mr. Norman's "Tables" by-and-bye; and each gold dollar contains 23·22 grains of fine gold.

Alice: Then a dollar is worth ever so much less than a sovereign, father.

Mr. Bulllion: A good deal less, Alice. The first point you have to remember is that the figures 4·86¾ *must represent either American dollars or a British sovereign, or parts of a sovereign,* because the exchange is between the United States of America and England.

Will: This is dreadfully difficult, isnt it?

Mr. Bullion: Not a bit of it: you will understand all three quotations perfectly in the course of a few minutes, if you will give me your full attention. The money of account in England, a sovereign, contains 113 grains of fine gold; the American money of account—a gold dollar, contains 23·22 grains of fine gold. How many dollars do you think you could get for a sovereign? How many times will 23·22 go into 113?

Will: Quite four times, I should think.

Mr. Bullion: Very well. Then we will conclude that 4·86¾ represents the dollars and parts of a dollar that America was giving yesterday per British sovereign. We can soon prove it. Divide 4·86¾, that is, 4·8675, by 4·3066 cents, which is the denominational expression in America of a grain of fine gold. Give us the result, John, as soon as you can.

John Smith (after a few minutes' work): There are 113·024 grains of gold in 4·8675 dollars, sir.

Mr. Bullion: Quite right. The whole numbers, you see, are the same as those contained in our sovereign, subtract 113·001 from 113·024.

Alice (after scribbling in great haste): I've done it, father, ·023 remains.

Mr. Bullion: Very well: your result shows that yesterday America was paying England a very small premium—about ⅛ per mil—for gold. The quotation, therefore, reads thus: "At New York, yesterday, the exchange on London was at the rate of 113·024 grains of fine gold for 113·001 grains.

John Smith: But how did you get at the premium paid by America, which you say is about $\frac{1}{5}$ per mil?

Mr. Bullion: How do you multiply decimal figures by 1,000?

John Smith: By moving the point three places to the right.

Mr. Bullion: Quite so; this would convert ·023 into 23·000 grains. Divide the 23·000 grains by 113·001, the number of grains contained in a sovereign, and the result will be ·2 grains; that is, $\frac{1}{5}$th per mil.

Will: It is not so very difficult, after all.

Exchange on Berlin.

Mr. Bullion (smiling): Somehow, things never are so hard when once you understand them, Will. Sometimes, however, the rate will express grains of metal in a fractional part of the money of account of one country, for a definite number of the moneys of account of another country. This is the case when the exchange on Berlin is quoted. If you look at Mr. Norman's "Tables," you will see that the money of account of Germany is a gold mark containining 5·531 grains of fine gold; whereas, the American money of account contains 23·22 grains, more than four times as many grains. The quotation to-day is, "Exchange on Berlin, ·95¼." Let us conclude that New York was yesterday giving ·95¼ dollars, that is, nearly $\frac{1}{20}$th less than one dollar, for *four German marks.* Now, Will, find out how many grains of gold there are in 95¼ dollars?

Will: I know how to do that: divide ·95250 by the denominational expression of a grain of gold in America, that is, by 4·3066 cents.

Mr. Bullion: Make haste about it, then; and you, Alice meanwhile find out how many grains of fine gold there are in four German marks.

(Alice was ready first, and was going to read out her figures; but Mr. Bullion held up a warning finger, and made her wait until Will's sum was completed.)

Mr. Bullion: Will's sum must come first. What do you bring it to, my boy?

Will: There are 22·117 grains of fine gold in ·95¼ dollars, father.

Alice (looking pleased): And there are 22·125 grains of fine gold in four German marks. Isn't that very nearly the same?

Mr. Bullion: Very nearly, indeed. Subtract the latter from the greater number of grains, and see what remains?

John Smith (after putting a few figures rapidly): ·008, or 8 per mil. Divide this by 22·117, and the result is ·3 per mil. That's the discount that America was charging Berlin, is it not, sir?

Mr. Bullion: You are quite right, John.

Exchange on Paris.

Alice (eagerly): And now, father, dear, do let me try to shew you what I have learnt. Please lend me the paper, and let me see what the "Exchange on Paris," is.

Mr. Bullion: Here it is, Alice; let us hear what you can make of it.

60 days' sight.

Alice (reading): "Exchange on Paris at 60 days' sight, 5.20." Oh! father, I do not know in the least what this means —"at 60 days' sight."

Mr. Bullion: It means nothing that will interfere with your calculations, Alice; but simply this: if a New York banker is sending money for one of his depositors to a Paris banker, he makes his money order payable *at* 60 *days' sight;* that is, the order (in whatever form it may be sent) cannot be cashed in Paris until 60 days after it was seen in New York. Now, go on with your interpretation of the quotation.

Alice: I find by Mr. Norman's "Tables" that there are 23·22 grains of fine gold in an American dollar; but only 4·480 grains of fine gold in a gold franc, which is the French money of account; so I think the quotation must mean 5·20 francs for an American dollar. John, please find out quickly for me how many grains of gold there are in 5·20 francs:—A franc is worth 100 cents., and the denominational expression for a grain of fine gold in France is 22·320 cents.

Mr. Bullion (laughing): I do not know that I ought to let John do your work for you.

Alice: Oh! it's quite fair, father; I know how to do it—divide 520 cents. by 22·320 cents.—only I should not do it nearly so quickly as John.

John Smith: Here you are, Miss Bullion. There are 23·29 grains; call it 23·30 grains of fine gold in 5·20 francs.

Alice (delighted): Then I *am* right, for that is as nearly as possible the same. America was paying 23·30 grains of gold for 23·22 grains; ·08 more grains for every dollar.

Will: And how much is that per mil, Allie? Come now, you will have to finish the sum, you know.

John Smith: 23·22 divided into 80; that is just 3 dollars per mil.

Alice: America was yesterday paying France a premium of 3 dollars per mil. Thank you for your help, John. Now, was I not quite right, father?

Mr. Bullion: Perfectly right, my dear. I am very much pleased at the manner in which you applied what I had just taught you. I believe I have now explained to you everything which you ought to know before undertaking the examination paper I have prepared for you. Here is a copy of questions for each one of you, and three copies of Mr. Norman's "Tables," by the help of which you will, I hope, be able to solve all the problems. Do them as carefully as you can, and take your time about them.

(*Exeunt* John Smith, and Alice and Will Bullion.)

GOLD.

TABLE showing the weight of Fine Gold in grains of the moneys of account of fifty-two countries of the world, at mint issue weight, with the values of a grain attached. Col. I., name of money of account ; II., grains of fine gold ; III., value of one grain ; IV., countries using the weights as moneys of account ; *b* attached to the money of account denotes that the money of account, or the multiple of it forming a coin, is not a token ; * attached to name of country denotes that gold is unlimited legal tender ; † denotes the possession of a mint ; ‡ denotes that the mint receives gold in unlimited quantities. It is sufficient to use the value of a grain to the third decimal place ; 2·124d. instead of 2·123863d. gives 1½d. per £100 more than 2·123863. Less than 20 years ago the currency of France, Italy and the United States consisted of inconvertible paper.

Col. I. Money of Account.	II. Grains Fine Gold.	III. Value of One Grain.	IV. Names of Countries.
I. £ or sovereign of 20s. or 240d. *b*	113·0016	2·124 pence	Great Britain,*†‡ Australasia,*†‡ Canada,* Bahamas,* South Africa,* Jamaica,* Malta,* Bermuda,* Newfoundland,* Falkland Isles,* Turk's Islands,* St. Vincent,* Granada,* Tobago, St. Lucia,* Leeward Islands,* Gibraltar,* Sierra Leone,* Gambia,* Gold Coast,* Lagos,* Cape of Good Hope,* Natal,* St. Helena,* Cyprus,* Labuan,* Fiji.*
II. Milreis of 1,000 reis *b*	25·088525	39·859 reis	Portugal.*†‡
III. Dollar of 100 cents *b*	23·539477	4·248 cents	Newfoundland.*
IV. Dollar of 100 cents *b*	23·22	4·307 cents	United States of America,*†‡ Liberia.*
V. Peso of 100 centavos *b*	23·148525	4·32 centavos	Argentine Republic,*†‡
VI. Peso of 100 centavos *b*	22·401753	4·464 centavos	Venezuela,*†‡
VII. Milreis of 1,000 reis *b*	12·681996	78·852 reis	Brazil.*†‡
VIII. Escudo of 100 centimos *b*	11·648955	8·584 centimos	Spain.*†‡
IX. Crown of 100 ores *b*	6·222709	16·07 ores	Denmark,*†‡ Sweden,*‡ Norway.*‡
X. Mark of 100 pfennings *b*	5·531340	18·079 pfennings	Germany,*†‡ Heligoland.*
XI. Franc of 100 cents *b*	4·480350	22·32 cents	France,*†‡ Belgium,*†‡ Switzerland (francs),*†‡ Italy (liras),*†‡ Greece (drachmas),*‡ Servia (dinars),*‡ Roumania (leys),*‡ Bulgaria (lews),*‡ Finland.
XII. Piastre of 40 paras *b*	1·156693	34·581 paras	Egypt.*
XIII. Piastre of 40 paras *b*	1·020063	39·213 paras	Ottoman Empire.*†

SILVER.

(Concluded.)

TABLE showing the weights of Fine Silver in grains of the moneys of account of thirty-seven countries of the world, at mint issue weight, with the values of a grain attached. Col. I., name of money of account; II., grains of fine silver; III., value of one grain; IV., countries using the weights as moneys of account; *b* attached to the money of account denotes that the money of account, or the multiple of it forming a coin, is not a token; * attached to the name of country denotes that silver is unlimited legal tender; † denotes the possession of a mint; ‡ denotes that the mint receives silver in unlimited quantities.

Col. I. Money of Account.	II. Grains Fine Silver.	III. Value of One Grain.	IV. Names of Countries.
I. Tael of 1,000 cash *b*	508·5	1·966 cash	Shanghai.*
II. Trade Piastre of 100 cents *b*	378·	·264 cents	Cochin China* and elsewhere in the East (trade dollar).
III. Peso of 100 centavos *b*	377·058607	·265 centavos	Mexico,*†‡ Falkland Islands,* Turk's Islands,* British Honduras,* British Guiana,*Bahamas,* Trinidad,* Barbadoes,* Leeward Island,* Labuan.*
IV. Yen of 100 sen *b*	374·399613	·267 sen	Japan,*†‡ Hong Kong* and Straits Settlements* (dollar).
V. Peso of 100 centavos *b*	360·561024	·277 centavos	Philippine Islands.*
VI. Peso of 100 centavos *b*	347·227875	·288 centavos	Bolivia,* Chili,*† Ecuador,* Peru,*† Guatemala,* United States Columbia,*† Uruguay, Hayti.*
VII. Peso of 100 centavos *b*	322·150306	·310 centavos	Costa Rica.*
VIII. Rouble of 100 kopecks *b*	277·72243	·36 kopecks	Russia.*†
IX. Tecal of 8 fuangs *b*	212·142	·038 fuangs	Siam.*†‡
X. Florin of 100 kreutzers *b*	171·470384	·583 kreutzers	Austria-Hungary.*†
XI. Rupee of 16 annas or 192 pies *b*	165·	1·164 pies	India,*†‡ Burmah,* Ceylon,* Mauritus.*
XII. Florin of 100 cents *b*	145·835707	·686 cents	Netherlands,*† Java.*
XIII. Keran of 2 panabats or 20 shaheis.	70·83448	·282 shaheis	Persia.*†‡
XIV. Piastre of 16 karobs *b*	43·014589	·372 karobs	Tunis.

The currency of five countries—viz., Russia, Austria-Hungary, the Argentine Republic, Brazil and Chili—consists at present of inconvertible paper. All these countries possess mints.

The following questions were published May 12, 1888, *in the "Children's Page" of "The Co-operative News." Prizes were offered for the three best sets of answers, the competition being open to those sons and daughters of co-operators who were under* 20 *years of age:—*

QUESTIONS.

Examination questions.

1. Explain the meanings of the following three terms:—(1) Unit of value; (2) money of account; (3) unlimited legal tender.

2. What is the difference between standard and token coins? Explain this fully.

3. What is the difference between a mono-metallic and a bi-metallic currency?

4. Give your definitions of the words "price" and "value."

5. Prove that the denominational expression for 1 grain of fine gold in Great Britain is 2·123863 pence.

6. Prove that the denominational expression for 440 grains of fine gold is £3 17s. 10½d.

7. What is the denominational expression for 7,000 grains troy, or 1 lb. avoirdupois of fine gold?

8. Find the denominational expression for a grain of gold in a gold-standard country (not Great Britain).

9. Find the denominational expression for a grain of silver in a silver-standard country (not India).

10. Find the price of a grain of gold in a silver-standard country, and the price of a grain of silver in a gold-standard country, on the price of 35 pence per standard ounce of silver.

11. Find the proportion established between gold and silver in a gold-standard country, and between silver and gold in a silver-standard country, on the price of 42 pence per standard ounce of silver.

12. Work out in grains of the standard metals the commissions given by Mr. Bullion to his son and daughter and to John

Smith, in chapters iv. and v., second series. Show the loss or gain per cent. on each transaction.

13. Work out the same commissions as those referred to in question 12, in the same manner, at the following prices:—

Piece Goods (shirtings) bought in Manchester.

3,000 pieces, at 7s. 10$\frac{7}{8}$d. per piece, including all charges to India.

Sale of Shirtings in India.

3,000 pieces sold over the ship's side, at Rs.5 11as. 11ps. per piece. A rupee to be reckoned worth 16$\frac{1}{2}$d. English money.

Purchase of Wheat in India.

784$\frac{1}{2}$ quarters of wheat, at Rs.19 1a. 2ps. per quarter. Freight to Great Britain, 4s. per quarter.

Sale of Wheat in Great Britain.

784$\frac{1}{2}$ quarters of wheat over the ship's side, at 31s. 6d. per quarter.

14. Give the price of a British sovereign in ten silver-standard countries; and the price of a Mexican peso in ten gold-standard countries, on the price of 58$\frac{1}{2}$ pence per standard ounce of silver.

15. Look out in a recent daily newspaper (of which you should give the date) the three quotations of exchange given under the head of "American Markets," namely, (1) Exchange on London; (2) Exchange on Berlin; (3) Exchange on Paris. Two prices will be quoted in each case for two successive days. Work out the three quotations, and give the six weights of fine metal indicated by them.

Answers to Examination Questions.

Answers to examination questions.

1. (1) "Unit of value" is a certain weight of a standard metal, but it is not always made up into a standard coin. (2) "Money of Account" is a number by which we may express the worth or value of an article. Suppose a two-shilling piece were the money of account in England, and we wished to express the value of an article, we should say that the article was worth

so many florins, or parts of a florin. (3) "Unlimited legal tender" is the name which is given to a metal when it is made the monetary standard of a country; but it must be received in unlimited quantities at the mint, and must be fitted for regular currency. (No. 78, Class I., J.D.)

3. Gold is the standard metal of England; the silver and bronze coins are tokens, *i.e.*, they only represent so much standard metal. A token only represents so much standard metal, whilst a standard coin really contains what it represents. (No. 83, Class I. J.D.)

3. A mono-metallic currency means having a single standard coin, that is, adopting one standard metal, either gold or silver, for coinage of unlimited legal tender. A bi-metallic currency means having a double standard coin, that is. allowing both gold and silver to circulate freely, and to be coined in unlimited quantities. (No. 1, Class II., J.D.)

4. "Price" means a definite weight of standard metal, represented by standard coins or their tokens. An article may or may not be worth the price given or demanded for it. (E. C. S.) "Value": This can be defined as the relation of a commodity, article, or utility possessed by one individual to the need of another person. For instance, suppose a man has a pair of boots that he wants to get rid of, and changes them for two pairs of shoes. He makes an interchange without having anything to do with price. Barter is largely practised in the world still, and is always the basis of trade, though price be the instrument. There is a cost value and an exchange value, measured by value-giving factors (such as labour, interest on capital, machinery, &c.) apart from price. The two pairs of shoes may have cost less than the one pair of boots, or *vice versa*, but the exchange value of them was the pair of boots. Again, price may vary immensely, but the exchange relation of substances embodying value-giving factors may remain constant. (The first sentence is by No. 1, Class II., S.D.; the rest of the answer by Mr. Norman.)

5. A sovereign contains 240 pence, and, according to Mr. Norman's "Tables," it contains about 113·0016 grains of fine gold. Therefore, the denominational expression for one grain of fine gold will be the number of pence (240) divided by the number of grains (113·0016), which comes to 2·123863 pence.

6. The denominational expression for 440 grains of fine gold is obtained by multiplying 2·123863 pence by 440. Answer: £3. 17s. 10½d., nearly.

7. The denominational expression for 7,000 grains of fine gold will be 2·123863 pence multiplied by 7,000. Answer: £61. 18s. 11·041d. (Answers 5, 6 and 7 by No. 1, Class II., J.D.)

8. In the United States of America, there are 23·22 grains of fine gold in one dollar, the value of a dollar being equivalent to 100 cents. Divide 100 cents by 23·22 grains. The answer is 4·3066 cents, which is the denominational expression for a grain of fine gold in the United States of America.

9. In Cochin China, there are 378 grains of fine silver in one piastre, the value of a piastre being equivalent to 100 cents. Divide 100 cents by 378 grains. The answer is ·2645 cents, which is the denominational expression in Cochin China for a grain of silver.

10. (1.) The price of a grain of gold in a silver-standard country depends upon the market price of gold in that country. If we suppose the market price of gold in India to be Rs.19 1a. 2p. per tola (or 180 grains of fine gold), then one grain of gold in India would be worth 20·34 pies. To do this, reduce Rs.19 1a. 2p. to pies, and divide the pies by 180. (2.) We may find the price of a grain of silver in a gold-standard country thus: Take the market price of silver in England to be 35 pence per standard ounce, or 444 grains of fine silver. Divide 35 pence by 444, and the result is ·07882 pence, which is the price of one grain of silver.

11. (1.) Taking the value of silver in London at 42d. per standard ounce (or 444 grains of fine silver), 42d. divided by 2·123863d. gives 19·77, *i.e.*, 19·77 grains of gold for 444 grains of silver. Therefore, 444 divided by 19·77 gives the proportion of 22·45 grains of silver to one grain of gold. (2.) Supposing the price of gold in India to be Rs.19 1a. 2p. per tola, and a tola equals 180 grains of fine gold: Rs.19 1a. 2p. equals 3,662 pies. Therefore, 3,662 pies divided by 1·16363 pies (*i.e.*, the denominational expression for a grain of silver in India) gives 3,147 grains of silver; and this divided by 180 gives the proportion of 17·48 grains of fine silver to one grain of fine gold. (By No. 1, Class II., J.D.)

12. *Alice Bullion's commission:* The right way to do this is to find out how many grains of gold were given for 3,000 pieces of Manchester shirtings: the answer is 134,542·576 grains. Then add 6,000 grains to the cost of the shirtings—being the sum spent on charges for shipping, &c.—this brings the number of grains of gold to 140,542·576. For the second part of Alice's commission, 3,000 pieces of shirtings sold at the rate of Rs.5, or 825 grains of silver. This comes to 2,475,000 grains of silver. Deduct 3 per cent. for Indian charges (that is, 74,250 grains of silver), and the result is 2,400,750·5 grains; then deduct one per cent. for shipping, &c. (24,007·5 grains) and 2,376,742·5 grains of fine silver remain. A rupee is worth 22·65d., or 10·664 grains of gold per 165 grains of silver. Divide 165 by 10·664, and the proportion will be 15·472 grains of silver to one grain of gold. Divide 2,376,742·5 grains of silver by 15·472, and the result will be 153,615·72 grains of fine gold. This is what the 3,000 pieces of Manchester shirtings realised in India, when all expenses had been deducted, including remitting the money to Mr. Bullion from Calcutta. What was the gain per cent.? The difference between 153,615·72 grains of gold, and 140,542·57 grains (the price of the Manchester shirtings in England, including all costs) is 13,073·15 grains; this latter amount of grains multiplied by 100 comes to 1,307,315. Divide by 140,542·57, and the result will be 9·3 per cent.

Will Bullion's commission: Rs.14,550—2,400,750 grains of silver, to be invested in Indian wheat, at the rate of Rs,16·12, or 2,659·8 grains of silver per quarter; 2,400,750 divided by 2,659·8, shows that 902·6 quarters of wheat were bought at this price, all expenses included. The wheat was to be sold in England at 35s. per quarter, and 2 per cent. deducted for London charges. Divide 35s. or 420d. by the denominational expression for a grain of gold. This comes to 197·942 grains of gold. 902·6 quarters of wheat at 197·942 grains of gold per quarter realise 178,662·4492 grains of gold. Deduct 2 per cent. (3,573·2488 grains of gold), and 175,089·2 grains remain. What is the gain per cent.? 140,542·576 deducted from 175,089·2 leaves 34,546·624 grains of gold. Multiply 34,546·624 by 100, and divide the result by 140·542·576: this shows that the profit made on the Manchester shirtings was 24·5, or 24½ per cent.

John Smith's commission: 2,707·62 quarters of Indian wheat, at 2,660 grains of silver per quarter, equals 7,202,269·2 grains of silver. Divide this by 15·472—the proportion established between gold and silver—and the result will be 465,503·438 grains of gold. This, divided by 113·0016 (the number of grains of gold in a sovereign), brings £4,119·44, that is, about £4,119 8s. To bring the sum out in rupees, divide the grains of silver by 165, and the result will be Rs.43,650. 2,707·62 quarters of wheat to be sold in England at the rate of 197·572 grains of gold. This sale realises 534,949·89864 grains of gold. Divide by 113·0016, and you will have £4,733 12s. as nearly as possible. What is the gain per cent.? Deduct £4,119 8s. from £4,733 12s.; the result will be £614 4s. or 614·2. Multiply this by 100, and divide the result by 4,119·4. This will show a profit of 14·9 per cent. Divide the sum total into three equal parts. 534,949·89864 grains of gold, divided by 3, equals 178,316·632 grains of gold, or £1,578. One-third of the sum total is to be remitted to John Smith in the form of gold through a London banker, less ¾ per cent. for carriage and other charges; and the gold will have to be converted into silver. To deduct ¾ per cent., divide 1,783·166 (which equals 1 per cent.) by 4, and subtract the result from 1,783·166. The result will be 1,337·376 grains of gold, to be subtracted from the original one-third. This will leave 176,979·256 grains of gold, and this, divided by 113,00·16, gives £1,566·16, or £1·566 4s. Multiply by 15·472 to convert the gold into silver grains: the result will be 2,748,222·948 grains of silver, or Rs.16,655·8. One-third was to be invested in silver by the London agent, and shipped to Calcutta. £1,578, or 178,316·632 grains of gold, equals 2,758,914·93 grains of silver. Deduct ⅞ per cent. for shipping, brokerage, &c., and you have 2,755,466·54 grains. Deduct 2¼ per cent. for Indian coinage, charge, &c.: the result will be 2,689,329·88 grains, or Rs.16,280. 2,689,329·88, multiplied by 15,472, equals 173,819·35 grains of gold; and this, divided by 113·0016, gives £1,538·2, or £1,538 4s. One-third of the money was to be invested in Manchester shirtings, at 46·8475 grains of fine gold per piece, the price to include freight and all charges to India. £1,578, or 178,316·632 grains of gold, to be invested in Manchester shirtings, at 46·8475 grains of gold per piece, equals 3,808 pieces of shirtings. These, sold at the rate of 825 grains of silver, or Rs.5 per piece, realise 3,141,600 grains of silver, or Rs.12,979·339. Less 3 per cent. for Indian charges, equals 3,047,352 grains of silver, or Rs.12,587·9; or 197,605·48 grains of gold, or £1,748·6, or £1,748 12s. And now we want to find out the gain per cent. on the whole of the transaction.

	£	s.	d.
First sum, remitted to Calcutta in the form of gold	1,566	4	0
Second sum, remitted to Calcutta in the form of gold	1,538	4	0
Third sum, invested in Manchester shirtings, which were sold at Calcutta	1,748	12	0
	£4,853	0	0

Deduct the original sum invested in Indian wheat, namely, £4,119 8s. from £4,853. £733 12s. is the profit made. What is the gain per cent.? To find this, reduce the two sums, £4,853 and £4,119 8s. to pence; multiply the former by 100, and divide it by the latter sum. The result will show a gain of 17·8 per cent. on John Smith's transactions.

Question 13 was not correctly worked out by any of the competitors.

14. (1.) The price of a British sovereign in ten silver-standard countries: The right way to do this is first to find the proportion established between gold and silver on the price of 58½ pence per standard ounce of silver: this will be 16·119 grains of silver to one grain of gold. Multiply 113·0016 grains of gold (the contents of a sovereign) by 16·119, and you will find that the price of a sovereign in grains of silver is 1821·472 grains of fine silver in England. Look out in Mr. Norman's "Tables" the denominational expression of a grain of silver in each of the ten silver-standard countries you choose for your examples. Multiply 1821·472 by the denominational expression of a grain of silver in each of those countries, and the results in each case will be the price of a British sovereign in the standard money of account of that country. None of the competitors worked these sums quite in the right way, though I hoped that the working of question 11 would have led to their doing so. Agnes Obee worked out the prices of the sovereign

rightly, though she did not get at the value of a sovereign in grains of silver by the best and shortest rules. Walter Ansell's answers to this question were also well done, and William English's fairly well.

(2) To find the value of a Mexican peso in ten gold-standard countries: Divide 377·058 (the contents of a Mexican peso in grains of silver) by 16·119, and you will find that the gold price of a Mexican peso is 23·392 grains of fine gold. Look out in Mr. Norman's "Tables" the denominational expression of a grain of gold in each of the ten gold-standard countries you choose for your examples: Multiply 23·392 by the denominational expression of each of those countries, and the result in in each case will be the price of a Mexican peso in the standard money of account of that country. These problems have been worked out quite correctly by Agnes Obee; and although Walter Ansell went to work in a more round-about way, he has brought out good results.

15. Agnes Obee and Margaret Riddell worked out the exchanges on London and Paris quite correctly. William English was right as far as he went, but did not say what was the premium given or discount charged by America. I think it will gratify all those who took part in this examination to hear that Mr. Norman has asked to be allowed to keep all the papers sent in, so that he may be able to shew them to the friends who are interested in the subject.

E. C. SHARLAND.

Report of the Examination taken part in by Members of the Junior Co-operative Club, Midsummer, 1888.

[S.D. means "Senior Division," and is used by members over 14 and under 20 years of age. J.D. means "Junior Division," and is used by members under 14, but over 8 years of age.]

Report of examination.

First Prize: "Advanced Studies of Flower Painting," by Ada Hanbury. Won by Agnes Obee, of Plumstead, Kent (aged 12 years).

Second Prize: "Money," by Professor S. Jevons; and "The Old Curiosity Shop," by Charles Dickens. Won by Walter Ansell, of Coventry (aged 13½ years).

Third Prize: Scott's Poetical Works. Won by Margaret Riddell, of Landport, Portsmouth (aged 12¾ years).

Marks Gained.

No. 1,	Class II.,	J.D.	(last term)	40 marks.
No. 3,	" I.,	"	"	31 "
No. 86,	" I.,	"	"	30 "
No. 83,	" I.,	"	"	20 "
No. 1,	" II.,	S.D.	"	18 "
No. 78,	" I.,	J.D.	"	17 "
No. 32,	" I.,	"	"	13 "
No. 34,	" III.,	S.D.	"	10 "

The result of the examination on the whole has given both Mr. J. H. Norman and myself great pleasure and satisfaction Agnes Obee's papers are remarkably good. It was really not to be expected that so young a girl should take up the papers; but she has done by far the best set of answers. Walter Ansell and Margaret Riddell have also done splendidly; and the papers by William English, of Hopedale, by Falkirk, N.B. —a non-prize competitor—deserves very special commendation.

APPENDIX.

CONTENTS OF APPENDIX,

To the General Reader, pages 131 to 135.

Quotation from Mr. Wm. Horsley's introduction to the "Universal Merchant" on the importance of legislators possessing a masterly skill in bullion and coin—The duty and privilege of all to add to monetary science—Baron Cotton on Queen Elizabeth and her edict on conquering the monster, *i.e.*, the variation of the standard—The foundation of monetary metallism, the difference between value and price and the necessary conditions of a standard, within the grasp of children—The method of quoting exchanges, baffling and perplexing—No alteration expected—The exchange calculus of great value as an educational instrument, for travellers, merchants, sailors, and soldiers—Mr. Alex. L. Glencross's constants—The importance of thoroughly understanding the concrete case of the interchange of Manchester piece goods for Indian wheat—Four-fold object of the pamphlet—What are the differences between the raising of the coins, bi-metallism, and the excessive issue of inconvertible paper?—Dr. Patrick Kelly's Universal Cambist—Sir John Sinclair's opinion upon Kruse's Hambro Contorist.

An Antidote to Bi-metallism, or Local Dual Standards, written for the Inaugural Meeting of the Bi-metallic League, held in the Mansion House, London, in March, 1882, by John Henry Norman, pages 136 to 140.

Definition of Bi-metallism and Mono-metallism—Ricardo on the exchange value of gold and silver being governed by their cost value—J. S. Mill on the same—A simple common sense axiom to guide the mind clear of the Bi-metallic theory—Twelve reasons against the practicability of working partially or universally the local dual standard theory—The views of Professor Stanley Jevons, and Bonamy Price upon the subject.

Memorandum on the Cause or Causes of; 1st. The world-wide fall in the gold price of silver and the rise in the silver price of Gold. 2nd. The fall in the prices of Commodities generally in Great Britain since 1873, prepared at the request of Lord Herschell by John Henry Norman for the Gold and Silver Commission of 1886-8 in November, 1887, pages 141 to 152.

Professor Dr. A. Soetbeer's opinion of the "elemental might" of weights of standard metals—Results of an effective metal standard—Concrete case of exchange of Manchester piece goods for Indian wheat through the instrumentality of gold and silver prices illustrating the elemental might of standard metals, the conditions of value, and the conditions of price—Reasons for asserting that the fall in gold price of silver is due to the closure of certain mints against the unlimited reception of silver—The present average comparative cost of the production of gold and silver—The evidence of Professor Roberts-Austen of the Royal Mint of the average gold cost of the production of silver — Canny provision in the Bland Bill — Annual absorption of silver in the monetary system of the United States of America—The asserted three distinct causes for the decline of prices in Great Britain since 1873—Reasons for believing that the fall in prices is due to the fall in the gold price of silver—Gold as a measure of value in Great Britain out of gear since 1873—High or low prices a matter of indifference in current operations—The position of the agricultural and pastoral interests of Great Britain since 1873—The Indian wheat shipper's expectation on a rise in the Indian exchange with Great Britain—The Manchester manufacturer's expectation on the fall of exchange between Great Britain and India—Until 1873 the debasing influence of the cheaper upon the dearer metal was masked by the action of bi-metallism in certain countries—Result of the United States opening their mints to the unlimited reception of silver at 16 parts of silver to 1 of gold—Result of the abrogation of the Bland Bill—The theory that in the event of a fall in the gold price of silver, prices would rise in silver standard countries proved to be wrong—Reasons against this erroneous theory to be found in the vast difference between the monetary systems of India and Great Britain and the elemental might of weights of standard metals—American estimate of India's silver circulation — Comparative sensitiveness of monetary systems. — Two currents of counteracting tendencies in India—The appreciation of gold theory as the cause of the decline in prices in Great Britain examined and refuted—The diminished cost of production of commodities generally theory, as the cause of the decline in prices in Great Britain, examined and refuted, to the extent of the decline in the gold price of silver—The position of debtors—Instance of lamentable ignorance even among educated people in official positions—Of 1,030,000,000 people composing the trading nations 700,000,000 most freely exchange any of their surplus productions for silver.

A LIST OF JOHN HENRY NORMAN'S WRITINGS SINCE 1883, PAGE 152.

THE PRESENT POSITION OF THE UNIVERSAL CURRENCY DILEMMA AND THE PROBABLE RESULTS OF THE POSSIBLE FUTURE ACTION IN CONNECTION WITH THE SAME, BY JOHN HENRY NORMAN, READ TO THE LONDON CHAMBER OF COMMERCE, 18TH JANUARY, 1888, THE RIGHT HONORABLE LORD BRAMWELL IN THE CHAIR. PAGES 153 TO 176.

Figures extracted chiefly from Professor Dr. Soetbeer's "Materialen"—Opinion of the present Chancellor of the Exchequer, the Rt. Hon. Mr. Goschen on Bi-metallism in 1878 and 1887—Production of gold and silver in the U.S.A., 1883/6—China first figures as a precious metal producing country in 1883—Estimated production of gold and silver in the world during 403 years, 1482-1885—Proportionate weight of output of silver to gold between 1493 and 1885 in eight periods—Future proportionate annual production of gold and silver—Comparative average cost of the production of gold and silver—Mr. Stewart Pixley's statements—Professor Roberts-Austen's statement—Professor Egleston's opinion—The result of information furnished by Americans, 97 parts of silver to one part of gold—Advocates of local ducal standards examined before the gold and silver commission of 1886-8, desire 15½ parts of silver to 1 of gold, to be the universal relation to be fixed by consentient legislation—Distribution of gold and silver—Messrs. Gibbs and Grenfell's erroneous statements in their book on Bi-metallism—£16,798,000 of £20,000,000 of gold produced per annum required for other than currency purposes—Professor Dr. Soetbeer's estimate of the gold reserves held by the Treasuries and Banking institutions of 13 countries of the world during the years 1877 to 1885—The same authority's estimate of the monetary supply of gold and silver in bullion and coin in 1885 in the chief countries of the world—Coinage during 35 years ended in 1885 in Europe, United States of America and Australia—Gold and silver in the monetary system of the United States of America, 1873-1887—Doubts expressed whether the estimate is not too high by £60,000,000 of gold—Foreign and colonial rates of exchange—

18 different expressions whereas one day there may be only 2—Under universal local dual standards the dearer currency might entirely disappear within 40 years from every monetary system in the world—The world's standard moneys of account—13 gold and 14 silver weights comprise the whole—Information needed in English, such as two German books contain—Changes in the gold value of silver and the silver value of gold between 1872 and 1887—The world should think of rates of exchange and prices as definite weights of standard metal—Ignorance of currency and the exchanges a disgrace to civilization—Area and population of countries using the gold standard, the silver standard, and the gold and silver standards prior to 1873—Five countries using inconvertible paper currency. Are there 5 countries in the world which have satisfactory automatic metal standard currencies out of the 103 which base their prices on gold, silver, or both?—The beneficent action of telegraphic communication—Goods sold before purchased—Change in the relative value of gold and silver has no effect to alter the relative quantities of commodities exchanged. Working classes no real interest in Bi-metallism—Revival of local dual standards—If the British Isles become bi-metallic in their currency the United States of America could discharge their cheap silver into them in payment for such properties and securities as they might be pleased to take in exchange—Danger to the United States of America in the rapid discharge of the debt of the country—Mr. Fairchild's statement of the monetary position of the United States of America in July, 1886, compared with November, 1887—His recommendation of terms upon which the Government purchase of silver should cease—Redemption of the silver dollar will be demanded in gold—Silver dollar in 1887 75 cents against gold 100 cents—United States Debt could be paid off in less than 10 years—Temptation to the United States of America to re-habilitate silver—Vain attempt to regulate the comparative values of gold and silver—Silver at its natural exchange value—Enhanced purchasing power of gold—Possibility of the United States of America to place their monetary system upon the basis of a single gold standard.

MONETARY STANDARDS, MONEY, AND MONETARY SYSTEMS BY JOHN HENRY NORMAN, RE-PUBLISHED FROM THE BANKERS' MAGAZINE FOR AUGUST AND OCTOBER, 1888, PAGES 177 TO 183.

An effective metal standard—Internal and international interchanges through the instrumentality of paper slips and leather strips only—Professor Huxley and a scientific automatic metal standard for monetary purposes—Tentative definition of the terms and conditions of a sound automatic metal standard currency—A standard of value must have correlative value with that for which it exchanges—Standard metal, whether as coin or bullion, can never command an agio either in token coin or paper so long as the monetary system of a country is sound, and there are no coinage charges on the standard metal—Peoples in countries where monetary systems were worked till 1873 on the local dual standard theory, are now living in a fool's monetary paradise—The financial secretary to the U.S.A., Mr. Fairchild, and other able men in these countries, are fully alive to this—The world-wide silver price of gold 44½ per cent. more than it was before the mints of Europe and the U.S.A. were closed against the unlimited reception of silver from the public—Money—The opinions of Professors H. Sidgwick, Dr. A. Soetbeer, F. A. Walker, and C. F. Bastable on money—Money and money tokens—Reasons why the definition of money should be confined to the standard substance—Monetary systems—Exhaustive investigation should be made into the, I. elemental might of weights of standard metals—II., Fresh rules (if such can be found) for the quantity theory of the standard — III. Fresh rules in connection with the value theory of the standard — IV., Comparisons of the monetary systems of the world — The probable unprepared state of the world to undertake the investigation, especially in the fourth particular. —Information needed.—Hindrances met with in seeking this information during the past 13 years, from Government and others.—Astounding opinion that gold and silver are only *small change*.—The second blue book issued by the Gold and Silver Commission a complete failure to elevate credit instruments to the same platform as standard metals.—Surprise at the appearance of Mr. Dunning Macleod's views of wealth appearing in the report.—The base of the present dilemma rests upon the value theory.—Impolicy of attempting to remove silver from one of the two monetary standards of the world.

American Opinion of Bi-Metallism and its Advocates. Extract from an Essay on Finance, by Posey S. Wilson, Esq. (Mem. Assoc. Econ. Soc.), Published in Rhodes Banking Journal, in July, 1888, pages 184 to 185.

A medium for exchange of materials, services, and rights, a matter of self-evident necessity. To avoid confusion, term dollar has been found and a concrete substance in 23·22 grains of fine gold appointed to correspond thereto. John Law admitted, "It is not the sound of the denomination, but the value of the metal which is to be considered." Misguided and designing men have sought in vain to prove that 23·22 grains of fine gold and $371\frac{1}{4}$ grains of fine silver are exactly equivalent, "if all would admit it." The double standard argument, the proof that one is equal to two. The clamour for the free coinage of silver in the United States of America merely a conspiracy on the part of mine-owners to keep silver, in spite of natural laws, at an arbitrary figure already set by themselves. Soon they will insist that gold and silver be made equal, ounce for ounce.

"Norman's Exchange Calculus," or "Single Grain System," pages 186 to 191.

Specimen of information which should be furnished annually by each country of the world to its people.—Gross and fine weights in grains of the chief gold and silver coins in the world, with the denominational expression for one grain of fine metal attached.—The value of the coins at 42 pence per ounce of silver. —A table of constants furnished by Mr. Alex. L. Glencross, being the value of each silver coin at $\frac{1}{16}$th of a penny, per 444 grains of fine silver, or one British standard ounce.—Two columns should be added to complete the calculus.

Table No. I.

Gross and fine weights in grammes and grains of the moneys of account, and the chief gold and silver coins in current use in the world.—The denominational expression for one grain of metal.—The proportion of silver to gold in the coinage.—The value of moneys of account in the proportion of 22·45 parts of silver to 1 of gold, in Great Britain, France, Germany, and the United States.

Tables No. II.

Tables showing the par values in Great Britain of the world's silver moneys of account, and the par values in India of the world's gold moneys of account, at proportions ranging from $15\frac{1}{2}$ parts of silver to 1 part of gold, to 100 parts of silver to 1 part of gold on "Norman's single grain system," with reasons for making the variation of silver to gold from $15\frac{1}{2}$ to 95 of silver to 1 of gold.

Table No. III.

The denominational expressions for equivalent weights of fine gold in 47 countries of the world, by Mr. Alex. L. Glencross.

October 20th, 1888.

TO THE GENERAL READER.

The following extract from Mr. William Horsley's introduction to the "Universal Merchant," written A.D. 1753, would appear as valuable and useful now, in this country and the world, as when it first appeared:—

"The acquaintance with the exchanges, however it may seem to some the business of merchants only, in commercial free States, falls properly under the cognizance of gentlemen, particularly those who have or intend having any share in the Legislature, and still more materially such who are in the immediate direction of public affairs, as without a masterly skill in bullion and coin it is impossible to understand exchanges, whence singular inconveniences may happen in delicate emergencies. There is not any article of trade in which the gentleman should not be a tolerable theorist, for many obvious reasons; but in bullion and coins, whereby other articles are usually adjusted, he should be practically skilful."

Every individual from the youngest to the oldest in each community of the world is interested with or without his knowledge, in the possession and preservation of a sound monetary system. It must supersede barter and become the instrument, under its operative term price, for the internal and international exchanges of services, properties, and commodities of every country. It is the duty and privilege of each, according to his or her ability, to aid in the acquirement of this knowledge by submitting their views to be threshed out by the world, that so perhaps little by little, monetary science may rest upon a solid basis of truth which no reasoning mind can consistently question or resist. It is not a subject for princes,* rulers, statesmen, legislators

---

* In Sir Thomas Rowe's famous speech on Money at the Council Table in 1640 he mentions the saying of Theodoret the Goth, alluding to the effiges upon coins, "Princes must not suffer their faces to warrant falsehood."

political economists, merchants and bankers only, but for all who are determined to understand the principles of the money they daily use.

It is not to be expected that every fairly-educated child and grown-up person who may peruse this pamphlet should, through its means, at once become a master of currency and the exchanges. The deficient education of past ages is not to be remedied quite so easily. Besides the inaptitude of many minds for figures, there is the reputed difficulty of the subject in hand to deter those who take pleasure in figures from attempting to master it. The former will say, "What is the use of all this botheration with decimals, long calculations and minutiæ of grains of fine metal? If I am going into a country, or going to do business with a country, I learn all that is necessary about its coinage and exchanges in a short way. I do not want to be bothered with all this stuff." The latter will say, "I do not want to run the chance of swelling the number in our lunatic asylums,* therefore I shall keep clear of the subjects." It is well that both classes should know that if they would entertain reasonable opinions upon mono-metallism, bi-metallism, tri-metallism, alternative-metallism and no-metallism, they must understand the foundation of metallism.

The "single grain system,"† herein made plain to the comprehension of children, effectually accomplishes this. The foundation thus exposed is not so difficult to master as the multiplication table and could be taught with advantage and interest in connection with geography in the schools of the world. The fundamental difference between value and price is quite within the power of children to grasp. It is easy to demonstrate that in all countries

---

He remarks "What renown is left to the posterity of Edward the 1st in amending the standard, both in purity and weight, from that of the older and barbarous times; it must needs stick as a blemish upon princes that do the contrary." Also "Queen Elizabeth in her edict telleth her people, that she had conquered now that monster that had so long devoured them," meaning the variation of the standard. Baron Cotton quoting this in 1626 added "and so long as that staid adviser lived she never (though often by Projectors importuned) could be drawn to any shift or change in the rate of her moneys."

* It is to be hoped we shall soon have heard the last of Sydney Smith's opinion that the subjects of currency and the exchanges, next to love and religion, fill our lunatic asylums.

† It will be seen in the appendix that three leading German political economists, Professors Soëtbeer, Lexis and Nasse, express their pleasure with Mr. Norman's system as a great simplification of the whole exchange calculus.

which possess effective metal standards, prices and rates of exchange are absolutely definite weights of standard metal. This knowledge is also easy to acquire and retain, and the necessary conditions of a metallic standard are quite as easy to understand.

It is very probable that the value of the new Exchange Calculus would have remained generally unrecognised for a long time to come, but for the exceedingly able manner in which Miss Sharland has elucidated it under the terms "single grain system," to the understanding of children, and the evidence that young persons have given that they can assimilate and reproduce her work. The following letter from Mr. H. J. Chaney, the keeper of the British standards, furnishes high testimony to the excellent work accomplished by Miss Sharland.

"*August* 27*th*, 1888.

"I beg to return by separate post the copies of the *Co-operative News* which you were so good as to leave with me. The answers given by the children to the questions on money are really surprising, for they evince powers of mind and application which could hardly be expected in children so young. The success has evidently had its origin in the able chapters on money which Miss Sharland had prepared for the children. In these chapters the actual relation between the standard of monetary measure in one or different countries is based on the simple unit of a grain of the standard substance, and so all the technical overloading always met with in the literature of this subject is quite swept away. The child has only a simple factor before him, and by successive gentle steps he has been taught to apply that factor to unravelling so many knotty problems in exchange and value. It has given me very great pleasure to read the papers which you have sent me, and I shall be glad at any time to receive further information on this important and interesting question of monetary values."

Though this Calculus may become of universal use, as an educational instrument; and of great value to the traveller, merchant, soldier and sailor, * it is not to be expected that there will be any altera-

---

* Certain benefit would oftentimes result to these classes from readily and easily ascertaining the par value of all moneys of account and gold and silver coins anywhere, whatever the gold price of silver or the silver price of gold might be. In Dr. Patrick Kelly's "Universal Cambist," published in 1811, it is stated that under regulation in Barbadoes a tenderer of light gold coins

tion in the present method of working or quoting the exchanges between the countries of the world, on the denominational expressions for weights of gold and silver. It may be true that if ingenuity had been set to work to devise a perplexing, baffling method of quotations of exchanges it could not have better succeeded than in the production of the present system. Now, however, any one desirous to know the weight of fine metals indicated by the quotations of exchange between countries possessing effective metal standards to be met with in the daily papers can easily ascertain them.

In Mr. Alex. L. Glencross's table which is attached, and the column of Constants which is added at his suggestion, to the exchange Calculus, there is gratifying evidence that the subject is one of growing interest.

It is well that possibilities should be faced, and for that purpose only, are the gold prices of silver coins and the silver prices of gold coins at proportions of silver to 1 of gold ranging from 15½ to 100 given in the Table II attached.

The concrete case of interchanges between Great Britain and India of Manchester piece goods for Indian wheat at altered rates of exchange, or the lower gold price of silver and the higher silver price of gold, given in the memorandum prepared for the Gold and Silver Commission, should be carefully studied and thoroughly understood. This demonstrates the "elemental might" of weights of standard substances, and the fundamental difference between

---

was compelled to receive 2¾d. per grain less for each grain short of the proper weight of the coin. The denominational expression for one grain of standard gold which contains $\frac{1}{12}$th part of copper is 1·947 pence. Comparing this with 2·75 pence, the difference is 41 per cent. upon the lower quotation. If the pence in Barbadoes were such as the pence now used here, *i.e.*, the 1/240th part of a pound, dealing in light gold coins was possibly a very profitable business there in those days. The same author mentions the high opinion Sir John Sinclair had of Kruse's Hambro Contorist, and that he recommended its translation, Sir John adding: "Till then we principally rely upon foreign merchants, who make fortunes from our ignorance of the nature of the exchanges." This book is in the British Museum, but there is no English translation of it. Thomas Hatton in his essay on gold coins published in 1774 mentions that the general value of gold is at the rate of twopence per grain. The eminent numismatist Thomas Snelling in his most valuable essay on gold coins in 1766 gives the denominational expressions for weights of British standard gold, ranging from one quarter of a grain to one pound troy. The denominational expression for one grain of fine gold in the British Isles has been, and always will be, within a minute fraction of 2·124 pence, so long as the sovereign is divided into 240 pence and there are 113·0016 grains of fine gold in it on its issue from the mint.

the interchange of commodities by barter and their interchange through the instrumentality of price, in so far as the weights of standard substances may be altered by causes which operate alone upon those substances and which do not alter the quantities of commodities interchanged, in this case wheat and piece goods.

Besides the subjects mentioned, the following pages contain, (1) A definition of money. (2) The terms and conditions of a scientific, automatic metal standard for currency purposes. (3) Remarks upon the importance of a thorough comprehension of the different monetary systems of the world. (4) Weighty and unanswered arguments agains tlocal dual standards or bi-metallism. (5) An American view of bi-metallism and its advocates.

Upon monetary subjects there is a very large admixture of error to be found in legislative enactments, state documents, the evidence and report of commissions, the 2,000 and more books and pamphlets and the utterances of statesmen, legislators, political economists and others throughout the world.

The objects of this pamphlet are, to bring the foundation of money within the comprehension of all, to promote the teaching of the subject with geography in the schools of the world; to stimulate the study of it, and to assist those whose desire it is to discriminate between truth and error in the past and current literature of the subjects.

Every student of money should read Locke "On the raising of coins." It might be well asked, what are the differences between the raising of coins, bi-metallism, and the excessive issue of inconvertible paper, in their respective effects on prices, the morality of such procedures, and the adequacy of the measures to accomplish the object in view ?*

It may shortly be more generally recognised than it is at present, that without a thorough understanding of the exchanges of gold, silver and inconvertible paper, it is impossible to form sound views upon Monetary Science, much less to become a master of it.

22, Lee Terrace, London, S.E.
October 4th, 1888.

---

* For an essay in reply to this question, besides Locke "On the Raising of Coins," resort might be had to Messrs. Cernuschi, Gibbs & Grenfell's writings on bi-metallism, and to F. A. Walker's "Money, and the History of the States of North America on the excessive issues of inconvertible paper."

AN ANTIDOTE TO BI-METALLISM; OR, LOCAL DUAL STANDARDS; WRITTEN IN 1882.

I.—Definition of Bi-metallism and Mono-metallism.

1. *Bi-metallism*—What it is.—The reception from and the coinage for the public under national law by the mints of the nation of any quantities of both gold and silver, and returning the same to the public at a fixed proportion of one to the other, the general approval being in the proportion of one part of pure gold to fifteen and half parts of pure silver; also the national appointment that both shall be legal tender to unlimited extent.

2. *Mono-metallism*—What it is.—The reception from and the coinage for the public under national law of either gold or silver (but not both), and returning the same to the public; also the national appointment that one metal only shall be legal tender to unlimited extent.

3. *Experience* of the markets of the world has shown that the variation between gold and silver has ranged between one part of pure gold to ten parts of pure silver, and one part of pure gold to twenty-two and half parts of pure silver.

II.—The Exchange value of Gold and Silver Governed by their Cost Value.

4. The precious metals, as currency, subject to the same laws of value as other substances and dependent upon cost of production—proved from the writings of Ricardo and J. S. Mill. The following quotations are from—

Ricardo—*On the rent of Mines.*—"It will be sufficient to remark that the same rule which regulates the value of raw produce and manufactured commodities is applicable also to the metals, their value depending not on the rate of profits, nor on the rate of wages, nor on the rent paid, but on the total quantity of labour necessary to obtain the metal and to bring it to market. It has, therefore, been justly observed, that however honestly the coin of a country may conform to its standard, money made of gold and silver is still liable to fluctuations in value, not only to accidental and temporary, but to permanent and natural, variations in the same manner as other commodities."

On Foreign Trade.—"Any improvement in the facility of working the mines by which the precious metals may be produced with a less quantity of labour will sink the value of money generally. The nations of the world must have been early convinced that there was no standard of value in nature to which they might unerringly refer, and therefore chose a medium which, on the whole, appeared to them less variable than any other commodity."

On Currency Banks.—"Gold and silver, like all other commodities, are valuable only in proportion to the quantity of labour necessary to produce them and bring them to market. Gold is about fifteen times dearer than silver, not because there is a greater demand for it, nor because the supply of silver is fifteen times greater than that of gold, but solely because fifteen times the quantity of labour is necessary to procure a given quantity of it."

On the influence of demand and supply upon prices.—"It is cost of production which must ultimately regulate the price of commodities, and not, as has been said, the proportion between the supply and the demand. The proportion between the supply and the demand may, indeed, for a time affect the market value of a commodity until it is supplied in greater or less abundance according as the demand may have increased or diminished, but this effect will be only of temporary duration."

On the high price of Bullion.—"Gold and silver, like commodities, have an intrinsic value which is not arbitrary, but is dependent on their scarcity, the quantity of labour bestowed in procuring them, and the value of the capital in the mines which produce them. If the quantity of gold and silver in the world employed as money were exceedingly small or abundantly great it would not in the least affect the proportions in which they would be divided among the different nations. The variation in their quantity would have produced no other effect than to make the commodities for which they exchanged comparatively dear or cheap. The smaller quantity of money would perform the functions of a circulating medium as well as the larger. However exact the conductors of the mint may be in proportioning the value of gold to silver in the coins, at the time when they fix the ratio, they cannot prevent one of these metals from rising while the other remains stationary or falls in value. Whenever this happens, one of the coins will be sold for the other. Mr. Locke, Lord Liverpool, and many other writers have ably considered this subject, and have all agreed that the only remedy for the evils in the currency proceeding from this source is to make one of the metals only the standard measure of value. Mr. Locke considered silver as the most proper metal for this purpose, and proposed that gold coins should be left to find their own value and pass for a greater or less number of shillings as the market price of gold might vary with respect to silver; Lord Liverpool, on the contrary, maintained that gold was not only the most proper metal for the general measure of value in this country, but that by the common consent of the people it has become so, was so considered by foreigners, and that it was best suited to the increased commerce and wealth of England."

J. S. MILL—*On the value of money as dependent upon the cost of production.*—"But money, no more than commodities in general, has its value definitely determined by demand and supply. The ultimate regulator of its value is cost of production. It is evident, however, that the cost of production, in the long run, regulates the quantity; and that every country (temporary fluctuations excepted) will possess, and have in circulation, just that quantity of money which will perform all the changes required of it consistently with maintaining a value conformable to its cost of production."

Of money considered as an imported commodity.—"In so far as the precious metals are imported in the ordinary way of commerce, their value must depend on the same causes and conform to the same laws as the value of any other foreign production. Money, then, like commodities in general, having a value dependent on, and proportional to, its cost and production, the theory of money is, by the admission of this principle, stripped of a great deal of the mystery which apparently surrounded it."

5. The conclusions of these writers have never been con-

troverted, nor the soundness of their theory, that the value of the precious metals is dependent on the cost of the production of them.

6. It would appear, therefore, to follow that, in the main, the historical fluctuations of the market value of the metals gold and silver, in the proportion one has borne to the other, is the measure of the variation of the comparative cost of the production of each, and confirms, with regard to these two substances, a theorem which universal experience commends, viz., that NO TWO DIFFERENT SUBSTANCES CAN BE PRODUCED FOR ANY LENGTH OF TIME ON PARALLEL LINES OF COST.

7. If this theorem be true with regard to the cost of the precious metals, bi-metallism is an unnatural and unscientific system which cannot possibly be established.

8. The unsoundness of the bi-metallic system is evidenced by the admission of its advocates that it cannot be adopted unless it becomes universal; but would the metal-producing countries, such as Australia, consent to it?

9. Bi-metallists must prove that the cost of production has no effect upon the value of the precious metals as circulating media, and those among them who say that it costs as much to produce an ounce of silver as it does to produce an ounce of gold, appear the most consistent, however erroneous they may be.

10. The more simple the laws affecting the currency, and the more the ebb and flow of the standard metal is left to automatic action, the better for the internal and foreign trade of that country.

11. To make a law which would act against nature cannot be the desire of bi-metallists, and could never accomplish the object for which it was intended.

12. If all the nations using metallic currency embraced bi-metallism at once, the proportion in the currency being fixed at one part of pure gold to fifteen and a half parts pure silver, there would commence an immediate debasement of the coinage of this country; and in process of time a higher range of prices from such action would ensue, which would be injurious to fundholders and persons enjoying fixed sterling annuities or incomes, from whom, as well as from others, a complaint would proceed that they were being impoverished by law.

13. Even by legalising bi-metallism it would not follow that

contracts would invariably be made on either gold or silver, one metal only might be specified.

14. Under an universal bi-metallic system what would be the relative quantities of production, and what the ratio of cost of production of gold and silver, at which the production of one of the metals for currency would cease? Would excessive quantities of gold, in the ratio of one part of pure gold to ten parts of pure silver, cause the production of silver to cease, or would excessive quantities of silver, in the ratio of one part of pure gold to twenty parts of pure silver, cause the production of gold to cease?

15. Bi-metallism would impose a tax on the general public in the nature of a monopoly of a most unjust kind, whereby the producer of the cheaper metal of the two on the established ratio would command the same value as the producer of the dearer metal.

16. The invariableness of a measure of value under the mono-metallic system is great, productive of loss and constant injury: the variableness under the bi-metallic system must prove eventually considerably greater.*

---

* This paper was read to the late Professor Stanley Jevons before it was printed in 1882, and was approved by him. The following is an extract on it, from a note received from the late Professor Bonamy Price in November, 1882. "Thanks, so many, for the paper you have sent me. It is excellent. I wish it was hung up in the study of every bi-metallist in Europe: it could not but do him endless good. The quotations are admirable."

MEMORANDUM on the cause or causes of: 1st. *The world-wide fall in the gold price of silver and the rise in the silver price of gold.* 2nd. *The fall in the prices of commodities generally in Great Britain since* 1873, *by* JOHN HENRY NORMAN, *November,* 1887, *for the gold and silver commission.*

---

1. I am convinced that the sole cause of the world-wide fall in the gold price of silver, amounting now to 25·57 per cent.,* and the rise in the silver price of gold, amounting now to 33·93 per cent., is the closure of the mints of the countries forming the Latin Union and the United States of America against the unlimited reception of silver from the public.

2. I am equally convinced that the chief cause of the fall in prices generally in Great Britain since 1873 is distinctly traceable to the fall in the gold price of silver.

3. Before advancing reasons for these opinions I would advert to a prominent and very important statement made by Professor A. Soetbeer in his excellent publication "Materialen," to the effect that the "elemental might" of weights of standard metals is seen in the rates of exchange and in the actual transmission of standard metal in satisfaction of international balances.† This so

---

* The average price of silver in London for the year 1873 was 59¼ pence per ounce, and it is now 44 pence per ounce.

† The following are the per-centage total imports and exports of gold and silver upon the total import and export trade of Great Britain in commodities, on figures furnished by the Board of Trade. Averages of periods of five years ended in 1863, 14·4; 1868, 9·; 1873, 9·1; 1878, 9·9; 1884, 5·9. The average yearly movements during these periods have ranged from £41,299,000 in the period ended in 1884 to £63,323,000 in the period ended in 1878. During the eight years ended in 1886 there has been an excess export over import of gold of £11,318,000, against an excess import over export of gold of £75,249,000 during the previous 20 years. In the 28 years the excess import has been £63,931,000. Taking the annual requirements of Great Britain for other than currency purposes at £2,500,000, it would amount to £70,000,000 in the 28 years.

entirely supports the view which I have long taken of the standard substance for currency purposes that I do not hesitate to make this statement, that wherever there is a monetary system which is based upon an *effective metal standard*,* there prices and rates of exchange are denominational expressions of definite weights of standard metals, and that these weights as weights alone constitute prices and rates of exchange, and are ordinarily the true measures of value and at all times the means of payment. All instruments of credit, including legal tender banknotes, are money tokens, and but signs of the standard substance which alone is true money.

4. To illustrate the elemental might of weights of standard metals, the working of exchanges of commodities through the instrumentality of price, and by means of barter, I present a concrete case of exchange between England and India of Manchester shirtings for wheat. I assume that prices for commodities have fallen in Great Britain, and that they have remained stationary in India, that the transport and all other charges are the same now as they were in 1873, but that the exchange in 1873 on India was 22·65 pence per rupee, and that it is now 16·75 pence per rupee.† This fall in exchange is 26 per cent. Under the fall

---

* I mean by an effective metal standard that all money tokens are readily convertible into the standard. I ventured to define the terms and conditions of a sound automatic standard currency. It is briefly this: The substance selected for the standard must be received in unlimited quantities, and coined and certified by the State, be appointed unlimited legal tender, and be preserved in an effective state. At a meeting of the London Chamber of Commerce, held on the 18th January last, at which I read a paper upon "The present position of the world-wide currency dilemma, &c.," Lord Bramwell who was in the chair, approved of this definition.

† In 1873.

	£	s.	d.		Grains of Fine Gold.
3,000 pieces of Manchester shirtings at 7s. 11½d., or 44·8475 grains of fine gold, per piece, with freight to India ...	1,190	12	6	or	134,542·5
Insurance on £1,200	4	10	0	,,	508·5
	1,195	2	6	,,	135,051·0

Exchange at 22·65 pence per rupee, or 10·664 grains of fine gold per 165 grains of fine silver. 135,051 grains of fine gold divided by 10·664 grains of fine gold gives 12,663·26, which is the number of rupees. These, multiplied by 165, give 2,089,438 grains of fine silver.

of exchange, before experience taught what the result would be, it was the wheat exporter's expectation that the rise in exchange would ensure him a profit upon his wheat shipment to Great Britain equal to the difference in the rise in the exchange; and the Manchester manufacturer uttered loud lamentations that the fall in exchange with India would cut him off from supplying the Indians with piece goods. In these two instances, of inter-

---

Sale of these Shirtings at Kurrachee.

	Rs.	a.	p.		Grains of Fine Silver.
3,000 pieces at 4 rs. 3 ann. 7 pies, or 696·479 grains of fine silver, per piece net price, less freight and all Indian charges	12,663	4	9	or	2,089,438
Say that this silver is invested in wheat for Great Britain:					
784·627 quarters wheat at 14 rs. 4 ann. 10 pies, or 2,359·725 grains of fine silver, per quarter, free on board					1,851,504
Freight to Great Britain, per quarter 3s. 7d. = 20·246 grains of gold, or 313·246 grains of silver					237,934
					2,089,438

The rate of exchange being 22·65 pence per rupee, or 10·664 grains of fine gold, for 165 grains of fine silver. 2,089,438, being divided by 165, gives 12,663·26 rupees, and these, divided by 10·664, gives £1,195 2s. 6d.

Sale of Wheat Free of all Charges over the Ship's side in Great Britain.

	£	s.	d.		Grains of Fine Gold.
784·627 quarters at £1 10s. 5½d., or 172·108 grains of fine gold per quarter	1,195	2	0	or	135,051

In this instance of exchange it is seen that 3,000 pieces of shirtings, costing 135,051 grains of fine gold, sold in India for 2,089,438 grains of fine silver, which, invested in wheat, &c., produced 784·627 quarters, which sold in the United Kingdom for 135,051 grains of fine gold. The rate of exchange for converting the gold into silver and the silver into gold being both the same, 22·65 pence per rupee, and one rupee for 22·65 pence.

In 1887.

	£	s.	d.		Grains of Fine Gold.
3,000 pieces of shirtings at 5s. 10½d., or 33·198 grains of fine gold per piece, with freight, &c., to India	881	5	0	or	99,596·97
Insurance	2	18	10	,,	332·88
	£884	3	10	,,	99,929·85

Exchange at 16·75 pence per rupee, or 7·886 grains of gold for 165 grains

changes of commodities in 1873 and 1887, which I have given at foot, we have powerfully illustrated, 1st. "The elemental might" of weights of standard metals, which is shown by the forced fall in the prices of piece goods and wheat in a gold standard country, to meet the fall in the gold price of silver. 2nd. The conditions of value. The same length of piece goods and the same weight of wheat of equivalent quality were exchanged in both cases, because these quantities depend upon the expenditure of value giving factors which might have retained the same relation in both instances. 3rd. The conditions of price. In the one case 135,051 grains of fine gold had to be given for 3,000 pieces of shirtings, and 784·627 quarters of wheat realised 135,051 grains of fine gold. In the other, 99,929·85 grains of fine gold had only to be given for 3,000 pieces of shirtings, and 784·627 quarters of wheat sold for 99,929·85 grains of fine gold. These changes in the gold standard country are accounted for by the measurable fall in the gold price of silver. In the silver standard country during the two periods 2,089,438 grains of silver made up the prices of the piece goods and the wheat respectively. The pressure for the adjustment of prices of goods whether in gold standard countries from silver standard countries, or in silver standard countries from gold standard countries necessary upon the fall in the gold price of silver and the rise in the silver price of gold found expression in the fall in gold prices of piece goods and wheat to meet the equivalent decline in the gold price of silver.

5. My reasons for asserting that the fall in the gold price of

---

of silver. Divide 99,929·85 by 7·886, and the result is 12,663·26 rupees; this, multiplied by 165, gives 2,089,438 grains of silver.

It is unnecessary to repeat the sale of the shirtings and purchase of wheat in India, the figures being the same as in 1873.

Sale of Wheat in Great Britain.

	£ s. d.	Grains of Gold.
784·627 quarters, over the ship's side, at £1 2s. 6½d., or 127·359 grains of gold, per quarter...	884 3 10	or 99,929·85

In this instance it is seen that 3,000 pieces of shirtings costing 99,929·85 grains of gold, sold in India for 2,089,438 grains of silver, and that 784·627 quarters of wheat, in which the proceeds were invested, sold in Great Britain for 99,929·85 grains of gold. The rate of exchange for converting the gold into silver and the silver into gold being both the same, say, 16·75 pence per rupee.

silver is due to the closure of certain mints against the unlimited reception of it from the public, are:

The certainty that if one country such as the United States of America—not Jersey—opened its mints to-morrow to the unlimited reception of silver from the public at the relation of 16 parts of silver to one of gold, exchange with India would immediately return to the rates prevailing between gold standard countries and that country before 1873.

The certainty that if the Bland Bill should be abrogated, the gold price of silver would at once further fall, possibly considerably below 30 pence per ounce in London.

The present comparative average cost of the production of gold and silver, so far as can be ascertained from American state printed documents, and testified to by the President of the Colorado Silver Alliance, with regard to silver in Colorado, and with reference to gold by the Mears' Chlorination Company of the United States of America for the whole world, is nearer 100 parts of silver to one part of gold; in which opinion a leading American expert concurs.

The evidence given by Professor Roberts-Austin before the Royal Commission last year that the average cost of producing silver measured by gold is 44 parts of silver to one part of gold. The absence of evidence that this sudden cheapening of the cost of the production of silver commenced in 1873. But there is evidence in the enormous wealth of the silver kings, and the anxious desire which existed in certain quarters long previous to 1873 to make Great Britain one of the dumping grounds of cheap silver, that the present proportion of 21·4 to 1 is vastly different from the true proportion.

The high probability that some silver Trust has been manipulating the British silver market ever since the Bland Bill contained the canny provision that the United States of America mints must buy $2,000,000 and not more than $4,000,000 of silver per month *on the London market price of the day.**

6. There may be many causes for the decline of prices generally

* Though the United States of America took into their currency £8,353,000 of silver last year against an average during the preceding five years of £5,621,000; the average price of silver was never lower than last year, and so far vastly lower prices do not appear to diminish the production of the article.

in Great Britain since 1873. Three among them which are on the surface have been much examined; and each has its advocates of ability and experience in monetary matters. The three are: 1st. The appreciation of gold, as caused by a diminished supply of that metal for currency purposes, together with a fresh distribution of it as between different countries using it for currency purposes. 2nd. A diminution of the cost value or over-production of commodities generally. The meaning of this is: That there has been a diminution of expenditure of value-giving factors such as labour, rent for land, or shelter, machinery, the use of capital and all other factors that give value, on the production of commodities. Or that commodities generally are being sold at an exchange value below their cost value. 3rd. That the fall in the gold price of silver has been the chief cause of the decline in prices generally in Great Britain since 1873.

After advancing reasons for holding the opinion that the fall in the gold price of silver is the prime factor and measurer of a large portion of the decline in prices in Great Britain, notice will be taken of the two other alleged causes.

7. Gold as a measure of value in Great Britain has since 1873 been completely thrown out of gear. Price, or a definite weight of gold, should be a measure of the cost and sale values of commodities within a narrow margin of fluctuation in ordinary times.* It was not so in the period of vast additions to the gold currencies of the world nor in previous periods of history when the standard was mostly silver, and vast additions of that metal were made to the currencies of the world. These were catastrophic periods to all States and peoples interested in deferred payments, but a matter of little moment to the working classes and all interested in current interchanges connected with industrial life. For if a high price was obtained a high price had to be paid. If a low price was obtained a low price had to be paid.† It did not affect to diminish

* This narrow margin results from the vast mass of metals as currency to be acted upon under the ordinary laws of supply and demand. The present dislocation between gold and silver is the result of the break-down of unwise legislation which assumed to control economic forces.

† If prices generally in Great Britain fall equally and at the same time with the fall in the gold price of silver—see *Economist* diagram of the prices of silver and commodities generally in the first report of the present Gold and Silver Commission—it is difficult to perceive how the current agricultural and pastoral interests are worse off than before the dislocation, provided there has been an equivalent fall in rent.

or increase quantities or lengths of commodities for quantities or lengths of commodities. Such is the position of this country's measure of value now in an inverse sense, and brought about by an entirely different cause. All the time that there has been an unnatural alliance between gold and silver produced by the legislation in a group of countries, that 15½ parts of silver shall be equal to one part of gold, and in another country that 16 parts of silver shall be equal to one part of gold, and the pressure of the cheaper metal at those relations did not overbear the law and destroy the action, the debasing influence of cheaper upon the dearer metal was masked. At the same time prices in the western world were based upon the joint action of both gold and silver. In the instance of exchange of piece goods for wheat we saw that the shipper of wheat expected that from the decline in the exchange he would be able to reap the benefit of that decline in securing the same or the approximate price for it in Great Britain as before the decline. He found that he got no more than his ordinary profit. The Manchester merchant, arguing upon the theory which he had been taught, that in the event of a decline in the gold price of silver there would be a corresponding rise in the silver price of commodities in silver standard countries, finding no rise in the value of his piece goods in India, in the midst of his lamentations discovered the gold price of his piece goods in Manchester declining to an adjustment with the stationary price in India, and his business proceed as before. These adjustments are due to the elemental might of weights of standard metals. Assume that the United States of America open their mints to the unlimited reception of silver in the proportion of 16 parts of silver to one part of gold. The London remitting rate on India would at once become approximately 1s. 11d. per rupee. On this the pressure for the re-adjustment of prices of a very large number of articles—all those from silver standard countries—would immediately commence. This pressure might result in a return, in large measure, to the prices of 1873 in this country. This might be the pressure in one direction. But for the past six years it has been the general impression in London, that on the abrogation of the Bland Bill, silver would decline to 30 pence per ounce or 31·43 parts of silver to one of gold. It is most probable that the fall in price would be much more. Assume, however, that this last buttress of silver, the Bland Bill, goes, and the gold price of that metal becomes 30 pence per ounce. This means another fall in the gold value of silver of 32·66 per cent. It may be a matter of opinion how the pressure for the adjustment of prices would operate, whether by a further fall in gold prices generally or a rise in silver prices in silver standard countries, but that an adjustment would take place cannot be doubted if the experience of the past is to be our guide.

We have theorised that in the event of a decline in the gold price of silver, prices of commodities generally would experience a corresponding rise in silver standard countries. This theory may be false. Our fathers and grandfathers lived in the gold and silver fixed relation period, and their theories are based upon their surroundings. Their forefathers knew next to nothing about the subject. We are witnessing the tremendous might of gold and silver under a less constrained legislative relationship than existed 14 years ago, and we may possibly have to abandon some monetary theories and modify others.

The difference between the positions of gold standard countries such as Great Britain and silver standard countries is enormous. A gold standard country wherein barter has ceased to be practised, the monetary system of the first order affecting each unit of the whole population, wherein the quantity of the standard metal is sought to be maintained at a tolerably uniform level such as Great Britain possesses, cannot be compared with a silver standard country wherein barter most extensively prevails, where the monetary system, though of first class automatic order, affects only a minimum of the population, where the quantity of the standard metal as currency fluctuates with prosperous and unprosperous seasons, owing to the customs of the people and not to the condition of its external trade, such as India.* Would it not be unnatural to suppose that changes in currency matters would be equally rapid in two such countries?

---

* It is stated in "Tooke on Prices" that before the middle of this century it was estimated that India had absorbed £400,000,000 of silver, and that the loss by abrasion, &c., on this equalled £4,000,000 per annum. At the same time the French loss by abrasion on their silver circulation was estimated at £1,000,000 per annum. Baboo Tin Coorey Doss, of Calcutta, who in the main has written very sensibly upon the present currency dilemma, estimates the silver circulation of India at £75,000,000. Official documents of the United States of America place the circulation of that country at £200,000,000, but this is a calm doubling of the information received from their representative in Calcutta.

Surely the sensitiveness of the gold standard country must be vastly greater than that of such a silver standard country.* It would certainly appear to be a sounder theory, that given a fall in the gold price of silver in such a country, gold prices generally should fall there rather than silver prices should rise in such a silver standard country.

8. With regard to the first cause assigned for the fall in prices generally in Great Britain since 1873. If the theory is sound and applicable to the whole world† that owing to diminished supply and fresh distribution of gold for currency purposes, an appreciation of this metal has taken place, and that in consequence gold prices generally have fallen 30 per cent., then the purchasing power of gold instead of being as it was in 1873, £700,000,000, is now for the whole world £910,000,000. It might be asked whether this increase of purchasing power is only commensurate with the increase of interchanges. If it is more it should have the effect of raising prices. But as we have traced a decline of 26 per cent. to the dislocation between gold and silver, it appears only right to add this 30 per cent. fall which is due to another cause to that amount, and it becomes 56 per cent.; a total fall which facts disprove. The result of the operation of that which appears to me to be the true cause, is the appreciation of gold. But it would not be true to attribute the alteration in prices to the appreciation of gold in the sense described under the first alleged cause. The true cause of the change in prices in Great Britain would be the decline in the gold price of silver, in other words the dislocation between gold and silver.

9. With regard to the second of the alleged causes of the decline of prices generally in Great Britain since 1873, viz., the diminished cost, or over production of commodities generally. It is stated to account for declining prices in Great Britain, that

---

* The difference between the sensitiveness of the monetary systems of the two countries may be compared in the one case to a well-strung Eolian harp which responds to every breath of wind, whereas in the other case the harp is at best but ineffectively strung.

† In one of the Numbers of the "Fortnightly Review" for 1872, Cliffe Leslie gives his opinion that the value of money is a local affiair, even in Prussia. I have not the material on which to form an opinion whether or not in this catastrophic period since 1873, gold has preserved a level of value in Great Britain, the United States of America, and Western Europe. The conditions of the monetary systems of Great Britain compared with the other countries alluded to, present some wide and characteristic differences.

between two periods 1873 and 1887, the outlay of value giving factors necessary to produce a given weight or length of anything possessing exchange value has diminished to the extent of 30 per cent. in the fourteen years. It would appear to be exceedingly difficult to estimate changes in a good many of the items which make up the value giving factors embodied in anything without using the measure of price. There is one, however, and that the chief factor, viz., labour, upon which manual labour saving machinery must have had a very considerable effect, but whether it has had anything like an equivalent effect to the fall in the gold price of silver during the past fourteen years I am quite unable to judge. I should be disposed to think it has not. But as this is a perfectly distinct cause to the dislocation between gold and silver, the 30 per cent. attributable to this must be added to the 26 per cent. due to the dislocation, which makes a general fall of 56 per cent. in British prices. Facts do not confirm this. Besides, if there have been economies in the production, &c., of wheat in India,* have there not been corresponding economies in the production, &c., of Manchester shirtings?

10. With regard to these last two reputed causes, I feel no diffidence in asserting that if the gold price of silver should become 44 parts of silver to one of gold there must be a pressure to adjust prices generally to that relation, and that in all probability it would take the shape of a further decline of prices in gold standard countries. In that case I venture to affirm that there can neither be an appreciation of gold in the sense of the first cause, nor proportionate economies in the expenditure of value giving factors on the production of commodities, which will cause any one to question whether the fall in the gold price of silver was the true cause of the decline in gold prices generally in Great Britain.

11. Is there any remedy for debtors—states or individuals—of deferred obligations. Some advocates of local dual standards insist upon the world or so many countries as they think may give per-

* For centuries past there have been two currents of counteracting tendencies in India which have been very largely intensified since the introduction of railways into that country. One is the extension of the monetary system to vast numbers of the people, the tendency of which should be to reduce prices there. And the other the cheapened cost value of commodities, chiefly attributable to diminished cost of carriage and the rendering accessible to trade fresh tracts of country which would tend to raise prices there through the greater work the same amount of standard metal could perform.

manence to the arrangement, endeavouring to carry out their theory on the proportion of 15½ of silver to one of gold. Other advocates of the same system desire to engage the world or less to endeavour to carry out the fixed relation theory on the present relation. Many advocates of the system admit the truth of the aphorism* at foot, and the possibility of the cheaper metal becoming the only standard, but add that such an event would not signify as the world does its business on paper, and that it should carry that about rather than metal. To all this, the answer is that the additional knowledge gained during the past fourteen years of the principles which must govern a sound monetary system based upon an effective metal standard, precludes the attempt. It is likely that, for a long time to come, whilst silver is finding its exchange value in nearer relation to its cost value, that general prices will be fallacious guides to values. We may hope that when the last vestige of protection is removed from silver, that in consequence of the fall in its gold price, production will be so curtailed as to save it from the very great fall which to some people, at present, appears inevitable.

The genius who may devise some means, without an overt or covert attempt at a fixed relation between gold and silver, to relieve debtors from the additional burden which the break down of the

---

* "No two different substances can be exchanged for any length of time on parallel lines of quantities or values, neither can they be produced for any length of time on parallel lines of cost." The conclusion from this is that local dual standards are unnatural, unscientific, and unworkable. It has been pointed out more than once that if periods in history recurred just now with regard to the comparative output of gold and silver and on the present comparative cost of the two metals, within forty years there would not be any gold currency, it would have been driven out by silver even though all the world had embraced bi-metallism.

As an instance of lamentable ignorance, even among educated people in official positions, where a better understanding might be expected, the definition given of double standards or bi-metallism in the last valuable report issued by the Mint Master of the United States of America is "where its standard silver coins are unlimited legal tender, the same as its gold coins." This is the distributive side of bi-metallism. Without the receptive side as well which is that the metal must be received in unlimited quantities, there is no bi-metallism. As a fact it does not exist in the world at present.

It is hardly a fair representation of the monetary position of the world to assert that silver is discredited because certain countries in Western Europe and North America have ceased their efforts to combine that metal with gold as their standards. Of the 1,030,000,000 people within the comity of trading nations, whose interchanges as separate communities among themselves are measured by a more or less effective metal standard, 700,000,000 people most freely exchange any of their productions for silver.

montrous delusion of bi-metallism has entailed, and without injuring the residents of Great Britain and other countries which may be similarly situated, will earn a very prominent niche in the Walhalla of the nations of the world.*

The following are Mr. Norman's writings on monetary subjects since 1883. The articles which subsequently appeared in "Local Dual Standards," printed by Cassell's, have [1] attached. Those in this present pamphlet have [2] attached.

---

* In the columns of the London *Chamber of Commerce Journal.* A demonstration that Professor Stanley Jevons was not a Bi-metallist, August, 1883. "Function of gold and silver currency in the internal and international transactions of countries, international indebtedness, and the simplification of exchange," in the numbers for July,[1 2] August, September, October, November, and December, 1883; March and May, 1884. A refutation of the views of Mr. Dunning M'Leod, that the sole essence of wealth is exchangeability, January, 1884. A letter on the proposed degradation of the half-sovereign to a token, May, 1884. "On Coinage Charges," May, 1884. "On the production of gold and silver in the United States of America," January and March, 1885. The "Comparative cost of the production of gold and silver, and the comparative yield of grains of gold and silver per ton of ore," June, July, August, September, and December, 1885; February, May,[1] July,[1] and October,[1] 1886; January[1] and May, 1887. A letter on decimal currency, August, 1887. "A scientific automatic physical standard currency, September 1885. On the question whether the "Dislocation between gold and silver, or the appreciation of gold, produced the disturbance in gold prices," October, November, and December, 1887. "On the present position of the universal currency dilemma, and the probable results of the possible future action in connection with the same," March,[2] April,[2] May,[2] June,[2] 1888. Lecture read at the London Institute of Bankers, reported in the March, 1887, number of the *Institutes Journal*, namely, "An elucidation of the metallic bases of the colonial and foreign exchanges, and the simplification of exchange." "Norman's Exchange Calculus," November,[2] 1888. In the *Bankers' Magazine*, "Norman's Single Grain System," for determining the par value of all moneys of account and gold and silver coins between all countries: also, for ascertaining the comparative weights of fine gold or silver indicated by relative prices throughout the world; May, 1887. Appreciation of gold, July, 1887; on Professor Nicholson's "Money and monetary problems," July, 1888; "An effective metal standard," August,[2] 1888; "Money and monetary systems," October,[2] 1888; "Norman's Single Grain System," September,[2] 1888. "A memorandum prepared for the Royal Gold and Silver Commission of 1886-8, on the cause or causes of—(1) the world-wide fall in the gold price of silver, and the rise in silver price of gold, and (2) the fall in the prices of commodities generally in Great Britain since 1873," November,[2] 1887.

THE PRESENT POSITION OF THE UNIVERSAL CURRENCY DILEMMA AND THE PROBABLE RESULTS OF THE POSSIBLE FUTURE ACTION IN CONNECTION WITH THE SAME.

January, 1888.

By John Henry Norman.

In attempting to depict the present position of the currency dilemma, I make use of the first report of the Commissioners on currency issued last year, Dr. Soetbeer's "Materialien," the proceedings of the British Association at their meeting last year at Manchester, the reports of the Directors of Mints, U.S.A., and the utterances of responsible Statesmen on the subject. I shall work into this article the material furnished by the Director of Mints, U.S.A., in his report for the calendar year, 1886, received by me on the 9th August.

Utterances of Responsible Statesmen.

Among the followers of the leaders of the advocates of local dual standards, I meet with a good many who claim the present Chancellor of the Exchequer as among those who are in favour of bi-metallism. Since many of these gentlemen are not, like their leaders, at home with the opinions expressed by the Right Honourable G. J. Goschen on this matter, I would, in justice to this learned and high authority upon currency matters, make the following quotations from the proceedings of the International Conference held in Paris in 1878.

Remarking on facts submitted by Mr. Feer-Herzog and a proposition made by Mr. Horton, Mr. Goschen said, "What Mr.

Horton has asked was that the Conference should pronounce on the utility of the relation irrespective of the present possibilities or impossibilities of establishing it. Now he did not consider it necessary to give a categorical reply to a question thus hypothetically put; but, if the character of the question were changed by the question of principle being no longer separated from the question of execution, he would modify also the character of his answer, and would not in that case hesitate to affirm, as Mr. Feer-Herzog had done, *the entire and absolute impossibility of the establishment of a fixed ratio*, and this for many reasons of a scientific and economic nature, which he need not enter into in detail." Again at the same conference, he is reported to have said, "I merely desired to combat the theory of the economists who demand the universal adoption of the single gold standard, a measure which, in my view, might be the cause of the greatest disasters. I maintain my assertions in this connection absolutely. I believe that it would be a great misfortune if a propaganda against silver should succeed, and I protest against the theory, according to which this metal must be excluded from the monetary systems of the world. But from my words no opinion ought to be deduced in favour of the adoption of the double standard—*a system to which my colleagues and myself are entirely opposed, and which has against it the public opinion of the nation which I have the honour to represent.* As for the desire which has been expressed that the hope be left open that some day a fixed relation may be established between gold and silver, and an international value given to them, the English delegate declared that in his view it was impossible to realise this, impossible to maintain it in theory, and that it was contrary to the principles of science." (Extract from the International Monetary Conference, August, 1878, Washington Government Printing Press, 1879.) However great the dilemma the world is in, or however great any course of action may cause it to become, it is not likely that these decisive opinions on questions of principles could be changed by anyone holding them on the strength of honest conviction, and we may be sure from all Mr. Goschen has said upon the subject since 1878, that his views are not changed. In support of this, reference can be made to his speech to his constituents, at St. James's Hall, London, on the 7th July of last year, when he placed "this fierce controversy" about the fixed ratio third to light gold and £1 notes, and stated that the Government "could not allow these questions to drift without bringing them at last to a real authoritative decision," after studying them in the autumn.

I know of no responsible statesmen who has said anything to favour the aspirations of the advocates of local dual standards.

Production of Gold and Silver.

The production of gold and silver in the United States of America during 1886 is returned by the Mint authorities of that country as follows in the 22 States.

The following Table gives the amount yielded in each State against the yield of 1885, 1884 and 1883 Exchange at \$4·86 per £. 000 omitted.

	1886.		1885.		1884.		1883.	
	Gold.	Silver.	Gold.	Silver.	Gold.	Silver.	Gold.	Silver.
Alaska . .	90	1	62	1	41	0	61	0
Arizona . .	228	697	180	780	191	925	195	1,070
California .	3,018	287	2,606	513	2,070	615	2,905	300
Colorado . .	912	3,280	862	3,246	871	3,280	843	3,574
Dakota . .	553	86	657	20	676	31	658	31
Georgia . .	31	0	27	—	28	0	40	0
Idaho . .	369	738	370	709	256	569	288	432
Montana . .	907	2,542	666	2,067	443	1,435	371	1,235
Nevada . .	633	1,025	637	1,233	717	1,147	518	1,118
New Mexico .	82	471	164	616	61	615	57	580
North Carolina	35	1	31	1	32	1	34	0
Oregon . .	203	1	164	2	135	4	136	4
South Carolina	3	0	9	—	12	0	12	0
Utah . .	44	1,332	37	1,386	27	1,394	28	1,158
Washington .	30	16	25	14	18	0	17	0
Texas, Alabama, Tennessee, Virginia, Vermont, Michigan and Wyoming . .	1	42	18	1	18	2	7	0
	7,130	10,519	6,525	10,588	6,196	10,018	6,170	9,602
	£17,658,000		£17,113,000		£16,214,000		£15,672,000	

This shows an increase in gold over 1885 of 9·4 per cent., and a decrease of silver of 0·6 per cent. This sudden check to the previous yearly advance of the output of silver is not prominently dealt with, but may be due to the decreasing gold value of the metal. Reasons are stated why reliable information of the quantities of silver produced cannot be obtained, and why its value in gold should be estimated at 16 parts of silver to 1 part of gold.

It was Dr. Soetbeer's suggestion that the weight of silver should be measured by the gold dollar according to its market value. In reply to the arguments advanced against adopting Dr. Soetbeer's suggestion, I would say that so long as countries meet their international engagements in gold their standard is gold, and such silver as they possess in circulation or reserves is but the token of the standard, and therefore should not be taken at a value greater than the market value in estimating the reserves. I would recommend that statisticians should treat weights rather than denominational values in dealing with gold and silver if one only is used.

On the world's production of gold and silver there is no return for any later year than in the preceding report. There is a readjustment for the years 1883-5: this readjustment shows the following changes, 000 omitted:—

	1885.		1884.		1883.	
	Gold.	Silver.	Gold.	Silver.	Gold.	Silver.
	£	£	£	£	£	£
This report .	21,702	25,406	21,076	23,759	19,652	23,398
Last ,, .	20,883	25,667	19,535	23,605	19,312	23,969
	£819 +	261 −	1,541 +	154 +	340 −	571 −

I had remarked in my epitome in sterling of the United States Mint Report for 1885, published in the LONDON CHAMBER OF COMMERCE JOURNAL, that I had heard that the East, India, China and Borneo, produced £1,500,000 precious metals per annum. For the first time China figures in these revised returns as contributing £1,087,000 of gold in 1883, £1,276,000 in 1884, and £953,000 in 1885. The annual weights of gold and silver produced in these three years were—Gold, 1883, 147·050 tons; 1884, 155·652 tons; 1885, 161·846 tons; silver, 1883, 2,792·239 tons; 1884, 2,833·489 tons; 1885, 3,041·867 tons.

Estimated Production of Gold and Silver in Tons and Cwts. Avoirdupois and Pounds Sterling: Silver 15½ parts to 1 of Gold, during 403 years, 1482-1885.

Years.	Gold.		Silver.	
	Cwt.	£	Cwt.	£
98 ended 1580 .	11,926	82,750,420	283,965	127,030,000
100 ,, 1680 .	16,591	115,110,000	761,634	340,961,500
100 ,, 1780 .	34,564	239,800,000	909,301	407,018,085
50 ,, 1830 .	15,521	107,672,000	717,671	321,243,290
50 ,, 1880 .	123,070	853,855,000	1,073,712	480,667,920
5 ,, 1885 .	14,948	103,706,076	257,500	115,257,000
	216,620	1,502,893,496	4,003,783	1,792,177,795
	10,831 tons of gold.		200,189 tons of silver.	

The silver is not taken at its present market value. That would be £1,322,849,903. One hundredweight avoirdupois of fine gold is £6,938. What the production of gold and silver had been from the earliest times to A.D. 1481 is entirely conjectural. There must have been a very considerable weight of gold and silver in one form or another upon the surface of the earth in the service of man, or hoarded, before 1481. For the 52 years ended in 1544 the recorded annual average output of gold was 126$\frac{7}{25}$ cwts., £877,128; and of silver, 1,315 cwts.; or at 15½ parts of silver to 1 of gold, £590,636. The following is the recorded proportionate weight of output of gold and silver during the periods mentioned: fluctuating weight of silver to 1 of gold:—

	Years.	Silver to Gold.		Years.	Silver to Gold.
1493 to 1544	= 52	10·41 = 1	1851 to 1870	= 20	5·42 = 1
1601 ,, 1700	=100	40·81 = 1	1871 ,, 1880	= 10	12·24 = 1
1701 ,, 1800	=100	25·71 = 1	1493 ,, 1840	=348	33·70 = 1
1801 ,, 1840	= 40	39·10 = 1	1881 ,, 1885	= 5	22·23 = 1

Proportionate Annual Production of Gold and Silver.

Enthusiastic adherents to the theory of local dual standards have advanced the statement that the proportion of 15½ parts of silver to 1 part of gold is a natural relation. The foregoing return of the statistical position of this matter must entirely dissipate such an idea. Dr. Soetbeer's tables show that there was a period of 40 years ended in 1620 when the annual average proportion between the output of gold and silver was 53 parts of the latter to 1 of the former. With regard to the future, I believe that a great number of experts connected with gold and silver mining consider that these industries are but just out of their infancy, and that what with deep mining and cheapened methods of the separation of the metals from their surrounding ores, the annual yield will be greatly increased.

Professor Nicholson, in his evidence before the Royal Currency Commission, stated the opinion of Professor Geikie (Question 5524), which is, "I see no reason for believing that the production of silver will become relatively greater than it is at present. The average annual yield of gold may increase as fresh mining districts are opened up, and the same may be the case with silver. But over a number of years the relative proportion of the two metals will probably not vary much." This opinion is not shared in by experts who are quoted by Dr. Soetbeer in his "Materialen," nor by speakers on the subject at the recent meeting of the British Association. I should conclude from their statements that they might hazard some opinion with regard to the output of gold, but that they could not do so with regard to the output of silver, the possible supplies of which appear to them inexhaustible.

Comparative cost of the Production of Gold and Silver.

In the evidence given by Mr. S. Pixley before the Select Committee of the House of Commons in March, 1876, question 213, he stated that, in new mines in Mexico, he believed that silver could be got out at 1s. 6d. per ounce, which is at the proportion of 52·4 parts of silver to one part of gold. Mr. Pixley has also given evidence before the Royal Commission, 1886-8, and in answer to questions 232-236, he stated that "very few mines can produce silver for less than 85·4 cents., which is equal to 3s. 6d. per ounce. One or two large mines were shut down because the workmen refused to reduce their pay; he was allowed to mention that the Blue Bird mine, in Butte city, can produce silver at 1s. 2·9d. per ounce, and he quoted what the chairman of one of the largest mines in Montana stated, which was, "we can produce our silver at 1s. 6·3d. per ounce." He assumes that his correspondent took the cost of production at 3s. 6d. per ounce for the general country of America, north and south. (Question 243.) Professor Roberts-Austen, of the Royal Mint, London, presented a statement to the Commissioners on Currency in 1886, showing the weight of silver obtained from the four different sources in 1883, and the average cost of the same at 20 pence per ounce, on which, if 15 per cent. is taken for interest on capital, the cost is brought up to 23 pence per ounce, or forty-four parts of silver to one of gold.*

It must be noticed that these statements of Messrs. Pixley and Roberts-Austen are the gold values of silver. A comparative statement of the cost of the production of gold and silver would be a very different return, and I should expect that Mr. Roberts-Austen's promised comparative cost of the two metals at the present time will show proportions of something like from eighty to a hundred parts of silver to one part of gold. I have taken great pains with the quotations of actual yields of gold per ton of ore, in California, and of silver per ton of ore in Colorado, as recorded by the Mint authorities of the United States of America for the years 1883 and 1884. I am not aware that any error has been found in them; I am, on the contrary, under the impression that our London Mint authorities have gone through them without discovering any discrepancies to which they could draw my attention. It is true that the President of the Colorado Silver Alliance considered that there was no truth in the statements I drew up in connection with these figures, and therefore none in the conclusions I arrived at, and he was kind enough to furnish me with information of yields of silver, and cost of production in Colorado. Having this, and also information with respect to gold, from the Mears Chlorination Company, I made a comparative statement of the cost of gold and silver, with the result given in detail in the January, 1887, number of the London Chamber of Commerce Journal, viz., ninety-seven parts of silver to one of gold. There are advocates of the local dual standards theory, who now desire that no definite

* The Professor's estimate is, I believe, confirmed by Professor Egleston, of the School of Mines, New York. Professor Egleston, who has manifested much interest from the first in my investigations into the present comparative average cost of the production of gold and silver, considers that my estimates are likely to prove not far from the mark.

conclusion should be arrived at in this country or elsewhere, until this question of relative cost of production is settled. The bi-metallists examined by the Royal Commission advocated the relation of fifteen-and-a-half to one. There are some bi-metallists who declare, that rather than adopt fifteen-and-a-half to one, when the market rate is twenty-one to one, they would become mono-metallists. The proposition to wait until the present relative cost of the production of gold and silver is determined, is utterly puerile, for it may be one proportion this year, and something quite different five years hence. That thoughtful men could make such a proposition only shows the delusive straits into which unsound theories lead people.

Distribution of Gold and Silver.

We have seen under the head of production of the precious metals, that during the 403 years, 1482-1885, the weight and value of gold and silver produced in the world, according to the accepted statistics, *for what they are worth*, was at fifteen-and-a-half parts of silver to one of gold.

Gold.

	Tons.	
Production in 403 years	10,831	£1,502,893,496
Estimated currency, circulation, and reserves of the whole world ... say		£700,000,000
Balance for other than currency purposes besides Stocks in 1481		£802,893,496

Silver.

	Tons.	
Production in 403 years	203,926	£1,792,177,795
Estimated currency circulation, and reserves of the whole world ... say		£650,000,000
Balance for other than currency purposes besides Stocks in 1481		£1,142,177,795

Dr. Soetbeer estimates the gold currency and reserves of the civilised countries of the world at £657,000,000, and the silver currencies and reserves of the civilised countries of the world at £384,000,000. In a return of the United States of America Mint authorities for the year 1883, the gold, silver, and paper circulation of thirty-nine countries of the world is given at, gold £677,698,000; silver £566,791,000; notes £811,470,000.* In this return India

* See London Chamber of Commerce Journal for June, 1885.

is put down for £213,620,000 of silver. But there is no silver for Russia or any part of the East, except India and Japan.

Messrs. Gibbs and Grenfell, in their book on bi-metallism, assert that gold and silver would not have the value they possess if they were not used as currency, in fact they deny that these substances are merchandise because they are used as currency. These tables show that much the larger portion of these substances is used for other than currency purposes. At the same time these gentlemen complain that there is not enough gold for currency purposes, and might adduce the fact that at least three-fourths of the present annual supply of gold goes for other than currency purposes.* In fact the present annual supply of gold continued for 35 years would be sufficient to furnish a sum equal to the world's present gold currency. Dr. Soetbeer estimates the annual industrial use of gold in the world at about 90 tons, or £12,291,030. India absorbs gold annually at the average of £4,587,000. These two sources alone take for other than currency purposes £16,798,000 per annum.

The Doctor's estimate of the gold reserves held by the Treasuries and Banks of Great Britain, the United States of America, Australia, France, Belgium, Italy, Netherlands, Austria-Hungary Russia, and Sweden, Norway, Denmark, and Switzerland.

000 OMITTED.

	£		£
1877 . .	141,330	1882 . .	199,050
1878 . .	139,390	1883 . .	224,940
1879 . .	171,150	1884 . .	228,860
1880 . .	185,340	1885 . .	246,460
1881 . .	190,710		

* In Gibbs and Grenfell's "Bi-metallic Controversy" on page 117, among the fundamental propositions of bi-metallists which Mr. Grenfell states they all assert, his first is the following: 1. "That the precious metals used for circulation are so large a proportion of the existing mass that the amount in use for any other purpose is too small to have any influence on their value." On page 369 Mr. Gibbs states that mono-metallists and bi-metallists must admit that gold and silver are differently conditioned from all other commodities in four ways. Under the head of the third he makes this astounding statement: "*Ninety per cent. of the demand for the precious metals being for one purpose only*, that of serving as money, the demand for either of them in any country, and consequently in all countries, is subject to be almost entirely and quite suddenly extinguished by the action of law." A quotation of Seyd's figures of the production and distribution of gold and silver on page 370 entirely disposes of these inaccurate assertions on the part of the leaders of the advocates of local dual standards.

The estimate of the gold and silver money and bullion given by the Doctor is as follows :—

MONETARY SUPPLY OF THE PRECIOUS METALS AT THE END OF 1885 IN £. 000 OMITTED.

	Gold.	Silver.	Total.
Great Britain	108,600	21,120	129,720
Great Britain's Colonies without India .	33,300	3,260	36,560
Netherlands	3,910	13,040	16,950
France, Italy, Belgium and Switzerland .	205,160	156,500	301,660
Austria-Hungary	7,820	18,190	26,000
Germany	85,280	43,620	128,908
Scandinavia	5,620	2,050	7,670
Russia	37,660	13,700	57,360
United States of America.	123,430	63,280	186,710
Other Countries in Europe and America .	45,770	48,900	94,670
	£656,550	383,660	1,040,210

During the 35 years which ended in 1885 the civilised states of the Western world, including the United States of America and Australia, coined £1,129,800,000 of gold and £367,050,000 of silver.

GOLD AND SILVER IN THE MONETARY SYSTEM OF THE UNITED STATES BULLION AND COIN, AS PER THE HON. JAMES A. KIMBALL'S MINT REPORT, 1887, IN £. 000 OMITTED.

	Gold.	Increase or Decrease.	Silver.	Increase or Decrease.
1873	27,675	...	1,260	...
1874	30,211	2,536	2,122	862
1875	24,832	5,379 –	3,970	1,848
1876	26,662	1,830	7,465	3,496
1877	34,346	7,684	11,575	4,110
1878	43,706	9,360	18,050	6,475
1879	50,377	6,671	24,092	6,042
1880	72,027	21,650	30,447	6,355
1881	98,089	26,062	35,954	5,507
1882	103,885	5,796	41,660	5,706
1883	110,260	7,385	47,561	5,901
1884	111,827	567	52,391	4,830
1885	120,683	8,856	58,113	5,722
1886	121,107	424	64,010	5,897
1887	134,177	13,070	72,363	8,353

This is a very remarkable statement. In three years 1880–81 and 1887 the United States is represented to have added £60,000,000 of gold to its monetary system. Doubts are expressed in the States as to whether the gold in the monetary system of that country is not over-estimated by £60,000,000.

Foreign and Colonial Rates of Exchange.

There are more than 103 empires, kingdoms, states and islands, which conduct their international interchanges of commodities, &c., through the instrumentality of prices or definite weights of standard metal. In only a few of these countries has barter ceased to exist. If the world possessed but one satisfactory automatic metal standard, whether gold or silver, the rate of exchange would be the expression of a weight of standard metal in country A for a weight of the same standard metal in country B. If each country of the world had a satisfactory automatic metal standard gold here, and silver there, there would be six different expressions of the rates of exchange. In the present miserable condition of the currencies of the world, a quotation of exchange may mean one of 18 different things. The following 18 quotations, which are given as illustrations, should be the extreme or metal points, *i.e.*, the limits to the fluctuations of exchange. I am not, however, sufficiently acquainted with the charges in each case to attempt this; but in no instance have I taken a greater margin of fluctuation than 4½ per cent. The weight of fine metal in grains is for the rate quoted G denotes gold; S, silver; I P C, inconvertible paper currency.

	Exchange.	Examples.	Quotations.	Grains of Fine Metal for Fine Metal.
I.	G. for G.	England or Australia	1¼ % prem.	G. 114·27 for G. 113·0016.
II.	G. for G.	Australia or England	1¼ % dis.	G. 111·729 for G. 113·0016.
III.	S. for S.	India or China	Rs. 2·28 ⅌ Dollar	S. 375·466 for S. 374·3996.
IV.	S. for S.	China or India	Dollar ⅌ Rs. 2·22	S. 374·3996 for S. 366·302.
V.	G. for S.	England or India	1s. 4d. ⅌ Rupee	G. 7·533 for S. 165·.
VI.	S. for G.	India or England	Rupee ⅌ 1s. 3·45d.	S. 165· for G. 7·274.
VII.	G. for G. or S.	England or France	Sovereign ⅌ Francs 25·22	G. 113·0016 for G. 113·0016 or S. 1751·60.
VIII.	G. or S. for G.	France or England	Francs 25·32½ ⅌ Sovereign	G. 113·465 or S. 1758·70 for G. 113·0016.
IX.	S. for G. or S.	India or France	Rupee ⅌ Franc 1·624	S. 165· for G. 7·34 or S. 113·77.
X.	G. or S. for S.	France or India	Franc 1·67 ⅌ Rupee	G. 7·48 or S. 115·94 for S. 165.
XI.	I. P. C. for I. P. C.	Russia or Austria	I. P. C. for I. P. C.	I. P. C. for I. P. C.
XII.	I. P. C. for I. P. C.	Austria or Russia	I. P. C. for I. P. C.	I. P. C. for I. P. C.
XIII.	G. for I. P. C.	England or Russia.	1s. 10½d. ⅌ Rouble	G. 10·59 for I. P. C.
XIV.	I. P. C. for G.	Russia or England	Rouble ⅌ 1s. 10d.	I. P. C. for G. 10·36.
XV.	S. for I. P. C.	India or Russia	Rupee ⅌ Rouble 1·66	S. 267·30 for I. P. C.
XVI.	I. P. C. for S.	Russia or India	Rouble ⅌ Rupee 1·57	I. P. C. for S. 259·05.
XVII.	G. or S. for I. P. C.	France or Russia	Franc 2·74 ⅌ Rouble	G. 12·27 or S. 190·18 for I. P. C.
XVIII.	I. P. C. for G. or S.	Russia or France	Rouble ⅌ Franc 2·68	I. P. C. for G. 12·00 or S. 186·.

I am disposed to think that there are at present not more than five countries in the world in the possession of satisfactory automatic metal standard currencies, viz., Great Britain, Australasia, India, Germany, and the Scandinavian Union.

Under Universal Local Dual Standards could Gold disappear from the Currencies of the World?

It would be too much to expect that bi-metallists should read the writings of mono-metallists, or that mono-metallists should read the writings of bi-metallists. Their systems start from such diametrically opposite bases that there has hitherto been little in common between them. The exposition of some of the views of bi-metallists under the strong light of the Currency Commission cannot fail to have done much good, though no prominence was given to some of their extreme opinions such as I pointed out in the May, 1886, number of the London Chamber of Commerce Journal. I find at question 4,581 of the Royal Commission on Currency in 1887, this statement by Mr. H. H. Gibbs: "I have always asked the question, whither would the metal go, and nobody has ventured to answer it." It was this very question that I essayed to answer in the November, 1883, and May, 1886, numbers of the Journal, and the reply was briefly this. I assume that all the world has embraced local dual standards. That the 40 years which ended in 1620, during which time the output of silver, according to Dr. Soetbeer's tables, was in the proportion of 53 parts of silver* to one part of gold, at once recurs upon the present yield of gold, not an impossible event being based on history. That the proportion fixed between the gold and silver is the old relation, or one not in conformity with the actual comparative cost of production, but much less silver to gold than should be. Then the production of silver being unnaturally stimulated, the mass of silver equal to £2,640,000,000 at 15½ parts of silver to 1 of gold would so saturate and inflate the currencies of the world—all gold-yielding countries included—that it might cost 30, 60, 80, or 100 parts of silver to produce 1 part of gold from the earth, whilst 1 part of gold could be taken from the currency for 15½ parts of silver, and before the end of the forty years there would be no gold currency. It would all have gone for other than currency purposes.

---

* There is another period of forty years ended in 1811, in which according to the same returns the proportionate output of silver to gold was 48·5 parts of the former to one of the latter.

The World's Standard Monies of Account.

I believe that all the exchanges of the world are commanded by the knowledge of 13 gold and 14 silver weights. I give them with the names of the countries attached, in which they are standards.

Noback's work, published in Leipzig in 1879, gives the gross and fine weights in grammes of 637 gold and 1,452 silver coins. A work published in a cheap form in Bremerhaven in 1875 contains the fac-similes of 426 gold and 824 silver coins, of which there are for Europe 316 gold and 663 silver; for Asia, 22 gold and 37 silver; for Africa, 5 gold and 1 silver; for America, 79 gold and 116 silver; and for Australia, 2 gold. The weights of the gold and silver coins at present current in the world will be found in the table at the end.

England, I suppose, may yet be considered the centre of the world's exchange operations, and, to its disgrace, be it said, that anyone desiring such information as I have here endeavoured to present must resort to foreign books for it, where he will find the weights given in grammes. Noback, the German authority, and Costes, the French authority, do not agree in the weights in grammes for all coins. In a lecture which I gave at the Bankers' Institute in February, 1887, I endeavoured to stir up the bankers to produce a cheap authentic work on the subject as a fitting jubilee memorial of Her Most Gracious Majesty's reign. I am not aware that anything at present has come of the suggestion.

The Changes in the Gold Value of Silver and the Silver Value of Gold between 1872 and 1887.

Gold for Silver.

1872. Grains of Fine Gold.	1887. Grains of Fine Gold.	Money of Account.	Grains of Fine Silver.
10·556	7·857	Rupee	165·
32·533	24·214	Tael	508·5
23·953	17·927	Yen	374·399613
24·184	18·00	Trade dollar	378·
24·132	17·954	Mexican dollar.	377·058607
22·215	16·533	South American peso	347·227875
13·572	10·102	Tical	212·142

Silver for Gold.

1872. Grains of Fine Silver.	1877. Grains of Fine Silver.	Money of Account.	Grains of Fine Gold.
1766·21	2373·03	Pound Sterling	113·0016
362·92	487·62	U.S.A. dollar	23·22
146·07	196·26	Florin	9·345985
97·26	130·67	Crown	6·222709
86·45	116·15	Mark	5·531340
70·04	94·08	Franc	4·480350

The world has not yet commenced to think of colonial and foreign exchanges as an interchange of weights of metals or their tokens, nor of prices as definite weights of standard metal or its tokens for the commodities priced. I believe this to be of great importance for the thorough understanding of the subject.

It is not my intention to repeat here what I have written upon automatic and autocratic metal currencies, nor upon the terms and conditions of a sound automatic metal standard currency. Suffice it to say that I have treated of these in the numbers of the London Chamber of Commerce Journal for July and October, 1886, and for September, 1887.

I am of opinion that the general ignorance which exists upon currency and the exchanges is a disgrace to civilisation and a serious reflection upon the politico-economic and lower educational teaching of the world. Governments in free countries should see to it that this state of things shall be remedied, the means for effecting which appear simple to me.

The Currencies of the World.

I have stated the currencies for 103 countries of the world in the May number of the London Chamber of Commerce Journal for last year. I shall not name them here, but will only group them under gold standard (1), silver standard (2), gold and silver standard before 1873 (3). £ 000 omitted.

	Area of miles.	Population.	
(1) Gold standard . . .	12,134,027	132,890,000	Gold £236,000
(2) Silver standard . . .	19,504,172	842,450,000	Silver 229,000
(3) Gold and silver prior to 1873	5,809,722	183,743,000	Gold 530,000 Silver 338,000
			£1,333,000

There are thirteen countries of minor importance at present containing 923,303 square miles and with a population of 17,570,000, the standards of which I am unable to ascertain. Among the three classes above given there are certainly five countries with inconvertible paper currencies, two on a professedly gold standard, Brazil and the Argentine Republic; and three on a professedly silver standard, Russia* Austria-Hungary and Chili. How many of these 103 countries have satisfactory automatic metal standard currencies? There are at present only twenty-six which possess mints, and four of the twenty-six are countries with inconvertible paper currencies. How many of these 103 countries have a good circulating medium sufficient for their internal interchanges? How many have only just such a medium on the seaboard as enables them to manage their international interchanges?

The countries which before 1873 ostensibly practised the local dual standard theory, viz., France, Italy, Belgium, Switzerland, and Greece, together with the United States of America, who perhaps may be said to have covertly practised the same theory, are now credited with possessing £530,000,000 of gold and £338,000,000 of silver, at 15½ to 16 parts of silver to 1 part of gold. These countries estimate their silver for currency and reserves against notes at 28¼ per cent. greater value than it is. I am not sure that Germany does not practise the same monstrous delusion with a good portion of her £43,620,000 of silver. To the extent that

* There was an intimation in the *Economist* of the 22nd October that on the 1st November, 1887, Russia would issue two new gold coins for 10 and 5 roubles, the fine gold in which would be four times the weight of 10 and 5 francs respectively. The British mint authorities have not received any official information with regard to these coins. It is said to be the intention of Russia to have a gold standard.

this silver is overvalued in gold, these countries might as well hold as reserves against their notes lands in the Sahara desert or South Sea stocks. Have any of these countries satisfactory automatic metal standard currencies?

Would London continue to be the exchange centre of the world if, as is done in some central cities, a presenter of notes for gold was asked whether the gold was intended for export, and if so, be made to pay a premium for it?

When we are asked to change our currency all these matters have great weight and should be most carefully considered. They require also to be generally known and kept prominently in view.

The Beneficent Action of Telegraphic Communication.

The ordinary method of conducting international transactions, in other words of effecting purchases and sales of goods, &c., between countries is to effect sales before effecting purchases. This is strongly brought out by the Royal Commission on currency. Under this system all the items, viz., cost, carriage, exchange, commissions and interest, constituting the cost value of any commodity at the point of sale are determined when it is known that a certain price or weight of standard metal can be obtained for the commodity. I take this fact in connection with another fact which the Royal Commission has given prominence to, viz., that whatever change takes place in the relative value of gold and silver it has no effect to alter the relative quantities of commodities exchanged; in other words, it matters not in current transactions whether prices are high or low, it will not alter in one country, or between two countries, the quantities, say of piece goods for wheat, or tea for iron. With regard to wages, the working classes need instruction in this matter, and it should be dinned into the trading and middle classes of this country. For my part, I feel grateful to the Royal Commissioners that these two most important facts respecting current interchanges have been so well brought out by their examination of the witnesses they have had before them, and I think them particularly happy in eliciting one of these facts from such an able, cautious, and staunch bi-metallist as the secretary to the Indian Council in the Financial department.

I do not hesitate to express my firm conviction that if these two truths penetrate the understanding of the trading and working classes, we shall hear no more of the importence of local dual standards, as in the remotest degree competent to improve their position. For, unfortunately at present, few of the population of these islands are at all interested in deferred payments: and such as are interested in Savings Banks, Club Funds, &c., are benefitted by the fall in the gold value of silver. I would urge my brother associates of the Chambers of Commerce of this country to be up and doing, with the view of promoting the cause of truth in this currency controversy.

The World's Great Currency Dilemma.

In what then does the dilemma consist? It consists in the uncertain course of action which may be adopted by countries which are heavily loaded with silver, at an unnatural valuation, and the uncertainty of the relative values of silver and gold.

Revival of Local Dual Standards.

It is two years ago that in conversation with an American upon this subject, he told me that in his opinion it was a big dilemma, but that his mind was more occupied with the rapid payment of the American debt, since the completion of this would leave little but speculative stocks in his country for prudent people to invest in. I have often since thought that if this country joined a bi-metallic convention at fifteen-and-a-half to sixteen parts of silver to one of gold, and the natural relation became fifty to one or even more, how our cousins might load us up with silver at the convention arrangement, and take their pick of such securities as Great Britain and her colonies afford in exchange for the same.

But in the discharge of the American debt, does there not appear to be great danger in connection with their currency system? The gold and silver for general currency and reserves in the United States is estimated at £142,501,000 of gold, and £74,548,000 of silver, at sixteen parts of silver to one part of gold, together £217,049,000.

The following is a statement of the position of the currency of the United States presented by Mr. Charles S. Fairchild, the Secretary to the Treasury, to the Speaker of the House of Representatives, in December, 1887:—

COMPARATIVE STATEMENT OF METAL (GOLD AND SILVER) AND NOTE CURRENCY IN THE UNITED STATES OF AMERICA IN JULY, 1886, AND NOVEMBER, 1887. £ 000 OMITTED.

IN THE COUNTRY EXCLUSIVE OF THE TREASURY.

	July 1886.	Nov. 1887.	Increase or Decrease.	
Gold Coin	73,552	80,480	+	6,928
Silver Coin	10,756	12,717	+	1,961
,, ,, subsidiary .	9,462	10,514	+	1,052
	93,770	103,711	+	9,941
Gold Certificates . . .	15,590	20,525	+	4,935
Silver ,, . . .	18,063	32,946	+	14,883
	33,653	53,471	+	19,818
United States Notes .	66,320	67,941	+	1,621
National Bank ,, .	62,418	54,816	–	7,602
	128,738	122,757	–	5,891
Total . .	£256,161	279,939	+	23,778

HELD BY THE TREASURY.

	July 1886.	Nov. 1887.	Increase or Decrease.	
Gold Coin	38,854	37,380	–	1,474
Standard Silver	37,156	43,906	+	6,750
Silver Coin (subsidiary) . . .	5,965	5,016	–	949
Gold Bullion	8,878	24,641	+	15,763
Silver ,, ...	623	968	+	345
Trade dollars	...	1,427	+	1,427
	91,476	113,338	+	21,862
United States Notes . .	4,687	3,133	–	1,554
National Bank ,, . .	827	852	+	25
	5,514	3,985	–	1,529
Total . .	£96,990	117,323	+	20,333

TOTAL IN THE COUNTRY.

	July, 1886.	Nov. 1887.	Increase or Decrease.
Gold Coin and Bullion . . .	121,284	142,501	+ 21,217
Silver " . . .	63,962	74,548	+ 10,586
	185,246	217,049	+ 31,803
Gold Certificates . .	15,590	20,525	+ 4,935
Silver " . .	18,063	32,946	+ 14,883
	33,653	53,471	+ 19,818
United States Notes .	71,007	71,074	+ 67
National Bank " .	63,245	55,668	- 7,577
	134,252	126,742	- 7,510
Total .	£353,151	397,262	+ 44,111

This is a remarkable statement. It shows that in sixteen months the gold and silver added to currency purposes in the U.S.A. increased by £31,803,000, namely, £21,217,000 gold and £10,586,000 silver, nearly equal to three-fourths of the world's present annual production of these metals. That the Treasury obtained about £15,000,000 additional gold during the period, and £6,000,000 additional silver. That the people increased their use of gold and silver metal and notes, including metal certificates, by £23,778,000, besides diminishing their use of National Bank notes to the extent of £7,602,000. That they increased the use of gold certificates by £4,935,000, and of silver certificates by £14,883,000.

Adverting to the discredit cast upon the Government returns of the amount of gold in the hands of the public by the *Commercial and Financial Chronicle* in July, 1887, wherein it was estimated that they had placed the figures too high by £60,000,000, the present returns may be prudently examined with great caution.*

Mr. Fairchild, in the document we are examining, recommends

* Accepting these figures of the gold and silver currency of the country, one-third is silver and two-thirds gold. Should there be £60,000,000 less of gold in the country than this statement shows, then the proportion of gold to silver would be about half and half.

to Government that measures should be adopted to prevent the loading up of the Treasuries with useless silver, and suggests that when a prudent reserve of that metal is exceeded by £1,025,000, the purchase of silver should cease altogether. He remarks: "If ever the time comes when the standard dollar goes to a discount, the people, in the pockets of almost every one of whom will be found more or less of these dollars, will emphatically demand that they too shall be redeemed in gold, or made as good as when issued, and that the purchase of silver bullion be stopped. If the plan above suggested were now adopted, they would probably never go to a discount—surely not, except under altogether extraordinary circumstances—and yet the public would have a supply of them, limited only by the need and demand of the people for them."

As Mr. Fairchild admits that the silver dollar is only worth 75 cents., he alludes, I suppose, to the time when the American people generally will know as much about it as he does. He knows that the coin must be a token, but appears to vainly crave after making it a standard without a fixed relation to gold.

The question arises, when the National Debt of the United States is paid off, £198,235,000,* which could be done in less than ten years, assuming that the same policy with regard to it is carried on, what can they take as security for their note issues? Can they face the present and prospective decline in the gold value of silver? I give them credit for knowing pretty well the comparative cost of the production of gold and silver, and the possible output of the world, even at a greatly reduced cost of the production of gold. Were silver to go down to 30 pence per ounce, they would have to rate their silver at its true gold value if they desire to preserve a true gold basis, which would be a total decline of 50 per cent., or at £37,274,000. Now, with a metal currency of £142,501,000 gold, and silver £37,274,000, total £179,775,000, and no government securities as a backing for notes, there will be a strong temptation to them to open their mints to the unlimited reception of silver at the present relation in their currency. They may argue, what have we better than silver to take? The measure will re-habilitate the white metal. France and the other nations of the Latin Union will follow suit, and

* £26,160,000 of the debt was paid off last year.

there will be an abundance of oil for the wheels of commerce, high prices, no distress, and all the world jubilant.

This violent reaction could be accomplished, and would have a tremendous disturbing influence for a time, the production of silver would be stimulated, but most likely in the end, the countries attempting this unnatural juggle would find silver their sole standard ultimately, and be no better off than if they at once acknowledge the apparent inevitable, and adjust their currencies to it as best they can. They may restore the old relation for a little season. They may mask again for a time the debasing influence of the cheaper upon the dearer metal. They may create a revolution in gold prices throughout the world. But they can no more alter the course of nature, with reference to the comparative cost of gold aud silver, and their relative quantities in the crust of the earth, than they can alter the course of the planet on which we live.

If the Americans were to act as I have supposed, what effect would it have upon the rest of the world? In the first place, all those who desire to exchange silver for gold, would have the opportunity of doing so through the local dual standard mints, gold would find its way into gold standard countries, and prices in these countries might rise in consequence. The exchange between gold standard countries and silver standard countries would return to the approximate par it retained previous to 1872. The Government of India, and the salaried classes there in connection with Great Britain, and holders of Indian securities would rejoice, the only drawback to all being higher prices in England, which must accompany this change, as we have before seen.

Silver at its Natural Exchange Value.

But what will be the position if the Americans carry out their threat to the nations of the Latin Union, that unless they will help them to keep up the fictitious value of silver, they will let it go? This, that silver must yet fall, and no one can say how much. And the fall will have a very serious and trying effect upon silver standard debtor countries to gold standard creditor countries. Take India as an instance, say silver falls to 30d. per ounce, or another 5d. per rupee, this would necessitate providing in India Rs.50,000,000 to secure the same amount of gold as before the fall, which is requisite to meet India's sterling obligations in London. I would ask, if twelve years ago it had been predicted that by this time India would have to bear such a saddle, would not every one have said, Impossible? Will it be impossible for India to carry such another burden in the future? How some of the other silver standard debtor states are to bear the burden of their gold obligations I can form no opinion, as I know next to nothing about them; but I should think it might become beyond the ability of some of them to meet them.

It may be of some comfort to the salaried classes of India connected with this country, and to holders of silver securities, that gold will go proportionately further in gold standard countries in consequence of the fall in the gold value of silver.

There is an important factor to which I would draw attention. Let us assume that the fall of gold prices in these islands is due, as Messrs. Goschen, Giffen and other competent authorities maintain it is, to diminished supplies and fresh distribution of gold. It would be fair to assume, if there be no change in action or gold market rates of silver that either this appreciation of gold will become universal or will be rectified to some extent in this country through its exchanges with other countries, supposing that those countries have not experienced the same appreciation. Let us assume that they experience the same appreciation. Then the £700,000,000 of gold currency of the world becomes equal in purchasing power to £910,000,000, a rise of 30 per cent. during the past 14 years, and whilst at the same time there has been a great increase in the use of credit instruments both in Europe and America. On the assumption that the relative values of gold and silver may become 31 parts of silver to one of gold, the comparative purchasing power of silver measured by gold would be only one-half of what it now is. That is to say, it would be in the United States of America £37,274,000 against £74,548,000; in the nations of the Latin Union, £78,250,000 against £156,500,000; in Germany, £21,810,000 against £43,620,000; in Great Britain £10,560,000 against £21,120,000. Taking the rise in gold at 30 per cent., the purchasing power of gold held by these same countries would be as follows:—The United States of America, £185,251,000 against £142,501,000: the nations of the Latin Union, £266,708,000 against £206,160,000; Germany, £110,840,000 against £85,280,000; Great Britain, £141,180,000 against £108,600,000. These changes, if it is fair to assume them, place the United States of America in the following contrasted position :—Purchasing power—Gold, £185,251,000 ; silver, £37,274,000 ; together, £222,525,000; by weight at present—gold, £142,501,000 ; silver (16 parts of silver to 1 of gold), £74,548,000 ; together, £217,049,000.

This statement does not contain the full force of the future possible position. I have assumed a further fall in the gold value of silver, but I have only taken the purchasing power of gold at its present rate. On the assumption that the gold value of commodities, services, &c., must become equal to the gold value of silver, the position would become something like this, taking the rise in the purchasing power of gold at 50 per cent. more than in 1873, the £700,000,000 of gold in the currency of the world would be equal to £1,050,000,000, and the currency of the United States would equal—Gold, £213,751,000; silver, £37,274,000; together, £251,025,000; against the circulation, as at present valued, of £217,049,000.

If the late Secretary of the United States Treasury, Mr. Manning, considered that the country possessed ample gold and silver to discontinue the coinage of silver and abrogate the Bland Act, this statement does not show such an alteration as would render it necessary to delay such an operation. The high aim which Mr. Secretary Manning held out to his countrymen of possessing a sound automatic metal standard currency, with every state note having a backing of metal to ensure its payment, may yet, and speedily be realised in a country rich in gold and silver. That this can only be attained through sufferings caused by changes in prices none can deny, but they would be sufferings worthy of the people and of lasting benefit to their posterity.

MONETARY STANDARDS, MONEY AND MONETARY SYSTEMS.

(*From the* Bankers' Magazine, *August and October*, 1888.)

An Effective Metal Standard.*

The commercial history of most countries is strewn with the wrecks which have either been caused or aggravated by ignorance of sound currency laws. The past fourteen years have served to throw a flood of light upon the subject of currency for the benefit of the thoughtful student of the same. Upon Professor Huxley declaring, at a meeting held in the Mansion House in connection with the Imperial Institute, last year, that the Jubilee year of the Queen inaugurated the marriage of science with commerce, his trained mind—possibly a virgin one on the subject, and therefore perhaps the better—was sought to assist in determining the terms and conditions of a scientific automatic metal standard currency. Commerce has cause to regret that as yet neither his nor any other fully qualified mind has, so far as the world knows, been

* Suppose countries A and B possess equally well organised banking systems but no intrinsically valuable currency or reserves. That in A the unlimited legal tender and final discharger of debts consists of excessive issues by the State of stamped pieces of paper; whilst in B it consists of moderate issues by the State of stamped pieces of leather. Within certain limits interchanges of raw or manufactured articles, stocks, shares, bonds, &c., could be as freely effected as though the instrumentality of gold and silver were employed. The larger quantity of stamped paper in A, constituting price, than of stamped leather in B, would have no deterrent effect upon the interchanges. The high prices for which the goods, &c., of B sold in A would have to be given for the goods, &c., desired by B, and *vice versa* with regard to the goods, &c., of A in country B. The impediment to commerce would arise when the goods, &c., of one country are required by the other in excess of demand for goods, &c., on the part of the country of whom the requirement is made, since the paper in A would have no value in B, nor the leather of B in A. There could be no such exchange relation between these countries as substances of value embodied, say, in gold and silver at present affords.

brought to bear upon the subject. In the meantime, I may perhaps be permitted to state my views of what the requisite conditions are, premising that the standard must possess intrinsic value.

1st.—The substance selected must be suitable as far as possible to the wants and habits of the people, in considerable use as an intermediary in exchanges among them, and such as is generally desired by large populations of the earth for other than currency purposes. It must be received in unlimited quantities by the State authorities fitted for circulation by them, and made unlimited legal tender.

2nd.—All State notes and other credit instruments which form part of the currency must be encashable without question or delay, and for the actual weight of the standard metal indicated upon the face of such documents.

These conditions would appear to secure an effective automatic metal standard for currency purposes. If any one of these conditions is wanting, there would not be an effective metal currency, neither for the conduct of internal nor for international interchanges. These conditions imply, as essential, that the substance must be largely possessed and freely exchanged both for currency and other purposes; and that a true standard can never bear an agio or premium, in the terms of either another metal or inconvertible paper.

Most of the leaders among the advocates of local dual standards maintain the importance of the substance or substances selected possessing intrinsic value. Not in the sense that a £10 note contains the intrinsic value of something less than a farthing, but a value which it is intended should be of near relation to those things for which it exchanges. This is the distinction between standard and token metal. The latter does not possess the intrinsic value for which it exchanges for the former. The first is received by the Mints in unlimited quantities, and is constituted unlimited legal tender, whilst the second is neither the one nor the other. Does a legal enactment that 15½ parts of silver shall be equal to 1 part of gold—when the comparative intrinsic worth, measured by value giving factors, is in the proportion of 25 parts of silver to 1 part of gold—make 1 part of gold worth only 15½ parts of silver? It may be made to circulate in currencies for a time near the forced relationship; but on the testimony of competent judges, the underrated metal has commanded, and would command, an agio or premium in the overrated metal in spite of the law. When this takes place, some would conclude, and with good reason, that the standard would become the overrated metal, and of an autocratic nature resembling inconvertible paper. If the definitions of a standard which I have given are sound, and it is considered to be of importance that the different peoples of the earth should possess suitable sound automatic metal standards to the extent to which they can use them, for their own benefit *primarily*, it might appear that a great deal which some desire to attempt, especially with reference to Indian currency (and a few advocate in journals dealing with the subject), is a simple beating of the air, and both imprudent and impracticable.

France and the United States of America, as peoples, are reposing in a fool's monetary paradise, which springs from the delusion that they possess local dual standards. The first insist that in their currency 15½ grains of fine silver shall be worth 1 grain of fine gold, the second insist that in their currency 16 grains of fine silver shall be worth 1 grain of fine gold, whilst for other than currency purposes the wide world over more than 22 grains of fine silver have to be given for 1 grain of fine gold. Mr. Fairchild, the financial secretary of the United States, and doubtless many other men in both countries who understand the subject, are fully alive to the great danger of the position. All the world now, when it requires gold for currency or other purposes and has silver alone to give in exchange for it, has to pay an agio or premium of 44½ per cent. to command it. Such an agio as this in silver for gold will, in all probability, come to be paid by the monetary institutions of these two countries.

Money.

In an article in the *Contemporary Review* in 1879, entitled "What is Money?" Professor H. Sidgwick, of Cambridge, wrote:—"Though we have all of us something to do with money, most of us are painfully conscious that our acquaintance with it is very limited." After treating of various things which have been called money, he states "that the definition which includes bank notes generally, and excludes other bankers' liabilities, is least of all to be accepted." Professor Dr. A. Soetbeer, in his *Materialen*, wrote:—"I have in the customary way specified the circulation of notes according to the official reports; it must not be omitted, however, that endorsed bills and deposits at the banks payable on demand have as great an influence on the quantity of the circulating medium, and of facility for trade, as bank notes. In this matter it would be more exact to couple these obligations with the notes issued, and then to compare them with the stock of the precious metals." Professor C. F. Bastable, of Dublin, in his article on money in the *Encyclopædia Britannica*, quotes with approval the definition of money given by Professor F. A. Walker, of the John Hopkins University of the U.S.A., as follows:—"Money is that which passes freely from hand to hand throughout the community in final discharge of debts and full payment for commodities, etc., being accepted equally without reference to the character or credit of the person who offers it, and without the intention of the person who receives it to consume it or enjoy it, or apply it to any other use than in turn to tender it to others in discharge of debts or payment for commodities." I would remark upon this definition that a forced paper currency satisfies these conditions. A valueless *media* cannot be a satisfactory international measure; nor can corn, tea, salt, hides or cowries be so. Nothing as yet known equals gold and silver. The above definition applied to this country would embrace the standard substance, which is gold, Bank of England notes, silver and copper coins to a limited extent. This assumes, however, that at no time the credit of the bank, or the Government at the back of the bank, could be questioned. This definition does not satisfy me. I submit that there is money and that there are money tokens. In my opinion money is simply and solely the standard substance, as gold in this country and silver in India. The tokens of money are all those instruments used in exchanges and affecting price, which are known in this country as silver and copper coins, bank notes, cheques, bills of exchange, promises to pay, book credits—in fact, all instruments, of whatever nature, apart from the standard substance used in a country, purporting to pay money at once or at any future time, are tokens of the standard substance, and true economisers of the use of the standard substance. I would support this opinion by the following reasons:—

1. The standard substance is ordinarily—as it is intended to be—a measure of general and particular values, though itself of

variable value. It has an exchange value in some near relation t its cost value. Other instruments of exchange have not and not intended to have a correlative value with those thir which they exchange. The standard substance may be wı. hides, salt, or cowries, provided they are conditioned as standards.

2. The "elemental might" of weights of standard metal defined by Professor Soetbeer is not only manifest in the settlem of international balances of indebtedness, by the transmission the standard metal—as for instance, gold to this country, silver ı India, but also in prices and rates of exchange throughout the world.

It is no exaggeration to say that in every transaction into which price enters, where there is an effective gold or silver standard, either the actual weight of standard metal indicated by the price, or one or other of the tokens of the standard metal plays a part. And further, but for these tokens of the standard substance the weight of standard metal itself would have to pass unless a return were made to barter.

Monetary Systems.

In the event of the views expressed by me as to the chief cause of the decline in prices in this country since 1873 being found correct an exhaustive investigation into the different monetary systems of the world, in connection with the present world-wide monetary dilemma, seems imperative. I am disposed to doubt whether any country, even the United States of America, is in possession of the necessary facts to enable it to carry out this investigation to a satisfactory conclusion. During the past thirteen years all my efforts to get such information as I consider essential have failed. In the columns of the *London Chamber of Commerce Journal* I have more than once appealed to its readers to furnish the information, which is of the following nature:—Are the financial operations of the Government conducted through their own treasuries or through the public banks? Through what machinery is the standard metal added to the monetary system of a country? Has the country a mint? What are the mint regulations? If there is no mint there cannot be an effective automatic currency, unless some such arrangement exists as that which prevails in China, where an authoritative stamp on masses of silver indicates its purity, and thereby such confidence in it is engendered among the people as to ensure its currency. But unless this is unlimited, both in reception and circulation, automatic action would not be secured. Are there institutions through the instrumentality of which the equivalent of the standard metal can be obtained before the bullion is converted into coin? What are the laws and habits of the people in connection with bank notes, cheques, bills of exchange, and other credit instruments? How are interchanges effected?—by barter or through the instrumentality of price, or a definite weight of standard metal? Not being able to get this information from any of my mercantile or banking acquaintances, I sought to interest the Government—first a Conservative, then a Liberal one—through the Foreign Office, and prepared a series of questions which I thought our consular representatives in other countries should be asked by the Foreign Office to answer. I was, however, informed that our consuls had too much to do, and that it was such a delicate subject that it could not well be placed in their hands. In the two blue books which the Gold and Silver Commission has issued containing the evidences of the advocates of a local single standard and of local dual standards, this subject does not appear to have been touched. By examiners and examinees of this Commission the quantity theory has been made much of by some, and little of by others. And that which is astounding is that so many who would generally be thought to be possessed of competent knowledge on such a subject speak of gold and silver as *small change.** As to the value theory of gold and silver, beyond the evidence of Dr. Roberts Austen, of the Royal Mints, on the subject, few questions have been asked, or apparently little thought of the matter by the Commission. In October, 1883, I wrote in the *London Chamber af Commerce Journal*—"These questions of relation of quantities and relation of exchange values of the

---

* The impression left on my mind by the perusal of the second blue book issued by the Gold and Silver Commission is, that it is a complete failure of an attempt to elevate credit instruments to the same platform as standard substances. That Mr. Dunning Macleod's views of wealth should have been brought forward at all, will surprise a good many readers of the report. It is to be hoped that in the remaining work of the Commission, which is yet to appear, expositions will be found of the "Elemental might" of weights of standard substances; the value theory of them; and the different monetary systems of the world.

precious metals are the very kernel of bi-metallism, and further elucidation under this head of production is requisite." For my part I cannot arrive at any other conclusion upon this monetary dilemma than that its base rests upon the value theory. Silver is sold for what it now fetches because it pays to produce it, and most likely would pay at present at a much less gold price. It is not the quantity which has lowered its price. We are told that there are no stores of silver. If the production does not continue to pay, then its price must rise, or production must cease. The question might be asked:—If we are to have this greatly further fall in the gold price of silver with which you threaten us, would it not be better to make an effort to remove the silver standard from the world? I would reply:—Are we able to make the vaguest guess as to the gold and silver in the bowels of the earth, their proportionate output in the distant future, or their proportionate cost value? The idea of attempting to remove silver from the world as a monetary standard is surely not worth a moment's thought. It is neither practical nor prudent.

AN AMERICAN VIEW OF BI-METALLISM AND ITS ADVOCATES.

Extract from "FINANCE."

An Essay by POSEY S. WILSON (*Member Am. Econ. Soc.*), *published in* RHODES'S JOURNAL OF BANKING *for July*, 1888, *New York.*

"THAT in the interchange of material things for material things, of services for services, rights for rights, or any one of these for any part or more of the others, a medium is necessary is self-evident.

The inter-relation of these three classes of wealth are infinite in their permutation, as they vary through the agency of demand, and it is the function of money to indicate these relations when they are referred to it.

To avoid the confusion which would result from each man's using a term of his own as "lots," or "heaps," or "chunks," the statute makes a general term, "dollar." It ordains that contracts shall be expressed in dollars, and when tendered in payment for any past transaction, or proposed interchange, an offer of dollars shall be final. To complete its work, the statute which has named dollar as an unit of value, or divisor of value, in the abstract goes into the material world and selects that which shall be the dollar in concrete. This, it decrees, shall be a given quantity of gold of certain fineness, with a Government mark indicating these attributes. This, in our financial system, is the standard of its characteristics: $23\frac{22}{100}$ of fine gold or $25\frac{4}{5}$ grains of gold $\frac{9}{10}$ fine; *i.e.*, standard gold. Actually, this may vary a little, owing to our faculties being finite, but theoretically, it cannot vary in the smallest degree. Even in practice, there must be a relation as close as possible between the quantity and fineness, or value, of the bullion in coins, and the stamp, or denomination—the mint value as to gold, the market value as to silver. Even so wild a financier as John Law admitted "it is not the sound of the denomination, but the value of the metal which is to be considered," and the metal in coin derives its value solely from demand, and the demand grows out of its fitnesss to stand as the material sign of the abstract unit of value, though it would, without doubt, have a value for use even if it were not used as money.

Many misguided, as well as many designing men, sometimes called by the inexact term, bi-metallists, have sought in vain to prove that this concrete sign of the unit of value, which is incidentally the measure of value, standard of value, and medium of exchange—or as Voltaire calls it, "the pledge and agent of exchange," and as Turgot called it, "the certificate that the holder is entitled to something in return for some act or thing"—is exactly equal to 371¼ grains of pure, or 412½ grains of standard silver "if all would admit it." Hence they argue that two standards, or tests of the attributes of this concrete sign of the unit of value are possible; and also, because debt is large, necessary.

For want of space, I refer the double standard argument; the three tailed cat argument; the argument that black is white; and the proof that one is equal to two—by means of $a2 - a2 = a2 - a2$—to a later time, for the double standard argument assumes that things which are not equal to the same thing, may be made, by law, equal to each other; and, conversely, that things which are not equal to each other may be made equal to the same thing.

Besides, in the United States, the clamour for free coinage of silver, as the question now stands, does not represent the opinion of intelligent students and disinterested men, but is merely a conspiracy on the part of mine owners, their agents and allies, to induce the people to consent that through perpetual Governmental interference, an artificial demand for silver shall be created, and through that demand, the price of this metal placed beyond the influence of the natural laws of value, and the price thereby kept at an arbitrary figure already set by themselves.

If let alone, they will probably insist, after a while, that silver be made the equal of gold, ounce for ounce, and, indeed, that is the logical end of their demand."

"NORMAN'S EXCHANGE CALCULUS."*

OR AN UNIT SYSTEM, AS A GRAIN IN THE BRITISH ISLES, &c.; A GRAMME IN FRANCE, &c.; A RUTTEE IN BRITISH INDIA, &c.; FOR DETERMINING THE PARS OF EXCHANGE BETWEEN ALL COUNTRIES: ALSO FOR ASCERTAINING THE WEIGHT OF FINE GOLD OR SILVER INDICATED BY PRICES IN ALL COUNTRIES POSSESSING EFFECTIVE METAL STANDARDS.

Specimen of information which should be furnished annually by the Mint, or other State Department, of each country of the World to its people, in its own weights and monetary denominations. Gross weights are all important to such—bankers and others—as use scales.

BRITISH ISLES, &c.

EXPRESSIONS are used throughout the world for definite weights of fine gold and fine silver. One grain of fine gold in Great Britain, Australasia, Canada and many parts of the Empire is 2·123863 pence; because the weight of fine gold in the sovereign on its issue from the Mint is 113·0016 grains. 240 pence, divided by 113·0016, gives as nearly as possible 2·123863 pence. It is sufficient to take the expression for one grain of fine gold or fine silver to the third decimal point, since 2·124 instead of 2·123863 pence gives only 1½d. too much upon £100. So long as any country has an *effective* metal standard, be it gold or silver, the metal standard will not command a premium in any other metal or credit instrument. Attached to the chief gold or silver coin of each country will be found the weight of fine gold or silver which it contains on issue from the Mints

---

* "I think that your "Single Grain System" is most useful for all practical purposes, and simplifies very much the whole exchange calculus."—Professor Dr. W. Lexis, Gottingen, September, 17th, 1888."

also the denominational expression* for one grain of fine gold or silver. These used as multipliers of the weight of fine gold for the gold or silver for the silver in any of the world's moneys of account or coins gives the expressions for the weights thus multiplied. To find the gold price of silver and the silver price of gold, ascertain the proportion established between the two metals by the market price of silver in a gold standard country, or of gold in a silver standard country, thus: say, the ounce of silver (444 grains of fine silver) commands 42 pence in London; divide 42 by 444, and the result is ·0946 of one penny, which is the gold price of one grain of silver; divide 2·124 pence, the fixed expression for one grain of fine gold in Great Britain, ·0946 of one penny, and we get the proportion at this price between gold and silver, viz., 22·45 parts of silver to one part of gold. The fixed expression for one grain of gold, being divided by this proportion, gives the gold price of one grain of fine silver. The fixed expression for one grain of fine silver, being multiplied by this proportion, gives the silver price of one grain of fine gold. Attached to the names of the countries in the following tables will be found—(*a*) which denotes the possession of a Mint; (*b*) that gold is received in unlimited quantities; (*c*) that gold is unlimited legal tender; (*d*) that silver is received in unlimited quantities; (*e*) that silver is unlimited legal tender. The British par value of the gold coins is attached, and the British price of the silver coins at 42 pence per standard ounce or 444 grains of fine silver. On the thoughtful suggestion of Mr. Alex. L. Glencross, a column of constants is attached; being the gold price in decimal parts of a penny of each silver coin at the proportion of one-sixteenth of a penny per standard ounce, or 444 grains of fine silver. One-sixteenth of one penny is the denominational expression for a trifle more than one thirty-fourth part of one grain of fine gold.

To find the price of the silver coins at more or less than 42 pence per ounce of standard silver, it is only necessary to add or subtract the sum of the constants representing the difference to or from the sterling value column attached to the coins.

---

* "Men in their bargains contract not for denominations or sounds, but for the intrinsic value, which is the quantity of silver or gold by publc authority warranted to be in pieces of such denominations."—Locke, 1695.

	Sterling Value.	Gross Weight on issue from the Mint.	Grains of fine Gold (G) or Silver (s) on issue from the Mint.	One Grain.
Europe and Dependencies.				
Great Britain (*a b c*), Australasia (*a b c*), Canada (*c*), Bahamas (*c*), South Africa (*c*), Jamaica (*c*), Malta (*c*), Bermuda (c), Newfoundland (*c*), Falkland Isles (*c*), Turk's Islands (*c*), St. Vincent (*c*), Granada (*c*), Tobago, St. Lucia (*c*), Leeward Isles (*c*), Gibraltar (*c*), Sierra Leone (*c*), Gambia (c), Gold Coast (*c*), Lagos (*c*), Cape of Good Hope (*c*), Natal *c*), St. Helena (*c*), Cyprus (*c*), Labuan (*c*) Fiji (*c*)—Sovereign or 20 shillings or 240 pence, d.	20/-	123·274	G113·0016	2·124d.
½ sovereign, ½ of above				
Shilling or twelve pence	-/7½	87·225	s80·72937	·149d.
Crown, 5/-; double florin, 4/-; half-crown, 2/6; florin, 2/-; sixpence, -/6; threepence -/3				
German Empire (*a b c*) Heligoland (*b c*)—20 marks or 2,000 pfennings, p., and 10 marks	19/7	122·917896	G110·6268	18·079p.
5 marks or 500 pfennings, 2, 1, ½, ⅕ marks	3/0½	428·679815	s385·80875	1·296p.
Denmark (*a b c*), Sweden (*a b c*), Norway (*a b c*)—20 crowns or 2,000 ores, o., 10 crowns	22/0⅕	138·283115	G124·4542	16.C7o.
Crown or 100 ores, o., 4, 2, ½, ¼, ⅒ .	-/8¾	115·742625	s92·5941	1·08o.
France (*a b c e*), Belgium (*a b c e*), Italy (*a b c e*), Switzerland (*a b c e*), Servia (*b c e*), Roumania (*b c e*), Bulgaria (*b c e*), —20 francs or 2,000 cents, c. 100, 50, 10, 5	15/10⅓	99·563349	G89·607	22·32c.
Franc or 100 cents, 5. 2, ½, ⅕ . .	-/6½	77·04177	s69·44557	1·44c.
Austria-Hungary (*a e*)—Florin or 100 kreutzers, k., 8, 4	1/11¾	12·445418	G11·20087	8·928k.
Florin or 100 kreutzers, 3, 2, 1½, ¼, ⅒, $\frac{1}{20}$	1/4¼	190·526163	s171·47038	·583k.
Netherlands (*a b c e*)—William or 10 florins or 1,000 cents, c.	16/6½	103·844283	G93·45985	10·67c.
Ducat, double ducat	9/4½	...	G53·00394	...
Gulden or 100 c., 2½, ¼, ⅒, $\frac{1}{20}$ . .	1/1¾	154 3235	s145·8357	·686c.
Russia (*a e*)—½ imperial or 5 roubles or 500 copecks, c.	16/4½	101·0	G92·57043	5.4c.
Rouble or 100 c., ½, ¼, ⅕, ⅒, $\frac{1}{20}$ . .	2/2¼	319·935764	s277·7221	·36c.
Spain (*a b c e*)—Isabella or 10 escudos or 1,000 centimos, c.	20/7$\frac{7}{16}$	129·189396	G116·48355	8·534c.
Dollar or 100 c., escudos or ½ dollar .	2 10⅛	400·625349	s 360·56296	·555c·
Peseta or ⅕ dollar, ⅒, $\frac{1}{20}$ dollar . .	-/6⅛	...	s64·90074	...
Portugal (*a b c e*)—Coroa or 10 milreis or 10,000 reis, r.	44/4¾	273·692727	G250·88525	39·859r.
½ coroa or 5 milreis or 500 reis . .	23/11$\frac{5}{16}$	...	G135·273807	...
¼ ,, 2½ ,, 250 ,, 1 milreis	3/2$\frac{5}{16}$	...	G18·03656	...
½ milreis or 500 reis, r., ¼, ⅒, $\frac{1}{20}$ . .	1/3	192·904375	s176·828496	2·828r.

	Sterling Value.	Gross Weight on issue from the Mint.	Grains of fine Gold (G) or Silver (s) on issue from the Mint.	One Grain.	Constants — Value of each Silver Coin at $\frac{1}{16}$th of a Penny ℘ Standard Ounce.
Europe and Dependencies—*continued.*					
reece (*b c e*)—20 drachmai or 2,000 lepta, l., 10, 5	14/2$\frac{2}{3}$	89·137254	G80·223528	24·918.	
5 drachmai or 500 lepta, 1, $\frac{1}{2}$, $\frac{1}{4}$ . .	2/5$\frac{7}{16}$	345·453154	s310·90783	1·6081.	·0437d.
inland—10 markkaa or 1,000 penni, p. 20	7/11$\frac{1}{8}$	49·784761	G44·806285	22·318p.	
1 markkaa or 100 penni, p., 2 . .	–/6$\frac{1}{2}$	79·984326	s69·425519	1·440p.	·0098d.
urkey (*a b c*)—Medjidie or 100 piastres or 4,000 paras, p.	18/0$\frac{3}{8}$	111·359837	G102·00629	39·213p.	
Medjidie or 800 paras, p., $\frac{1}{2}$, $\frac{1}{4}$, $\frac{1}{10}$, $\frac{1}{20}$.	2/5$\frac{1}{8}$	371·231352	s308·116898	2·596p.	·0434d.
Piastre	–/1$\frac{7}{16}$		s15·406		·0022d.
America.					
nited States (*a b c e*), Liberia (*b c e*)—Eagle or 10 dollars or 1,000 cents., c., 20, 5, 2$\frac{1}{2}$, 1	41/1	258·	G232·2	4·307c.	
Dollar or 100 c., $\frac{1}{2}$, $\frac{1}{4}$, $\frac{1}{10}$, $\frac{1}{20}$	2/11$\frac{1}{8}$	412·5	s371·257414	·269c.	·0523d.
:exico (*a d e*)—Doublon or 16 pesos or 1,600 centavos, c. 10	64/8$\frac{1}{8}$	417·66575	G365·457531	4·387c.	
Peso or 100 c., $\frac{1}{2}$, $\frac{1}{4}$, $\frac{1}{10}$, $\frac{1}{20}$	2/11$\frac{11}{16}$	417·66575	s377·058607	·265c.	·0531d.
razil (*a b c*)—10 Milreis or 10,000 reis, r. 20, 5	22/5$\frac{1}{3}$	138·347931	G126·81996	78·852r.	
2 Milreis or 2,000 reis, r., 1, $\frac{1}{2}$, $\frac{1}{5}$ . .	2/0$\frac{1}{8}$	393·524925	s360·731181	5·544r.	·0508d.
eru (*a b c e*)—10 sols or 1,000 centavos, c. 20, 5, 2 1	39/7$\frac{3}{4}$	248·908373	G224·017535	4·464c.	
1 sol or 100 centavos, $\frac{1}{2}$, $\frac{1}{5}$, $\frac{1}{10}$ . .	2/8$\frac{7}{8}$	385·20875	s347·227575	·288c.	·0489d.
hili (*a b c e*)— Condor or 10 pesos or 1,000 centavos, c. 5, 2, 1	37/5$\frac{3}{4}$	235·3882	G211·85066	4·72c.	
Silver as Peru in pesos.					
nited States Columbia (*d e*), pesos; Guatemala (*d e*), pesos; Venezuela (*a b c*), venesolanos; Hayti (*e*), gourde					
Both gold and silver same as Peru.					
ruguay (*e*)—4 patacon or 400 centavos, c. 2, 1 escudos	16/1	103·852	G90·8703	4·402c.	
5 real or 50 centavos, 2$\frac{1}{2}$, 1$\frac{1}{4}$	1/3$\frac{13}{16}$	200·781046	s167·31753	·299c.	·0235d.
olivia (*e*)—16 bolivanos or 1,600 centavos, c. $\frac{1}{2}$, $\frac{1}{4}$, $\frac{1}{8}$, $\frac{1}{16}$	61/4$\frac{3}{4}$	385·216047	G346·69545	4·615c.	
Silver same as Peru, $\frac{1}{2}$, $\frac{1}{4}$, $\frac{1}{8}$, $\frac{1}{16}$.					
rgentine Republic (*a b c e*)—5 pesos or 500 centavos, c.	19/7$\frac{13}{16}$	128·603173	G115·74262	4·32c.	
Silver same as Peru, $\frac{1}{2}$, $\frac{1}{4}$, $\frac{1}{8}$, $\frac{1}{16}$.					
osta Rica (*e*)—20 pesos or 2,000 centavos, c.	79/3$\frac{3}{5}$	497 816746	G448·03507	4·464c.	
$\frac{1}{2}$ pesos or 50 centavos	1/3$\frac{1}{4}$	192·904437	s161·07515	·310c.	·0227d.
cuador (*e*)—8 pesos or $\frac{1}{2}$ gold ounce or 800 centavos	31/2$\frac{2}{5}$	209·	G176·396	4·535c.	
Silver same as Peru.					
Asia.					
ersia (*a d e*)—1 toman or 200 shaheis, s. .	9/4$\frac{1}{2}$	53·490327	G52·96536	3·776s.	
1 keran or 2 panabats or 20 s. . .	–/6$\frac{3}{4}$	73·785923	s70·83448	·282s.	·0099d.

	Sterling Value.	Gross Weight on issue from the Mint.	Grains of fine Gold (G) or Silver (s) on issue from the Mint.	One Grain.
Asia—*continued.*				
India (*a d e*), Burma (*e*), Ceylon (*e*), Mauritius (*e*)—Mohur or 15 rupees or 2,880 pies, p.	29/2½	180·	G165·	17·454p.
Rupee or 16 annas or 192 p., ½, ¼, ⅛	1/3⅝	180·	s165·	1·164p.
China (*e*)—Tael or 1,000 cash, c.	4/0$\frac{1}{10}$	565·	s508·5	1·966c.
Japan (*a d e*)—10 yens or 1000 sen, s. 20, 5, 2, 1	40/11$\frac{1}{16}$	257·206347	G231·48525	4·320s.
1 yen or 100 sen, ½, ¼, ⅛, $\frac{1}{16}$	2/11⅖	416·	s374·399613	·267s.
Cochin-China (*e*)—Trade dollar or piastre or 100 cents, c. ½, ⅕, $\frac{1}{10}$	2/11¾	420·	s378·	·264c.
Siam (*a d e*)—Tical or 8 fuangs, f.	1/8	233·55	s212·142	·0377f.
Netherlands India (*e*)—25 cents, c. $\frac{1}{10}$, $\frac{1}{20}$	-/3⅓	49·07487	s35·339085	·707c.
Hong-Kong (*e*), Straits Settlements (*e*), Borneo (*e*)—Dollar or 100 cents, c. ½, ⅕, $\frac{1}{10}$, $\frac{1}{20}$	2/11⅖	416·	s374·399613	·267c.
Africa.				
Egypt (*b c*)—50 piastre or 2,000 paras, p., 100, 25	10/2$\frac{13}{16}$	66·096755	G57·83466	69·163p.
10 piastres or 400 paras, 5, 2½ 1	1/4$\frac{7}{16}$	192·904375	s173·613937	4·608p.
Tunis (*e*)—50 piastres or 800 karobs, k. 100, 25, 10, 5	24/-	150·619736	G135 557762	5·90k.
2 piastres or 32 karobs, 1	8/⅓	95·587976	s86·029178	·372k.
Philippine Islands (*e*)—Pesoduro or 100 centavos, c. 4, 2	4/0½	26·096103	G22·83705	4·379c.
50 centavos, 25, 10, 5	1/5	200·311903	s180·280712	·277c.
Antilles (*c e*) — Sovereign, dollar and piastre.				
Three half-pence	-/1¼	14·58357	s13·489737	

Two German books, one by Noback, of 1,234 pages, published in 1879, contains the gross and fine weights in grammes of 637 gold and 1,452 silver coins, together 2,089 coins of the world; the other of 114 pages, published in a cheap form in Bremerhaven in 1875, contains the fac-similes of 426 gold and 824 silver coins, together 1,250 coins, of which there are for Europe 316 gold and 663 silver, for Asia 22 gold and 37 silver, for Africa 5 gold and 1 silver, for America 79 gold and 116 silver, and for Australia 2 gold. Some countries have the same weights of money of account and coins but different denominations. If we confine the number of moneys of account or coins on which the exchanges of the world are at present regulated to 12 gold and 13 silver, 25 coins or moneys of account in all, then the 2,089 coins of which Noback gives the weights in grammes present 52,225 different values in the 103 countries of the world, all of which can be ascertained by the possession of Noback's book and my tables of values of one grain or gramme of fine gold and one grain or gramme of fine silver in the various countries of the world.

There is another German book, "Krusé Hambro Contorist," of which Dr. Patrick Kelly, in his Universal Cambist, written in 1811, makes mention, that Sir John Sinclair had a high opinion of it and recommended its translation into English. Sir John adds: "Till then we principally rely upon foreign merchants who make fortunes from our ignorance of the nature of the exchanges." There is a copy of this work in the British Museum, but it does not appear that any translation of it into English was ever made. It is not mentioned either by McCulloch or Stanley Jevons in their Bibliographies. I am disposed to think that Tate's Cambist now answers to this work.

The addition of two columns of charges per cent. or per mille would make such a table as the above complete. One column should contain the coinage charges of each country attached to the coin: these would be fixed charges. The other column should contain a minimum and maximum charge varying with the time occupied between securing the metal in one country and receiving the proceeds through the mint in another country, all transport charges and a fixed interest to be mentioned, say at the rate of five per cent. per annum. Illustration; Desired to know the equivalent gold price in London for a Bill on India on a price of 42 pence per standard ounce of silver. By one of the methods shown in this table the par value of the rupee would be found to be 15·60 pence. The first column would show 2 and $\frac{1}{8}$ per cent., the second say the maximum $\frac{7}{8}$ of one per cent., together 3 per cent., which added to 15·60 pence makes the price of the Bill 16·07 pence per rupee.

NORMAN'S

SINGLE GRAIN SYSTEM

FOR

DETERMINING THE PAR VALUE OF ALL MONEYS OF ACCOUNT AND GOLD AND SILVER COINS BETWEEN ALL COUNTRIES.

ALSO FOR

ASCERTAINING THE COMPARATIVE WEIGHTS OF FINE GOLD OR SILVER INDICATED BY RELATIVE PRICES THROUGHOUT THE WORLD.

BY JOHN HENRY NORMAN.

Reprinted from the "Bankers' Magazine" for May, 1887.

PRICE ONE PENNY.

LONDON:
—PRINTED BY WATERLOW AND SONS LIMITED, LONDON WALL, E.C.—
1887.

NORMAN'S SINGLE GRAIN SYSTEM FOR DETERMINING THE PAR VALUE OF ALL MONEYS OF ACCOUNT AND GOLD AND SILVER COINS BETWEEN ALL COUNTRIES. ALSO FOR ASCERTAINING THE COMPARATIVE WEIGHTS OF FINE GOLD OR SILVER INDICATED BY RELATIVE PRICES THROUGHOUT THE WORLD.

By John Henry Norman.

Many of my friends, among whom are a good number who have to do with foreign moneys of account and coins, are surprised when I tell them that I have a table and rules whereby I profess that any boy or girl who can work decimal multiplication and division is enabled to ascertain the par of exchange between all the countries of the world, and the values of the coins of any country in all other countries, whatever may be the gold value of silver or the silver value of gold.

Fourteen years' working of the exchanges in Calcutta made me thoroughly familiar with the subject, and before I left that city, in 1875, I had formed a table of the gross and fine weights of the standard and chief subsidiary coins of the world, with the value of one grain of fine metal attached to each in the currency of the country where the coin circulates. I pointed out that fine metal alone was that to be taken account of in the exchanges. This table fell perfectly flat in Calcutta, where the whole banking and mercantile community possessed it, and I am not aware that the issuers of credits in London, to whom copies were sent, ever saw anything in it worthy of their attention. I received a recognition of the merit of the compilation from the then Mint Master of the United States of America, Dr. Linderman, in 1875, but no practical use (so far as I have been able to ascertain) has been made of my method in the United States. Observing, in 1882, that the late Professor Stanley Jevons was studying the subject of legal weights of English coins, I sent him a copy, which led to my making the acquaintance of this emiment authority upon certain branches of currency. Since then I have fairly completed my system in tables, with directions in my pamphlet on *Local Dual Standards**, and my paper "An Elucidation of the metallic bases of the Colonial and Foreign Exchanges and the simplification of exchange," read before the Bankers' Institute on the 16th February, 1887.

---

* *Local Dual Standards*, published by Cassells.

Whether a person favours a "Local single standard" or "Local dual standards," this simplification of values and the exchanges is equally valuable to him, and it is not in my opinion necessary to wait until truth silences all dissentients on this disputed question before the adoption of my system. There is one statement which, however, I would advance here, which is—that a metal to become a monetary standard must be received in unlimited quantities by the Mint or other institution of a country, be fitted for currency, and be appointed unlimited legal tender. I believe that both schools of thought on currency now admit this, and consequently that where the receptive side of local dual standards is not practised, though the distributive side is, there no such thing as local dual standards exists, and that the real standard in those countries, so long as their international trade is conducted on the dearer metal, is the dearer metal.

The foundation of my system rests upon the value of one grain of fine metal in the standard money of account or coin of each country. I present in two tables, one of fine gold and the other of fine silver, twenty-five different gold weights of moneys of account, and twenty-five different silver weights of moneys of account. Of these fifty different weights I think that there are not more than twelve gold weights, and not more than thirteen silver weights that are not tokens. It would be with these therefore that calculations would have to be made in determining the par values of the moneys of account and the gold and silver coins of the world.

Having the value of one grain of fine gold in the currency of a gold standard country, the weight of fine gold in any gold coin being multiplied by this value the result will be the value of the coin in the currency of that country. The same with regard to silver. To find the gold value of silver coins in a gold standard country, the gold price of silver may be divided by the value of one grain, which will give the number of grains of gold indicated by the price, and this compared with the number of fine grains of silver procurable for the price, will show the proportion established between gold and silver; the fixed gold value of one grain of gold being divided by this gives the gold value of one grain of silver. The same process with regard to finding the silver value of gold coins in silver standard countries, but the proportion established between gold and silver must be multiplied by the fixed value of one grain of silver, and the result will be the silver value of one grain of gold.

The exchanges are always based upon Mint issue weights between countries possessing convertible paper currency. For actual weights scales are needed, and then resort should be made to my large tables in *Local Dual Standards*, wherein the gross weights, the alloy and the fine weights are given with the values of one gramme and one grain in each of fifty-four countries of the world of the 103 countries, the internal and international prices in which are based upon gold and silver.

The following are the tables, and the rules are appended. I recommend anyone who desires to master the system to work out the examples.

GOLD.

TABLE showing the weight of Fine Gold in grammes and grains of the moneys of account of 71 countries of the world, at Mint issue weight: with the values of a gramme and a grain attached. Col. I., Name of money of account; II., Nobacks, fine weights; III., Value of one gramme; IV., Grains of fine gold; V., Value of one grain; VI., Countries using the weights as moneys of account; [b] attached to the money of account denotes that the money of account or the multiple of it forming a coin is not a token; * attached to name of country denotes that gold is unlimited legal tender; † denotes the possession of a Mint; ‡ denotes the Mint receives gold in unlimited quantities.

Col. I. Money of Account.	II. Grammes fine gold.	III. Value of One Gramme.	IV. Grains fine gold.	V. Value of One Grain.	VI. Name of Countries.
I. £ or sovereign of 20*s*. or 240*d*.[b]	7·3224	32·766139 pence	113·0016	2·123863 pence	Great Britain,*†‡ Australasia,*†‡ Canada,* Bahamas,* South Africa,* Jamacia,* Malta,* Bermuda,* Newfoundland,* Falkland Isles,* Turk's Islands,* St. Vincent,* Granada,* Tobago, St. Lucia,* Leeward Islands,* Gibraltar,* Sierra Leone,* Gambia,* Gold Coast,* Lagos,* Cape of Good Hope,* Natal,* St. Helena,* Cyprus,* Labuan,* Fiji.*
II. Toman of 100 scahis[b]	3·4467	29·01326 scahis	53·190166	1·888 scahis	Persia.*†‡
III. Milreis of 1,000 reis[b]	1·62571	615·1158 reis	25·088525	39·8588 reis	Portugal.*†‡
IV. Peso of 100 centavos	1·55615	64·2611 centavos	24·09761	4·1498 centavos	Uruguay.
V. Dollar of 100 cents[b]	1·52535	65·5587 cents	23·539477	4·2481 cents	Newfoundland.*
VI. Dollar of 100 cents[b]	1·50463	66·52798 cents	23·22	4·3066 cents	United States of America,*†‡ Liberia.*
VII. Yen of 100 sen	1·5	66·66666 sen	23·148525	4·3199 sen	Japan.† Argentine Republic.[b] *†‡
VIII. Peso of 100 centavos	1·480081	67·56385 centavos	22·841095	4·3781 centavos	Mexico,† British Honduras,* British Guiana.*
IX. Pesoduro of 100 centavos	1·4796	67·5859 centavos	22·83409	4·3789 centavos	Philippine Islands.
X. Peso of 100 centavos	1·45161	68·8890 centavos	22·401753	4·4639 centavos	Guatemala, Peru, United States, Columbia, Hayti, Venezuela,*†‡ Costa Rica.
XI. Peso of 100 centavos	1·428787	69·9888 centavos	22·0495	4·5352 centavos	Ecuador.
XII. Boliviano of 100 centavos	1·404098	71·2192 centavos	21·668531	4·615 centavos	Bolivia.
XIII. Peso of 100 centavos	1·37278	72·8449 centavos	21·185221	4·7203 centavos	Chili.*
XIV. Rouble of 100 kopecks	1·19974	83·35139 kopecks	18·514807	5·4 kopecks	Russia.†
XV. Milreis of 1,000 reis[b]	·82178	1216·8069 reis	12·681996	78·8519 reis	Brazil.*†‡
XVI. Escudo of 100 centimos	·75484	132·4780 centimos	11·648955	8·58446 centimos	Spain.*†‡
XVII. Florin of 100 kreutzers	·725812	137·7766 kreutzers	11·200876	8·92787 kreutzers	Austria-Hungary.†
XVIII. Rupee of 16 ans. or 192 pies	·712786	269·3653 pies	11·	17·4545 pies	India.†
XIX. Florin of 100 cents	·60561	165·12276 cents	9·345985	10·6999 cents	Netherlands.*†‡
XX. Crown of 100 ores[b]	·403225	248· ores	6·222709	16·0701 ores	Denmark,*†‡ Sweden,*‡ Norway.*‡
XXI. Mark of 100 pfennings[b]	·358423	279· pfennings	5·531340	18·0788 pfennings	Germany.*†‡ Heligoland.*
XXII. Franc of 100 cents[b]	·290325	341·44157 cents	4·480350	22·3196 cents	France,*†‡ Belgium,*†‡ Switzerland, francs,*†‡ Itlay, liras,*†‡ Greece, drachmas,*‡ Servia, dinars,*‡ Roumania, leys,*‡ Bulgaria, lows,*‡ Finland.
XXIII. Paistre of 16 karobs	·17568	91·07468 karobs	2·7111552	5·9015 karobs	Tunis.
XXIV. Paistre of 40 paras[b]	·074952	533·6720 paras	1·156693	69·1626 paras	Egypt.*
XXV. Paistre of 40 paras[b]	·066099	605·14985 paras	1·020063	39·2133 paras	Ottoman Empire.*

SILVER.

TABLE showing the weights of Fine Silver, in grammes and grains, of the moneys of account of 65 countries of the world, at Mint issue weight: with the values of a gramme and a grain attached. Col. I., Name of money of account; II., Noback's fine weights in grammes; III., Value of one gramme; IV., Grains of fine silver; V., Value of one grain; VI., Countries using the weights as moneys of account; [b] attached to the money of account denotes that the money of account or the multiple of it forming a coin is not a token; * attached to the name of the country denotes that silver is unlimited legal tender; † denotes the possession of a Mint; ‡ denotes the Mint receives silver in unlimited quantities.

Col. I. Money of Account.	II. Grammes fine Silver.	III. Value of One Gramme.		IV. Grains fine Silver.	V. Value of One Grain.		VI. Names of Countries.
I. Tael of 1000 cash [b]	32·9502	30·34883	cash	508·5	1·9665	cash	Shanghai.*
II. Trade Piastre of 100 cents [b]	24·494	4·08263	cents	378·	·2645	cents	Cochin China* and elsewhere in the East, trade dollar.
III. Peso of 100 centavos [b]	24·433	4·09282	centavos	377·058607	·2652	centavos	Mexico,*†‡ Falkland Islands,* Turks Islands,* British Honduras,* British Guiana,* Bahamas,* Trinidad,* Barbados,* Leeward Islands,* Labuan.*
IV. Yen of 100 sen [b]	24·2607	4·12189	sen	374·399613	·2671	sen	Japan,*†‡ Hong Kong* and Straits Settlements,* dollar.
V. Dollar of 100 cents	24·0567	4·15684	cents	371·251414	·2693	cents	United States America.†*
VI. Peso of 100 centavos [b]	23·364	4·2801	centavos	360·561424	·2773	centavos	Philippine Islands.*
VII. Peso of 100 centavos [b]	22·5	4·4444	centavos	347·227875	·288	centavos	Argentine Republic,*† Bolivia,* Chili,* Ecuador,* Peru,* Guatemala,* United States Columbia,* Uruguay, Hayti,* Venezuela.*†
VIII. Peso of 100 centavos [b]	20·8750	4·7904	centavos	322·150306	·3104	centavos	Costa Rica.*
IX. Rouble of 100 kopecks [b]	17·9961	5·5587	kopecks	277·72243	·36007	kopecks	Russia.*†
X. Tecal of 8 fuangs [b]	13·7472	·58191	fuangs	212·142	·0377	fuangs	Siam.*
XI. Milreis of 1000 reis	11·6875	85·5615	reis	180·365590	5·5442	reis	Brazil.
XII. Florin of 100 kreutzers [b]	11·11111	9·	kreutzers	171·470384	·58313	kreutzers	Austria-Hungary.*†
XIII. Rupee of 16 ans. or 192 pies [b]	10·6918	17·9577	pies	165·	1·16363	pies	India,*†‡ Burmah,* Ceylon,* Mauritius.*
XIV. Florin of 100 cents [b]	9·450	10·58201	cents	145·835707	·6857	cents	Netherlands,*† Java.*
XV. Crown of 100 ores	6·0	16·6666	ores	92·5941	1·08	ores	Denmark,† Sweden and Norway.
XVI. Shilling or 12 pence	5·231	2·2940	pence	80·72937	·148644	pence	G. Britain,† Australasia,† Canada, Jamaica, Malta.
XVII. Mark of 100 pfennings	5.	20·	pfennings	77·16175	1·296	pfennings	Germany.†
XVIII. Franc of 100 cents	4·5	22·2222	cents	69·44557	1·44	cents	France,*† Belgium,*† Switzerland,*† Italy, liras,*† Greece, drachmas,* Servia, dinars,* Roumania, leys,* Bulgaria, lews,* Spain, peseta,* Sierra Leone,* Gambia.*
XIX. Markka of 100 penni	4·499	22·2227	penni	69·43014	1·4402	penni	Finland.
XX. Lew of 100 cents	4·175	23·9521	cents	64·430061	1·5517	cents	Bulgaria.*
XXI. Piastre of 16 karobs [b]	2·7875	5·73991	karobs	43·014589	·3719	karobs	Tunis.
XXII. Testoon of 100 reis	2·29166	43·6364	reis	35·3657	2·8276	reis	Portugal.†
XXIII. Piastre of 40 paras	1·125	35·5555	paras	17·36139	4·6079	paras	Egypt.
XXIV. Piastre of 40 paras	·99825	40·0702	paras	15·405845	2·5964	paras	Ottoman Empire.
XXV. Banabat 1/10th of Toman.	·468	2·13675	scahis	7·22234	·1384	scahis	Persia.†

The currency of four countries, viz., Russia, Austria Hungary, the Argentine Republic, and Brazil, consists at present of inconvertible paper. The three first-named possess Mints.

Rules and Examples.

Rules for Finding: First, the gold value of a grain of fine gold in countries where gold is the standard. Second, the silver value of a grain of fine silver in countries where silver is the standard. Third, the gold value of one grain of fine silver where gold is the standard. Fourth, the silver value of one grain of fine gold in countries where silver is the standard.

I. To find the gold value of a grain of fine gold in countries where gold is the standard: divide the units of the money of account in the country for which the investigation is made by the weight of fine gold in the money of account on issue from the Mint, and the result will be the answer.

Thus:—There are 240 pence in one sovereign, and there are 113·0016 grains of fine gold in a sovereign on its issue from the Mint; 240 divided by 113·0016 gives 2·123863, which are pence, and constitute the value of one grain of fine gold in the currency of the United Kingdom.

II. To find the silver value of a grain of fine silver in countries where silver is the standard: divide the units of the money of account in the country for which the investigation is made by the weight of fine silver in the money account on issue from the Mint, and the result will be the answer.

Thus:—There are 192 pies in one rupee, and there are 165 grains of fine silver in one rupee on its issue from the Mint. 192 divided by 165 gives 1·16363, which is one pie and parts thereof, and constitutes the value of one grain of fine silver in the currency of India.

III. To find the gold value of one grain of fine silver in countries where gold is the standard: the gold price of silver must be divided by the grains of fine silver for which the quotation is made, and the result will be the answer.

Thus:—Say the gold value of silver in London is 44 pence per ounce, or 444 grains of fine silver; 44 divided by 444 gives ·099099, and this decimal of one penny is the British gold value of one grain of fine silver.

IV. To find the silver value of one grain of fine gold in countries where silver is the standard: the silver price of gold must be divided by the grains of fine gold for which the quotation is made, and the result will be the answer.

Thus:—Say that the silver value of gold in India is Rs. 21. 8*a.* 1*p.* per tola, or 172½ grains of fine gold. Rs. 21. 8*a.* 1*p.*, or 4,129 pies divided by 172·5 gives 23·9362, and this number of pies constitutes the Indian silver value of one grain of fine gold.

As the tables contain the values of one grain of fine metal in the standard moneys of most countries of the world, it would be easy to find the gold value of silver, and the silver value of gold, by forming a table of the relative proportions of silver to gold established by a gradation of prices and applying these proportions as divisors of the gold value of one grain of fine gold to get the gold value of one grain of fine silver, and applying them as multipliers of the silver value of one grain of fine silver to get the silver value of one grain of fine gold.

V. To find the proportion established between gold and silver in a gold standard country, divide the gold price of silver by the fixed value of one grain of fine gold, the result will be grains of fine gold; compare these with the grains of fine silver commanded by the price, and the proportion will be at once shown by dividing the grains of silver by the grains of gold.

Thus:—Say the gold value of silver in London is 44 pence per ounce, or 444 grains of fine silver; 44 divided by 2·123,863 pence, the fixed value of one grain of fine gold gives 20·71 grains of fine gold, and this divided into 444 establishes a proportion of 21·43 parts of silver to 1 of gold.

VI. To find the proportion established between silver and gold in a silver standard country, divide the silver price of gold by the fixed value of one grain of fine silver, and the result will be grains of fine silver; compare these with the grains of fine gold commanded by the price, and the proportion will be at once shown by dividing the grains of silver by the grains of gold.

Thus:—Say the silver value of gold in India is Rs. 21. 8*a.* 1*p.* per tola, or 172½ grains of fine gold; Rs. 21. 8*a.* 1*p.*, or 4,129 pies, divided by 1·16,363 pies, the fixed value of one grain of fine silver, gives 3,548·3 grains of fine silver, and this divided by 172½ gives a proportion of 20·34 parts of silver to 1 part of gold.

Table of Proportions established between Gold and Silver by the fluctuating London price of one ounce of Silver, or 444 grains of fine Silver.

Col. I.	Col. II.	Col. I.	Col. II.	Col. I.	Col. II.	Col. I.	Col. II.
London Gold Value of Silver per ounce, or 444 grains of fine Silver.	Proportion of Silver to 1 of Gold.	London Gold Value of Gold per ounce, or 444 grains of fine Silver.	Proportion of Silver to 1 of Gold.	London Gold Value of Silver per ounce, or 444 grains of fine Silver.	Proportion of Silver to 1 of Gold.	London Gold Value of Silver per ounce, or 444 grains of fine Silver.	Proportion of Silver to 1 of Gold.
d.		*d.*		*d.*		*d.*	
64	14·73	45¾	20·61	43¼	21·80	40¾	23·14
62	15·28	½	20·77	43	21·93	½	23·28
60	15·71	¼	20·84	¾	22·05	¼	23·43
55	17·15	45	20·95	½	22·15	40	23·57
50	18·86	¾	21·07	¼	22·32	35	26·94
47	20·06	½	21·19	42	22·45	30	31·34
¾	20·17	¼	21 32	¾	22·59	25	37·71
½	20·28	44	21·43	½	22·72	20	47·15
¼	20·39	¾	21·55	¼	22·86	15	62·87
46	20·50	½	21·68	41	22·99	10	94·30

Pars of Exchange.

It is not through an oversight that this paper does not treat of the limits to the fluctuation of exchange, or metal points. To deal with this it would be requisite to know the conditions upon which each country can add to its standard metal currency and the cost of effecting the same. I am acquainted with these charges for a few countries only. They consist of coinage, packing, carriage, shipping, freight, insurance of the metal, interest, and a small commission if the business is undertaken by another. They will vary in total amount from ¼ to 3½ per cent. on the par of exchange, above or below the par. If I could present all these charges for each country in a percentage form on the par of exchange, this knowledge, together with the pars of exchange, could they be generally possessed, would not afford a sure guide to the rate of exchange of the day. This rate depends upon the state of the trade of the countries between which the rate is quoted. If the state of the country necessitates shipping standard metal, the rate will be one figure; if it necessitates the import of standard metal it will be another figure. None but those who are intimately acquainted with the trade can state accurately what the rate of exchange between two countries should be. It will, therefore, be seen that bankers, bullion, exchange dealers and brokers should offer no opposition to the spread of the knowledge of the pars of exchange, or to the limits to the fluctuation of exchange, as their functions are not trenched upon by the general possession of such knowledge.

A Traveller's Experience.

Travellers do not now take the coins of one country into another country; but, as a rule, they procure letters of credit under which a bill of exchange can be drawn and negotiated, and thus the traveller becomes possessed of the money of the country in which he is, according to his wants.

For my present purpose, as illustrations of my tables and rules, I assume that a traveller takes metal money—gold and silver—about with him.

A traveller from the United States of America has reached London with gold and silver dollars, and desires to exchange some of them for English money. He knows that both gold and silver dollars are unlimited legal tender in the country which he has left; he turns to my tables, and he finds that gold only is unlimited legal tender in England. Under the head of gold in England he finds the value of one grain of fine gold is 2·123,863 pence, and under the head of the United States A. he finds that the weight of fine gold in a dollar is 23·22 grains; he multiplies 2·123,863 by 23·22 and he gets 49·316 pence, or 4*s*. $1\frac{3}{10}$d. for one gold dollar; or for $5—246·58 pence, or £1 0*s*. $6\frac{1}{2}$*d*., or double this amount for a $10 piece. This is the intrinsic worth for his gold in English money at Mint issue weights. He should generally get about this sum for his unabrased gold coins, because the English Mint makes no charge for putting our Gracious Sovereign's effigy on the gold, and its appropriate alloy, in place of the effigy of the United States.

He also desires to convert some of his silver dollars into English money. He turns to my silver table and finds that the Mint is not open to the unlimited reception of silver in England, and consequently that he must sell his dollars at the gold market price of silver of the day, unless he can find some one to buy the silver dollars for remittance to the United States, in which case he should get a better price than for bar silver. He finds that the *Times* quotes the market value of silver as 47 pence per ounce, or 444 grains of fine silver; he divides 47 by 444 and gets ·105855 of a penny as the value of one grain of fine silver. He finds by the table that there are 371·2514 grains of fine silver in a dollar at Mint issue weight, and he multiplies that by ·105855 and gets 39·288 pence as the par value of his silver dollar. Even if his dollar be of the Mint issue weight, he should not expect to get quite this amount, as the risk, trouble, and profit of the money changer must be considered. If the money changer could see his way to buy the traveller's silver dollars at the proportion of 20·06 parts of silver for 1 of gold, and could freely dispose of them in America at the proportion of 16 of silver to 1 of gold, he could make a profit of 25·37 per cent., less the expenses attending the carriage and disposal of them on the other side of the Atlantic.

Our traveller proceeds to India, taking with him some gold and silver dollars, sovereigns and shillings. On arriving at Bombay he is desirous of exchanging some of his money for the metal currency of India. He consults the tables and finds that silver is unlimited legal tender, and that the Mints are open to the unlimited reception of silver from the public, in India. Against the silver rupee in my table he finds the value of one grain of fine silver to be 1·16363 pie; he multiplies 371·2514 grains of fine silver in the dollar, and 80·72937 grains of fine silver in the shilling, and gets respectively 432 pies, or Rs.2. 4*a*., as the value of one dollar, and 5 annas $10\frac{1}{2}$ pie as the value of the shilling—these are the par values in India of the dollar and shilling. He will learn that the Mint charge for coinage is $2\frac{1}{10}$ per cent.; he must therefore expect to get at least $2\frac{1}{10}$ per cent. less than the par value, even if the dollar and the shilling should be of Mint issue weight. He desires to convert some of his gold dollars and pounds into Indian money also. On reference to the gold table he finds that gold is not unlimited legal tender, and that the mints are not open to the unlimited reception of it. He will, therefore, have to sell his gold at the market value, which he finds to be Rs.21. 8*a*. 1*p*. per tola, or $172\frac{1}{2}$ grains of fine gold. He must find the proportion established between gold and silver by this quotation. To do this he divides 4,129 pies, which make Rs 21. 8*a*. 1*p*. by 1·16363 pie, the fixed value of one grain of fine silver, and gets 3548·3 grains of fine silver; this divided by 172·5 grains of fine gold gives 20·34 parts of silver to one part of gold. The Indian value of one grain of fine silver being multiplied by 20·34 gives the silver value of one grain of fine gold as 23·668 pies; 113·0016 grains of fine gold in the sovereign, and 23·22 grains of fine gold in the dollar being multiplied by 23·668 pies respectively gives

Rs.13. 14*a*. 10*p*. as the par value of the sovereign, and Rs.2. 13*a*. 9*p*. as the par value of the dollar, provided they are both of mint issue weight, and these are about the prices he should get for these coins.

Our traveller next proceeds to Shanghae, in China, and desires to exchange some of his gold and silver coins for the money of the country. He finds on reference to my tables that silver is unlimited legal tender, but that there is no mint in China. He learns, however, that it is the practice to stamp lumps of silver with the weight and fineness by authority, and that these lumps, as well as dollars, are unlimited legal tender. He desires to exchange some of his silver coins for China money, and on turning to my silver table he finds that the value of one grain of fine silver at Shanghae is 1·9665 cash; he, therefore, multiplies the 371·2514 grains of fine silver in the dollar, the 80·7297 grains of fine silver in the shilling, and the 165 grains of fine silver in the rupee, by 1·9665 respectively, and gets 730·065 cash for a dollar, 158·764 cash for a shilling, and 324·47 cash for a rupee. These are the par values provided the coins are of mint issue weight, and are about the values the coins would sell for in Shanghae. He desires to exchange some of his gold coins, and finds that he must sell them at their market value. The price of gold for the day is 22 taels 639 cash for 566 grains troy. The proportion established between gold and silver by this quotation is ascertained by dividing 22 taels 639 cash by 1·9665, the value of one grain of fine silver; this gives 11512·4 grains of silver, which divided by the weight of gold, 566 grains, gives a proportion of 20·34 parts of silver to 1 of gold. 1·9665 multiplied by 20·34 gives 40, which is the silver value in cash for one grain of fine gold. 113·0016 grains, 23·22 grains and 11 grains being multiplied by 40 cash, gives respectively 4 taels 520 cash as the value of a sovereign, 928 cash as the value of a dollar, 440 cash as the value of a rupee. These are the par values provided the coins are of mint issue weight, and should be about the China money obtained for them.

Our traveller now returns to the United States of America, and lands at San Francisco. He finds that he can there pass his United States silver dollars upon an equality with United States gold dollars, the legal tender proportion in the States being 16 parts of silver to 1 part of gold, though in England he had to sell them at the proportion of 20·06 parts of silver to 1 of gold. He desires to exchange his sovereigns and gold rupees into dollars. Finding by my gold table that the value of one grain of fine gold in America is 4·3066 cents, he multiplies 113·0016 grains of fine gold and 11 grains of fine gold by 4·3066 respectively, and gets \$4·866½ as the value of the sovereign and 47·37 cents as the value of the gold rupee. The coinage charge is one-fifth of 1 per cent., so that these gold coins should command about the values we have worked out, provided they are of mint issue weight. To convert his silver, consisting of some lumps from Shanghae stamped with the quantity of fine silver in them, his silver rupees and shillings, he must ascertain the rate the mints will buy silver at. This is the London price of the day, the Bland Bill providing that not more than \$4,000,000 and not less than \$2,000,000 should thus be purchased by the mints per month. I presume the market rate is judiciously adjusted to the Mint purchasing rate. We will say that the market rate is in the proportion of 20·06 parts of silver to 1 part of gold, the value of one grain of gold being 4·3066 cents in the States, 20·06 divided into 4·3066 gives ·214685 of a cent as the gold value of one grain of fine silver. Say the weight of the Shanghae lump is 20 ounces of fine silver, the rupee of 165 grains of fine silver, and the shilling of 80·72937 grains of fine silver, being multiplied respectively by ·214685, give \$20·61 for the Shanghae lump, 35·42 cents for the rupee, and 17·33 cents for the shilling, provided the coins are of mint issue weight. These rates are about the prices which would be obtained if the proportion of silver to gold is 20·06 of the former to 1 of the latter.

I have taken you through two gold and two silver standard countries. You can now, if you please, go through all the other countries of the world, exchanging the gold and silver moneys of all countries in each, as you proceed, with the assistance of my tables.

Two German books, one by Noback, of 1,234 pages, published in 1879, contains the gross and fine weights in grammes of 637 gold and 1,452 silver coins, together 2,089 coins of the world; the other of 114 pages, published in a cheap form in Bremerhaven in 1875, contains the fac-similes of 426 gold and 824 silver coins, together 1,250 coins, of which there are for Europe 316 gold and 663 silver, for Asia 22 gold and 37 silver, for Africa 5 gold and 1 silver, for America 79 gold and 116 silver, and for Australia 2 gold.

I can imagine that not a few readers of this article may say, "What is the use of all this botheration with decimals, long calculations and minutiæ of grains of fine metal? If I am going into a country or going to do business with a country I learn about its coinage in a short way, I do not want to be troubled with all this stuff." I reply that I have an end in view. I know the mode by which my own mind has found its way through the difficulties out of which no books that I know helped me, and I expect that my present experience may possibly be helpful to other students. If you would have reasonable opinions upon mono-metallism, bi-metallism, tri-metallism, alternative metallism, or no metallism, you must understand the foundations of metallism. If you cannot master, or care not to master, the system which I advocate, and which appears to be the very essence of metal currency, would it not be only prudently cautious to express ignorance of the subject? But if you can master them, is it not your duty to do so? seeing that every member of a civilised community is interested in the question of sound currency, and that all who can exercise any influence in the State may be called upon to express an opinion upon the matter.

I can name 103 countries in the world—and there are more—the prices in which are based upon gold and silver. Some of these countries have the same weights of money of account and coins but different denominations. If we confine the number of moneys of account or coins on which the exchanges of the world are at present regulated to 12 gold and 13 silver, 25 coins or moneys of account in all, then the 2,089 coins of which Noback gives the weights in grammes present 52,225 different values in the 103 countries of the world, all of which can be ascertained by the possession of Noback's book and my tables of values of one grain or gramme of fine gold and one grain or gramme of fine silver in the various countries of the world.

Standard Currency.

It is, in my opinion, absolutely necessary that an automatic standard currency for a country should be embodied in a substance having a correlative value to that for which it exchanges. This substance must have a cost value and a sale value, and be subject to the laws of supply and demand, just as other substances are which are produced under similar circumstances.* The errors and miseries resulting from the frequent over-issue of inconvertible paper money are due to the disregard of this truth. A currency standard cannot at the same time be both physical and metaphysical, real and ideal. It is due to the effort which has been made to combine these two that false opinions of currency are formed and the mind is led away into maze and mystery. Let it become firmly established that the basis of a sound automatic currency must be laid of a substance of correlative value with other substances, and through imperfection subject to variation in value in consequence of being produced and distributed under the laws of supply and demand; that all other instruments used in exchange are tokens of this substance; that the substance is constituted a standard by legal enactment based upon human needs; that these enactments provide for the unlimited reception of the substance and the fitting of it for currency by the State, and the appointment of that currency as unlimited legal tender; and we could never hear of such wild proposals as are current in the

---

* I have treated of these subjects in the columns of the *London Chamber of Commerce Journal* under the heads of "Function of Gold and Silver Currency in the Internal and International Transactions of Countries—International Indebtedness and Simplification of Exchange," July, August, September, October, November, December, 1883, March, May, 1884; "Production of Gold and Silver in the United States of America," January, March, 1885; "The Comparative Cost of the Production of Gold and Silver and the Comparative Yield of Grains of Gold and Silver per Ton of Ore," June, July, August, September, December, 1885, February, May, July, 1886, May, 1887.

United States of America, one of which is that the soundest and safest standard currency is notes composed of greenbacks.

Single Grain System, for finding the Weight of Fine Metal indicated by Relative Prices, and Mastering the Exchanges.

Relative prices and values in different civilised countries which are not under the slavery of inconvertible paper currencies, are the comparative weights of fine gold for fine gold, fine silver for fine silver, fine gold for fine silver, or fine silver for fine gold. Rates of exchange would also come under the same definition. My single grain system provides divisors for each country which resolve the weights of fine metal indicated by values, prices, and rates of exchange. Also multipliers, which yield in each country the values of the weights of metals in the moneys of account and the gold and silver coins in the world.

If I am credited with any knowledge of the principles of currency, or mastery of the exchanges, I am happy to explain that it is altogether due to possessing a firm hold on a few common sense axioms with regard to the first and the use of the single grain system applied to the second. I would assure every one that he can easily possess all the information which I have acquired. He may take different views of the principles of currency. But if he desires to be at home on the foundation of the exchanges and the international values of the world's moneys of account and gold and silver coins, he will find my system, which is contained in the tables and rules given herewith, all that is requisite to enable him to accomplish it. I am astonished that this single grain system has not been discovered and generally acted upon ages ago, for it has a simplicity, beauty and power which I feel confident will cause it to become of great general benefit to the world.

I trust that as each reader understands and appreciates this system he will do his utmost to extend the circulation of it, and assist others to understand it.

A good test of the knowledge of it consists in determining the monies of account meant by the three quotations of exchange under the head of American markets in the daily newspapers, and the weights of fine metal in the six quantities indicated by the three quotations.

I would that some millions of the more thoughtful of the inhabitants of the world could possess this table and rules at once.

All youths should work this system, and their elders of both sexes should understand it.

—Waterlow and Sons Limited, Printers, London Wall.—

TABLE I.

TABLE showing: Col. I.—Names of countries possessing actual and nominal monetary systems having letters attached denoting (a) the possession of a Mint; (b) that gold is received in unlimited quantities; (c) that gold is unlimited legal tender; (d) that silver is received in unlimited quantities; (e) that silver is unlimited legal tender. II.—Names of the principal current coins in the world attached to the countries wherein they circulate. III.—Gross weight in grammes. IV.—Fine weight of gold or silver in grammes. V.—Denominational expression for one gramme of fine metal. VI.—Gross weight in grains, Troy. VII.—Fine grains ℔ 1,000 grains. VIII.—Fine weight in grains on issue from the mint. IX.—Proportion of silver to 1 of gold in the coinage. X.—Moneys of account. XI.—Denominational expression for one grain of fine metal. XII.—Prices of moneys of account in pence, silver at 42 pence ℔ standard ounce. XIII.—Prices of moneys of account in French gold cents. Silver at 22·45 parts to 1 of gold. XIV.—Prices of moneys of account in gold cents of the United States of America. Silver at 22·45 parts to 1 of gold. XV.—Prices of moneys of account in German pfennings. Silver at 22·45 parts of silver to 1 of gold.

I.	II. Name of Coin.	III. Nobach's weights in grammes of metal.	IV. Nobach's weights in grammes of fine metal.	V. Value of one gramme of fine metal.	VI. Gross weight in grains Troy.	VII. Fine grains per 1,000.	VIII. Fine weight in grains on Mint issue	IX. Proportion of silver to 1 of gold in coinage.	X. Money of account.	XI. Value of one grain of fine metal.	XII. Value of money of account in pence. Silver at 42 pence per ounce.	XIII. Value of money of account in French gold cents. Silver at 22·45 parts of silver to 1 of gold.	XIV. Value of money of account in gold cents of the United States of America. Silver at 22·45 parts of silver to 1 of gold.	XV. Value of money of account in German pfennings. Silver at 22·45 parts of silver to 1 of gold.
British Empire—														
United Kingdom (a b c), Australasia (a b c), Cape of Good Hope (b c), and 75 other parts of the Empire (b c)	Sovereign G	7·9881	7·3221	32·77?139 pence	123·274	916·667	113·0016	14·287	Sovereign of 240 pence	G 2·122862 pence	240· 8d.	2522	486¾	2043
	Shilling S	5·6552	5·211	2·2910 pence	87·273	925·	80·72037	...	Shilling of 12 pence	S ·118644 "	7½	60½	15½	65
Canada (b c e), as Great Britain and United States of America...	50 cents S	11·620	10·7185	4·6318 cents	179·322807	925·	165·674011	...	50 cents	S ·30144 cents	15½	164	31½	133
India (a d e)...	15 rupees G	11·6635	10·6918	249·3553 pies	180·	916·667	165·	15·	1 rupee of 192 pies	G 77·4445 pies	23/36	249½	47½	108½
	Rupee S	11·6638	10·6915	17·9577 pies	180·	916·667	165·	...	... ...	S 1·10803 pies	15½	104	31½	132½
Burmah (d e), Ceylon (d e), and Mauritius (d e)	Rupee S		10·6916	17·9577 pies	180·	916·667	165·	...	1 rupee of 192 pies	S 1·16363 pies	..	104	...	...
Hong Kong (d e), Borneo (d e), and Straits Settlements (d e)...	Mexican dollar S	26·956	24·250	4·12181 cents	416·	900·	374·390613	...	Dollar of 100 cents	S ·26709 cents	35½	379½	71½	301½
Straits Settlements only...	20 cents S	...	...	...	85·813002	800·	67·860474	...	...	... ...	6½	66½	12½	
Newfoundland (b c e)	2 dollars G	3·328	3·0507	60·5587 cents	51·358??	916·667	47·078836	...	Dollar 480 to £100	G 4·2481 cents	49·79	515½	101¼	425½
	50 cents S	11·782	10·8983	4·5875 cents	181·823477	925·	168·187161	15·3	Dollar	S ·2372 cents	16	331½	32½	135½
France and Countries using the Franc basis—														
France (a b c e), Belgium (a b c e), and Switzerland (a b c e)	20 francs G	6·4516	5·8065	344·41167 cents	99·563349	900·	89·60701	15·5	Franc of 100 cents	G 22·3196 cents	9·31	100	19½	81½
	5 francs S	25·0	22·5	22·2222 cents	385·20875	900·	347·227875	...		S 1·44 cents	8½	69	13½	56
Italy (a b c e)	20 lires G; 5 lires S	Same as France.							Lira of 100 centesimi	See France.	...	See France.	See France.	See France.
Greece (b c e)	20 drachmai G; 5 drachmai S	Same as France.							Drachmai of 100 leptas	"	...	"	"	"
Servia (b c e)	20 dinars G; 5 dinars S	Same as France.							Dinar of 100 paras	"	...	"	"	"
Roumania (b c e)	20 leys G; 5 leys S	Same as France.							Ley of 100 banis	"	...	"	"	"
Bulgaria (b c e)	20 lews G	Same as France.							Lew of 100 cents	"	...	"	"	"
	1 lew S	...	4·175	23·0531	77·10175	835·	64·130061	14·3		S 1·5517 lews	6½	64	...	...
Austria-Hungary (a d e)	8 florins G	6·4516	5·8065	157·7?06 kreutzers	99·563349	900·	89·60701	...	Florin of 100 kreutzers	G 8·?217 kreutzers	22·79	250	48½	202½
	2 florins S	24·6914	22·2222	9· kreutzers	381·046326	900·	342·940706	15·3	...	S ·5833 kreutzers	16½	179½	33	138½
Spain (a b c e)	10 escudos G	8·3871	7·5484	132·?5 reals	129·436306	900·	116·492350	...	Escudo	G 8·56446 centimos	26·74	260	50½	210½
	5 pesetas S	...	...	See France, 5f.	385·20875	900·	347·227875	15·5	Peseta of 100 centimos	S 1·44 centimos	6½	69	13½	56
	2 escudos S	25·9601	23·3641	8·5603 centimos	400·628319	900·	360·562966	...	Escudo of 100 centimos	S ·55168 centimos	17½	179½	34½	145
Greece (b e)	20 drachmai G	[illegible]	5·1061	344·?170 leptas	99·137284	900·	89·223526	15·5	Drachmai of 100 leptas	G 24·91788 leptas	8·32	80½	17½	72½
	5 drachmai S	22·265	20·1465	24·91820	345·465154	900·	310·90784	...		S 1·6082 leptas	5½	61½	13	50½
Argentine Republic (a b c e)	5 pesos, 1 argentino G	[illegible]	7·50	centavos	128·603173	900·	115·74262	15·5	Peso of 100 centavos	G 4·3190 centavos	49·16	516½	96½	401½
	1 peso S	...	22·5	4·4146 centavos	See France.	See France.	Same as 5fr. piece.	...	... ...	S ·288 centavos	32½	345½	66½	280
Bolivia (d e)	16 bolivianos G	24·9610	22·4635	4·1512 centavos	385·210017	900·	346·69548	16·	Boliviano of 100 centavos	G 4·616 centavos	49·	483½	93½	391½
	1 boliviano S	...	22·5	4·4144 centavos	See France.	See France.	Same as 5fr. piece.	...	... ...	S ·288 centavos	32½	345½	66½	280
Chili (a d e)...	5 pesos G	7·6265	6·8639	72·8449 centavos	117·6951	900·	10[illegible]7533	16·39	Peso of 100 centavos	G 4·7213 centavos	46·99	472½	91½	381
	1 peso S	...	22·5	4·4446 centavos	See France.	See France.	Same as 5fr. piece.	...	...	S ·288 centavos	32½	345½	66½	280
Costa Rica (d e)	20 pesos G	32·255	29·032	344·1116 centavos	497·816746	900	448·035071	[illegible]	Peso of 1	G 4·4638 centavos	47·67	500	96½	404½
	1 peso S	12·5	10·4375	23·9520 centavos	192·904437	835·	161·075153	...	...	S ·3106 centavos	30½	320½	31½	260½
Ecuador (d e)	5 pesos or ½ gold ounce G	13·5430	11·4303	69·0588 centavos	209·	845·	176·3960	15·73	Peso of 10[illegible]	G 4·5352 centavos	47·57	492½	91½	396½
	1 peso S	25·0	22·5	4·4146 centavos	See France.	See France.	Same as 5fr. piece.	...	...	S ·288 centavos	33½	345½	66½	280
Guatemala (d e)	10 pesos G	16·129	14·5161	68·8890 centavos	248·906373	900·	224·017635	15·5	Peso of 10[illegible]	G 4·4639 centavos	47·57	500	96½	403½
	1 peso S	25·0	22·5	4·4144 centavos	See France.	See France.	Same as 5fr. piece.	...	...	S ·288 centavos	33½	345½	66½	280
Peru (a d e)...	10 sols G	16·129	...	...	...	...	...	...	...	... ...	...	...	...	...
	1 sol S	...	...	...	...	...	...	...	...	... ...	...	...	...	...
United States, Columbia (a d e)...	10 pesos G	16·129	...	...	...	...	...	...	...	... ...	...	...	...	...
	1 Venezolano S	...	...	...	...	...	...	...	...	... ...	...	...	...	...
Hayti (d e)...	10 gourdes G	...	...	...	...	...	...	...	...	... ...	...	...	...	...
	1 gourd S	...	...	...	...	...	...	...	...	... ...	...	...	...	...
Venezuela (a b c d)...	10 Venezolanos G	...	...	...	...	...	...	...	...	... ...	...	...	...	...
	1 Venezolano S	...	...	...	...	...	...	...	...	... ...	...	...	...	...
Uruguay (d e)	1 peso G	1·697	1·55115	64·5200 centavos	26·18869	917	24·00161	14·4	Peso of 100 [illegible]	G 4·1498 centavos	48·25	537½	103½	433½
	1 peso S	...	22·5	4·4144 centavos	See France.	See France.	Same as 5fr. piece.	...	...	S ·288 centavos	33½	345½	66½	280
Germany (a b c)	20 marks G	7·965	7·16846	279· pfennings	122·917500	900·	110·626301	15·98	Mark of 100 pfennings	G 18·0768 pfennings	11·74	123½	23½	100
	1 mark S	5·555	5·	20· pfennings	85·735363	900·	77·16175	...		S 1·296 pfennings	7½	69½	14½	69½
Russia (a b c e)	5 roubles G	6·541	5·9987	83·36129 copecks	101·	916·667	92·574027	15·	Rouble of 100 copecks	G 5·4 copecks	39·32	413½	79½	334½
	1 rouble S	20·7315	17·0961	5·5487 copecks	319·935781	868·056	277·722119	...		S ·36 copecks	26½	270	53½	223½
Finland (b c e)	10 markkaa G	3·226	2·9034	344·1341 penni	49·784761	900·	44·806??	15·5	Markkaa of 100 penni	G 22·316 penni	9·61	100	19½	80½
	1 markkaa S	5·1829	4·48575	22·7294 penni	79·961326	868·	69·436284	...		S 1·4403 penni	6½	69	13½	55½
Denmark (a b c), Sweden (a b c) and Norway (b c)	20 crowns G	8·9606	8·0645	248· ores	138·283116	900·	124·454185	[illegible]	Crown of 100 ores	G 16·0701 ores	13·21	138½	26½	112½
	2 crowns S	15·0	12·	16·6666 ores	231·485??	800·	185·188?	...		S 1·08 ores	8½	92	17½	75½
Netherlands (a b c d)	10 florins G	6·729	6·0561	165·13270 cents	103·844283	900·	93·459854	15·6	Florin of 100 cents	G 10·6999 cents	19·85	208½	40½	168½
	1 florin S	10·0	9·450	10·58201 cents	154·3236	945·	145·835707	...		S ·6857 cents	13½	145	28	117½
Portugal (a b c)	10 milreis G	17·735	16·2571	615·1164 reis	273·689737	916·667	250·882347	14·09	Milreis of 1,000 reis	G 39·8586 reis	53·28	560	108	453½
	5 testoons S	12·5	11·4583	43·6364 reis	192·904375	916·667	176·828490	...	Testoon of 100 reis	S 2·8256 reis	3½	33½	6½	28½
Ottoman Empire (a b c e)...	100 piastres G	7·216	6·6098	605·11985 paras	111·359837	916·667	10?·?0829	15·1	Piastre of 40 paras	G 39·3133 paras	2·16	22½	4½	18½
	20 piastres S	24·055	18·905	40·0702 paras	371·234362	830·	308·110808	...		S 2·5961 paras	1½	15½	3½	12½
Egypt (b e)...	50 piastres G	4·283	3·74762	533·6?20 paras	66·096155	875·	57·83166	15·	Piastre of 40 paras	G 34·5813 paras	2·46	25½	5	20½
	10 piastres S	12·5	11·25	35·5556 paras	192·904375	900·	173·613937	...		S 2·2820 paras	1½	17½	3½	14
Tunis	50 piastres G	9·700	8·731	91·01456 karubs	150·019736	900·	135·017762	15·66	Piastre of 16 karubs	G 5·9016 karubs	2·15	22½	4½	19
	2 piastres S	6·194	5·575	5·7301 karubs	95·587075	900·	86·028118	...		S ·3719 karubs	1½	27½	8	24½
Persia (a d e)	1 thoman G	3·4567	3·1321	58·27336 shahis	53·409937	900·	52·065368	15·37	Thoman of 200 shahis	G 3·77408 shahis	272·93	1682	328½	658½
	1 keran or 2 penabats or 20 shahis S	4·7612	4·69	4·2573 shahis	73·7569234	900·	79·83416	...	Keran of 20 shahis	S ·23234 shahis	3½	35½	6½	27
United States of America (a b c e)	10 dollars G	16·7181	15·0463	66·63706 cents	258·	900·	232·2	...	Dollar of 100 cents	G 4·3066 cents	49·31	516½	100	419½
	1 dollar S	26·729	24·0567	4·15685 cents	412·5	900·	371·281616	16·		S ·2693 cents	35½	369	81½	298½
Mexico (a d e)	16 pesos G	27·0643	23·6613	67·64266 centavos	417·66675	875·	365·457631	...	Peso of 100 centavos	G 4·3764 cents	48·51	509½	98½	412½
	1 peso S	27·0643	24·433	4·09288 centavos	417·66575	902·778	377·066607	16·5		S ·2652 cents	34½	374½	72½	303½
Brazil (a b c e)	10 milreis G	8·9648	8·2176	1216·1680 reis	138·317931	916·667	126·81996	15·25	Milreis of 1,000 reis	G 79·8610 reis	28·93	283	54½	231½
	2 milreis S	25·5	23·375	85·5615 reis	393·634925	916·666	360·731181	...		S 5·3442 reis	17½	179½	34½	118½
Philippine Islands (e)	1 peso G	1·6915	1·1706	67·5480 centavos	26·096103	875·	22·83705	15·70	Pesoduro of 100 centavos	G 4·3789 centavos	48·40	500½	98½	412½
	50 centavos S	12·980	11·682	4·2801 centavos	200·311903	900·	180·280712	...	Peso	S ·2713 centavos	34	356½	69½	289½
Shanghai (d e)	Tael S	36·6114	32·9502	30·34883 cash	565·	900·	508·5	...	Tael of 1,000 cash	S 1·9665 cash	48½	505	97½	409½
Japan (a d e)	10 yens G	16·6667	15·	66·6666 sen	257·206847	900·	231·48625	16·173	Yen of 100 sen	G 4·3199 sen	49·16	516½	99½	416½
	1 yen S	26·9564	24·2607	4·12188 sen	416·	900·	374·390613	...		S ·2671 sen	35½	372½	71½	301½
Cochin China (e)	Trade piastre S	27·216	24·494	4·08262 cents	420·	900·	378·	...	Mexican peso of 100 cents	S ·2645 cents	35½	375½	72½	303½
Siam (a d e)	Tical S	15·1338	13·7717	·65191 fuangs	233·55	910·	212·530	...	Tical of 8 fuangs	S ·0377 fuangs	20	209½	40½	171½
Netherlands India (e)	25 cents S	...	2·2860	10·91893 cents	40·07187	720·	28·330085	...	Florin—25 cent piece	S ·7055 cents	3½	35½	6½	28½
Antilles	Sovereign, dollar and piastre								Sovereign, piastre, dollar					
	Three halfpence S	...	·8743	...	14·38357	925·	13·189737	...	Three halfpence	S	1½	18½	3½	...
Trade Dollar	Dollar S	27·2156	24·494	4·08263 cents	420·	900·	378·	...	Dollar of 100 cents	S ·2645 cents	35½	375½	72½	303½

J. H. NORMAN.

TABLE II.

TABLES, showing at proportions ranging from 15½ parts of silver to 1 part of gold to 100 parts of silver to 1 part of gold, the par values in Great Britain of the world's silver moneys of account, and the par values in India of the world's gold moneys of account, worked out on "Norman's Single Grain System." It is assumed that the countries using these moneys of account have an effective metal standard. At present Russia, Austria-Hungary, Brazil, the Argentine Republic and Chili use inconvertible paper currencies. The monetary systems of the world, even such as are based upon effective metal standards, have varying degrees of comparative potency, the exhaustive exposition of which would be of great value at the present time.

So long as the sovereign contains, on its issue from the Mint, 113·0016 grains of fine gold, and there are 240 pence in the sovereign, a grain of gold is—not its worth, but is—2·123863 pence. The denominational expression of one grain of gold is 2·123863 pence; for 440 grains of gold it is £3. 17s. 10½d.; for 7,000 grains troy, or 1lb. avoirdupois, it is £61·94602. So long as the rupee contains, on its issue from the Mint, 165 grains of fine silver, and there are 192 pies in the rupee, a grain of fine silver is 1·16363 pie. The denominational expression for 440 grains of Silver is Rs. 2·66, for 1lb. avoirdupois it is Rs. 42·42.

TABLE I.—FINE GOLD FOR FINE SILVER.

Col. I.—Fluctuating proportions of silver to 1 of gold. Col. II.—Denominational expression D.E., for grains of fine gold G.G., for one ounce or 444 grains of fine silver. Col. III.—For 1lb. avoirdupois of fine silver. Col. IV.—For a Shanghai tael. Col. V.—For a trade piastre or dollar. Col. VI.—For a Mexican peso. Col. VII.—For a yen of Japan. Col. VIII.—For a peso of the Phillippine Islands. Col. IX.—For a Peruvian peso. Col. X.—For a peso of Costa Rica. Col. XI.—For a Russian rouble. Col. XII.—For a Siam tical. Col. XIII.—For a florin of Austria-Hungary. Col. XIV.—For an Indian rupee. Col. XV.—For a florin of Java. Col. XVI.—For a piastre of Tunis.

Col. I.	Col. II. 444 grains fine silver.		Col. III. 1lb. avoirdupois fine silver.		Col. IV. [illegible] grains fine silver.		Col. V. [illegible] grains fine silver.		Col. VI. [illegible] grains fine silver.		Col. VII. [illegible] grains fine silver.		Col. VIII. [illegible] grains fine silver.		Col. IX. [illegible] grains fine silver.		Col. X. [illegible] grains fine silver.		Col. XI. [illegible] grains fine silver.		Col. XII. [illegible] grains fine silver.		Col. XIII. [illegible] grains fine silver.		Col. XIV. 165 grains fine silver.		Col. XV. [illegible] grains fine silver.		Col. XVI. [illegible] grains fine silver.	
	D.E. pence.	G.G.	D.E. £	G.G.	D.E. D.	G.G.	D.E. D.	G.G.	D.E. D.	G.G.	D.E. D.	G.G.	D.E. D.	G.G.	D.E. D.	G.G.	D.E. D.	G.G.	D.E. D.	G.G.	D.E.	G.G.	D.E. D.	G.G.	D.E. D.	G.G.	D.E. D.	G.G.	D.E. D.	G.G.
15½ (a)	60·82	28·64	3·996	451·61	69·66	32·80	61·96	26·36	51·63	24·31	51·31	24·16	49·10	23·25	47·59	22·41	44·39	20·81	38·06	17·92	29·05	13·68	23·12	11·06	22·62	10·65	19·98	9·41	5·85	2·77
16 (b)	58·93	27·75	3·871	437·50	67·52	31·79	59·16	25·52	50·03	23·55	49·71	23·40	47·81	22·55	46·03	21·70	42·73	20·12	36·87	17·36	28·16	13·26	22·19	10·72	21·94	10·31	19·35	9·11	5·71	2·69
20 (c)	47·15	22·20	3·097	350·00	53·98	25·43	50·11	19·03	40·03	18·84	39·76	18·72	38·29	18·03	36·84	17·36	34·26	16·13	29·57	13·88	22·50	10·60	17·80	8·57	17·52	8·25	15·48	7·29	4·56	2·15
25	37·72	17·76	2·477	280·00	...	...	...	...	...	...	...	...	...	...	...	...	...	...	...	...	...	...	...	...	14·02	6·60	...	...	...	...
30 (d)	31·43	14·80	2·064	233·33	36·00	16·95	30·76	13·64	26·69	12·56	26·50	12·48	25·52	12·01	24·57	11·57	22·83	10·75	19·69	9·25	15·01	7·07	12·13	5·71	11·68	5·50	10·33	4·86	3·05	1·44
35	26·94	12·69	1·770	200·00	...	...	...	...	...	...	...	...	...	...	...	...	...	...	...	...	...	...	...	...	10·01	4·71	...	...	...	...
40	23·57	11·10	1·548	175·00	...	...	...	...	...	...	...	...	...	...	...	...	...	...	...	...	...	...	...	...	8·76	4·12	...	...	...	...
44 (e)	21·42	10·09	1·407	159·09	24·53	11·55	18·24	8·57	18·20	8·57	18·07	8·51	17·39	8·19	16·75	7·89	15·56	7·33	13·40	6·31	10·24	4·83	8·20	3·90	7·96	3·75	7·03	3·31	2·08	·98
50	18·86	8·88	1·239	140·00	...	...	...	...	...	...	...	...	...	...	...	...	...	...	...	...	...	...	...	...	7·01	3·30	...	...	...	...
55	17·14	8·07	1·126	127·27	...	...	...	...	...	...	...	...	...	...	...	...	...	...	...	...	...	...	...	...	6·37	3·00	...	...	...	...
60	15·71	7·40	1·032	116·66	...	...	...	...	...	...	...	...	...	...	...	...	...	...	...	...	...	...	...	...	5·84	2·75	...	...	...	...
65	14·50	6·83	·953	107·69	...	...	...	...	...	...	...	...	...	...	...	...	...	...	...	...	...	...	...	...	5·39	2·54	...	...	...	...
70	13·46	6·34	·885	100·00	...	...	...	...	...	...	...	...	...	...	...	...	...	...	...	...	...	...	...	...	5·01	2·36	...	...	...	...
75	12·57	5·92	·826	93·33	...	...	...	...	...	...	...	...	...	...	...	...	...	...	...	...	...	...	...	...	4·67	2·20	...	...	...	...
80	11·78	5·55	·774	87·50	...	...	...	...	...	...	...	...	...	...	...	...	...	...	...	...	...	...	...	...	4·38	2·06	...	...	...	...
85	11·09	5·22	·728	82·35	...	...	...	...	...	...	...	...	...	...	...	...	...	...	...	...	...	...	...	...	4·12	1·94	...	...	...	...
90	10·48	4·93	·688	77·77	...	...	...	...	...	...	...	...	...	...	...	...	...	...	...	...	...	...	...	...	3·88	1·83	...	...	...	...
95 (f)	9·92	4·67	·651	73·68	10·36	5·35	6·43	2·96	8·43	3·97	8·36	3·94	8·05	3·79	7·75	3·65	7·20	3·39	6·20	2·92	4·73	2·23	3·83	1·80	3·67	1·74	3·25	1·53	·95	·45
100	9·43	4·44	·619	70·00	...	...	...	...	...	...	...	...	...	...	...	...	...	...	...	...	...	...	...	...	3·48	1·65	...	...	...	...

(a.) 15½ parts of silver to 1 part of gold, or 60·82 pence ℔ ounce in Great Britain, is the proportion between silver and gold in the currencies of the nations of the Latin Union. (b.) 16 parts of silver to one part of gold, or 58·93 pence ℔ ounce in Great Britain, is the proportion between silver and gold in the United States of America. (c.) 20 parts of silver to one part of gold, or 47·15 pence ℔ ounce in Great Britain, is the highest price touched in the years 1886-7. (d.) 30 parts of silver to one of gold, or 31·43 pence ℔ ounce in Great Britain, is the price to which, in the opinion of the City of London, silver would decline if the Bland Bill were abrogated. (e.) 44 parts of silver to 1 part of gold, or 21·42 pence ℔ ounce in Great Britain, is the average cost of the production of silver measured by gold discovered by Professor Roberts-Austin of the Royal Mint. (f.) 95 parts of silver to one part of gold, or 9·92 pence ℔ ounce in Great Britain, is the comparative average cost of the production of the two metals, on information supplied to the compiler of this table by the President of the Colorado Silver Alliance of the average cost of silver in Colorado, and on the information of the Hunt Chlorination Co. of the United States of America of the average cost of the production of gold in the world.

TABLE II.—FINE SILVER FOR FINE GOLD.

Col. I. Fluctuating proportions of silver to one part of gold. Col. II. D.E. denominational expression, or G.S. grains of fine silver for one tola or 180 grains of fine gold. Col. III. for a sovereign of Great Britain. Col. IV. for a toman of Persia. Col. V. for a milreis of Portugal. Col. VI. for a dollar of Newfoundland. Col. VII. for a dollar of the United States, America. Col. VIII. for a peso of the Argentine Republic. Col. IX. for a milreis of Brazil. Col. X. for a Spanish escudo. Col. XI. for a florin of the Netherlands. Col. XII. for a crown of Denmark. Col. XIII. for a mark of Germany. Col. XIV. for a franc of France. Col. XV. for a piastre of Egypt. Col. XVI. for a piastre of the Ottoman Empire.

Col. I.	Col. II. 180 grains fine gold.		Col. III. 113·0016 grains fine gold.		Col. IV. [illegible] grains fine gold.		Col. V. [illegible] grains fine gold.		Col. VI. [illegible] grains fine gold.		Col. VII. [illegible] grains fine gold.		Col. VIII. [illegible] grains fine gold.		Col. IX. [illegible] grains fine gold.		Col. X. [illegible] grains fine gold.		Col. XI. [illegible] grains fine gold.		Col. XII. [illegible] grains fine gold.		Col. XIII. [illegible] grains fine gold.		Col. XIV. [illegible] grains fine gold.		Col. XV. [illegible] grains fine gold.		Col. XVI. [illegible] grains fine gold.	
	D.E. Rs.	G.S.	D.E. Rs.	G.S.	D.E. Rs.	G.S.	D.E. Rs.	G.S.	D.E. Rs.	G.S.	D.E. Rs.	G.S.	D.E. Rs.	G.S.	D.E. Rs.	G.S.	D.E. Rs.	G.S.	D.E. Rs.	G.S.	D.E. Rs.	G.S.	D.E. Rs.	G.S.	D.E. Rs.	G.S.	D.E. Rs.	G.S.	D.E. Rs.	G.S.
15·5 (a)	16·91	2,790	10·61	1,751·5	4·96	818·4	2·35	388·8	2·21	364·7	2·18	359·9	2·17	358·7	1·19	196·5	1·09	180·5	·87	144·8	·58	96·4	·52	85·7	·42	69·4	·11	17·8	·09	15·8
16 (b)	17·45	2,880	10·96	1,808·0	5·13	846·5	2·43	401·4	2·28	376·7	2·25	371·5	2·24	370·2	1·23	202·8	1·13	186·3	·91	149·5	·60	99·5	·54	88·5	·43	71·6	·11	18·4	·09	16·3
20 (c)	21·78	3,600	13·69	2,260·0	6·47	1,059·1	3·04	501·7	2·85	470·6	2·81	464·4	2·81	462·9	1·53	253·6	1·41	232·9	1·13	186·9	·76	124·4	·67	110·6	·54	89·6	·14	23·0	·12	20·4
30 (d)	32·73	5,400	20·54	3,390·0	9·63	1,588·9	4·56	752·6	4·27	706·2	4·22	696·6	4·21	694·4	2·30	380·4	2·11	349·1	1·70	280·1	1·15	186·6	1·01	165·9	·83	134·4	·21	34·5	·18	30·6
44 (e)	48·00	7,920	30·13	4,972·1	14·19	2,329·4	6·69	1,103·6	6·27	1,035·7	6·19	1,021·6	6·07	1,018·6	3·38	557·9	3·10	512·5	2·49	411·1	1·66	273·7	1·47	243·3	1·19	197·1	·31	50·6	·27	44·8
70	76·36	12,600	47·94	7,910·0	22·47	3,707·5	10·64	1,756·1	9·98	1,647·1	9·85	1,625·1	9·82	1,620·3	5·37	887·6	4·94	815·5	3·96	654·1	2·64	435·5	2·35	387·1	1·90	313·6	·49	80·5	·43	71·4
95 (f)	103·63	17,100	65·06	10,735·1	30·40	5,016·0	14·41	2,383·2	13·55	2,235·5	13·37	2,205·9	13·32	2,199·6	7·30	1,204·6	6·70	1,106·4	5·38	887·7	3·58	591·1	3·18	525·3	2·57	425·6	·66	109·2	·58	96·9
100	109·09	18,000	68·48	11,300·1	32·11	5,280·2	15·20	2,508·6	14·26	2,354·0	14·07	2,322·0	14·03	2,314·9	7·68	1,268·1	7·05	1,164·6	5·66	934·5	3·76	622·2	3·35	553·1	2·71	448·0	·70	115·0	·62	102·0

March, 1888.

a, b, c, d, e, f. For references see foot of Table I.

N.B.—To ascertain the silver price in India of one-tenth part of a sovereign, remove the decimal point one place to the left.

J. H. NORMAN.

Reprinted from the LONDON CHAMBER OF COMMERCE JOURNAL *for October*, 1888,
Mr. Kenric B. M

GOLD PAR

MR. ALEXANDER L. GLENCROSS'S TABLE OF DENOMINATIONAL EXPRESSIONS FOR EQUI
OF THE WORLD; ON NOBACK'S WEIGHTS, GIVEN BY MI

The following example shows the use of the table :—Q. How many francs a
Argentine Republic. In the left hand column find franc. Then at the point where t
be found the required equivalent, viz. 5.

	The Equivalent of One.	Sovereign.	Franc.	Mark.	Florin.		Rouble.	Escudo.	Kroner.	Milreis.		U. S. A.
					Austro-Hungarian.	Dutch.				Portuguese.	Brazilian.	
	Sovereign	...	0·0395	0·049	0·099	0·0327	0·164	0·103	0·0551	0·222	0·1123	0·2055
	Franc........................	25·22	...	1·24	2·500	2·086	4·133	2·600	1·3889	5·5997	2·8306	5·1826
	Mark	20·43	0·81	...	2·03	1·6898	3·35	2·106	1·125	4·5357	2·2928	4·1979
	Florin, A. H.	10·09	0·40	0·494	...	0·8344	1·653	1·04	0·5556	2·2399	1·1322	2·074
	„ Dutch	19·85	0·479	0·592	1·198	...	1·98	1·246	0·6658	2·6843	1·3560	2·4845
	Rouble	6·103	0·242	0·299	0·605	0·5047	...	0·629	0·3361	1·3551	0.6849	1·254
	Escudo	9·70	0·385	0·475	0·962	0·8023	1·59	...	0·5341	2·1538	1·0887	1·993
	Kroner	18·16	0·72	0·888	1·800	1·5021	2·975	1·872	...	4·0317	2·038	3·7319
	Milreis, ...	4·504	0·179	0·225	0·447	0·3725	0·738	0·4643	0·2481	...	0·5055	0·9255
	„ B.	8·91	0·3533	0·436	0·883	0·7369	1·46	0·919	0·4905	1·9712	...	1·831
	Dollar, U. S A.	4·867	0·1929	0·238	0·4824	0·4025	0·7999	0·5017	0·268	1·080	0·5461	...
	„ MEXICO	4·95	0·1962	0·242	0·491	0·4092	0·8106	0·51	0·2724	1·0984	0·5552	1·0165
IS	„ A. R.	5·044	0·2	0·247	0·500	0·4217	0·8266	0·52	0·2778	1·12	0·5661	1·0366
	„ CHILI	5·334	0·212	0·262	0·528	0·4412	0·874	0·55	0·2937	1·1317	0·5986	1·0961
	„ URUGUAY	4·69	0·186	0·23	0·465	0·3878	0·7683	0·4834	0·2582	1·0411	0·5262	0·9636
	„ VEN.	5·044	0.2	0·247	0·500	0·4172	0·827	0·52	0·2777	1·12	0·5661	1·0365
	„ BOL.	5·215	0·207	0·255	0·517	0·4313	0·855	0·538	0·2871	1·1578	0·5853	1·076
	„ ECUA.	5·125	0·203	0·251	0·508	0·4239	0·839	0·5283	0·2822	1·1377	0·5752	1·0539
	„ NFLD.	4·8	0·1903	0·235	0·476	0·397	0·7861	0·4949	0·2641	1·0658	0·5388	0·9864
	„ P. I.	4·948	0·1962	0·242	0·491	0·4092	0·817	0·5109	0·2726	1·0986	0·5553	1·0168
	Yen..........................	4·89	0·194	0·239	0·484	0·4037	0·800	0·503	0·2688	1·0838	0·5478	1·003
	Toman	2·124	0·0843	0·104	0·210	0·1757	0·3481	0·219	0·117	0·4717	0·2384	0·4366
	Rupee	10·273	0·4073	0·503	1·018	0·85	1·683	1·06	0·5657	2·2808	1·153	2·1109
	Piastre, Tunis............	41·68	1·650	2·04	4·132	3·4471	6·829	4·26	2·29	9·2539	4·6408	8·5646
	„ Egypt	97·69	3·87	4·782	9·683	8·0985	16·00	10·071	5·38	21·689	10·964	20·074
	„ Turkey	110·71	4·392	5·423	10·98	9·1571	18·15	11·42	6·1003	21·595	12·4375	22·763

N.B. 700,000,000 people of the earth effect their international interchanges on sil

III.

he kind permission of Mr. Alexander L. Glencross and the Secretary of the Chamber'
, F.R.G.S., F.S.S.)

UIVALENTS.

T WEIGHTS OF FINE GOLD ON ISSUE OF THE COINS FROM THE MINTS IN 47 COUNTRIES
N HENRY NORMAN, IN THIS JOURNAL FOR JULY 5TH, 1886.

ual to, at par, one dollar, Argentine Republic? A. In the top column find dollar
tical and horizontal columns, respectively, of these two denominations intersect will

Dollar.								Yen.	Toman.	Rupee.	Piastre.		
Argentine Republic.	Chilian.	Uruguay.	Venezuela.	Bolivia.	Ecuador.	Newfound-land.	Philippine Islands.				Tunis.	Egypt.	Turkey.
0·1982	0·1875	0·2133	0·1982	0·1917	0·1951	0·2083	0·2029	0·2048	0·4707	0·0974	0·024	0·01025	0·0090
5·0000	4·7284	5·3785	5·0000	4·8363	4·9214	5·2540	5·0971	5·1667	11·8720	2·4552	0·6051	0·2582	0·2277
4·05	3·9603	4·3566	4·05	3·9174	3·9863	4·2557	4·1287	4·1850	9·6161	1·9887	0·4901	0·2091	0·1844
1·9999	1·8918	2·1514	2·00	1·9345	1·9685	2·1016	2·0389	2·0667	4·7488	0·9821	0·2425	0·1033	0·0910
2·392	2·2667	2·5781	2·3960	2·3185	2·3592	2·5187	2·4435	2·4768	5·6912	1·1874	0·2900	0·1248	0·1091
1·21	1·1442	1·3015	1·2099	1·1703	1·1909	1·2714	1·2335	1·2503	2·8728	0·5941	0·1464	0·0624	0·0551
1·9229	1·8186	2·0686	1·923	1·8601	1·8928	2·0207	1·9605	1·9871	4·5661	0·9443	0·2329	0·0977	0·0876
3·6000	3·4045	3·8725	3·600	3·4822	3·5434	3·7827	3·6700	3·720	8·5477	1·7677	0·4357	0·1859	0·1639
0·8928	0·8444	0·9605	0·8929	0·8637	0·8788	0·9382	0·9143	0·9227	2·1201	0·4000	0·1081	0·0461	0·0407
1·7663	1·6704	1·9001	1·7856	1·7086	1·7386	1·8561	1·8007	1·8253	4·1942	0·8671	0·2138	0·0913	0·0804
0·9645	0·9124	1·0378	0·9648	0·9332	0·9496	1·0137	0·9835	0·9969	2·2908	0·4737	0·1167	0·0198	0·0439
0·9807	0·9275	1·055	0·9308	0·9487	0·9653	1·0305	0·9999	1·0134	2·3287	0·4816	0·1187	0·0506	0·0446
...	0·9458	1·0578	1·00006	0·9873	0·9343	1·0508	1·0195	1·0334	2·3745	0·4911	0·1210	0·0516	0·0455
1·0574	...	1·1375	1·0574	1·0223	1·0408	1·1111	1·0780	1·0927	2·5107	0·5191	0·1279	0·0546	0·0481
0·9295	0·8971	...	0·9296	0·8992	0·9510	0·9768	0·9477	0·9606	2·2073	0·4564	0·1125	0·0490	0·0423
0·9999	0·9457	1·0757	...	0·9673	0·9843	1·0508	1·0194	1·0333	2·3744	0·4909	0·1210	0·0516	0·0455
1·0338	0·9777	1·1121	1·0338	...	1·0130	1·0864	1·0503	1·0683	2·4548	0·5077	0·1251	0·0534	0·0471
1·016	0·9603	1·0929	1·0114	0·9603	...	1·0376	1·0357	1·0496	2·4123	0·4989	0·1229	0·0525	0·0463
0·9516	0·9	1·0203	0·9517	0·9205	0·9367	...	0·9701	0·9834	2·2979	0·4673	0·1152	0·0491	0·0433
0·9809	0·9277	1·0552	0·9809	0·9488	0·9655	1·0308	...	1·0136	2·3291	0·4817	0·1189	0·0507	0·0447
0·9677	0·9152	1·041	0·9677	0·9361	0·9525	1·0165	0·9865	...	2·2978	0·4752	0·1171	0·0499	0·0447
0·4211	0·3983	0·4528	0·4209	0·4074	0·4145	0·4435	0·4293	0·4352	...	0·2065	0·0509	0·0217	0·0192
2·04	1·926	2·1907	2·0365	1·9700	2·0045	2·1400	2·0760	2·1044	4·8356	...	0·2465	0·1052	0·0927
8·2623	7·14	8·8853	8·2623	7·9923	8·1329	8·6325	8·4234	8·5383	19·619	4·0573	...	0·4266	0·3762
9·366	18·315	20·8332	19·367	18·7331	19·0625	20·394	19·7431	20·059	45·9933	9·5100	2·3439	...	0·8819
1·9598	20·7085	23·6237	21·9611	21·2424	21·6158	23·0765	22·388	22·6232	52·144	10·7835	2·6578	1·134	...

es. Among these people gold forms no part of the monetary circulation.

INDEX TO CONTENTS.

PAGE
Adit level 46
Alice Bullion at the ironmonger's 88
Alice Bullion's definition of "Value and Price" 94
,, ,, commission 103
Alloy 18
Alluvial soil 37
Amalgamation, Gold 50
,, Silver 53
Amount of alloy allowed 68
Ancient coins stamped with seals 14
Answers to examination questions 117
Areometer, Baume's 67
Arrival at New York 62
Assayer, Duties of 64
Assay Office and its surroundings 63

Balloon, Dinner in the 31
Balloon starts, The 52
,, trip, Mr. Bullion and John Smith's 26
,, Up in a 27
Barometer, Price of 91
Bars, Gold 76
Bars or spikes 14
Bars per mil fine, Gold 69
,, ,, ,, Silver 71
Bars rolled and annealed, Gold 76
,, Silver 76
Barter and price illustrated 95
Barter, Monetary system not affected by 96
Bill at Coffee-house 91
Bills, Hat and coal 93
Bill, Tailor's 93
Blanks annealed and washed 77
Blanks, Making 77
,, Treatment of silver 77
Bohemia, Gold washing in 49
Brass and pewter 17
Brazil, Gold washing in 49
British coins, Value of all the 85
British money coined at Melbourne and Sydney 80

PAGE

British sovereign . . . 83
Bullion, Gold. . . . 59
Bullion, Gold and silver melted . . . 65
Bullion's definition of "Value and Price," Mr. . . . 95
Bullion's family, Mr. . . . 81
Bullion, Silver . . . 59
Burdon's gold ore pulverizer and amalgamator . . . 51
Buttons refined, Gold . . . 67

Capital, chattel and cattle, Origin of . . . 11
Cattle . . . 11
Cattle not indestructible . . . 20
Coffee-house luncheon . . . 89
Coinage, Bronze for . . . 71
,, Gold for . . . 71
,, Silver for . . . 71
Coins . . . 12
,, Divisibility of . . . 18
,, Indestructibility of . . . 20
,, Intrinsic value of. . . . 24
,, ,, ,, standard. . . . 25
,, ,, ,, token . . . 24
,, Light . . . 64
,, On the value of . . . 8
,, Perfect. . . . 79
,, Portability of . . . 18
,, Stamping the . . . 78
,, Weighing the . . . 78
Commercial dealings between India and England . . . 102
Comparative weights of standard metal seen at a glance . . . 109
Conditions of standard metal money . . . 86
Consol, Mr. . . . 75
Cookery, Some more . . . 55
Copper . . . 16
,, mines . . . 44
Corn . . . 13
Cornish mining rules . . . 29
Cost value . . . 95
Countries in which gold and silver are found . . . 42
Cradle rocking . . . 49
Crown pieces, James II.'s pewter . . . 17
Crushing, stamping, and grinding mills . . . 47
Cupellation . . . 56
Cupellation of gold samples . . . 66
Cupels . . . 66
Currency . . . 21
Cutting room . . . 77

Definition of money, John Smith's . . . 7
,, ,, ,, Miss Sweet's . . . 8
Denominational expression for a grain of gold in a gold standard country . . . 83
Denominational expression for a grain of silver in India . . . 97
Denominational expressions of British coins, with their real and representative weights in fine gold . . . 85
Description of gold and silver mining in quartz rocks . . . 46
Different kinds of metals used . . . 14
Difficulty of establishing a fair system of exchange . . . 10

PAGE
Doré gold 59
Drawback, that the value of metal is fluctuating 21
Dressing floors 47

Education of a miner, On the 25
Eliquation 58
Emigrants' landing station, New York 68
Examination questions 116
Exchange on Berlin 111
,, ,, London 110
,, ,, Paris 112
Exchange or barter 9
,, value 95
Explanation of technical terms 21

Fee, Origin of 11
Fifth Avenue Hotel and its surroundings 62
Fillets brought to right thickness 76
Finding of metals 36
Flux 69
Foreign exchanges 109
Formation of rock 31
,, ,, strata 32
Fragmentary deposits, Gold found in 37
Furs 11
,, not indestructible 20
Further treatment of silver 54

Geology 25
Gold and tin unaffected by water or air 41
,, dust 14
,, made up into ingots 51
,, more valuable than silver 20
,, not always native 37
,, samples tested 66
,, the only metal always found in a metallic state 40
,, washing 48
Government v. Private refiners 59
Granite 35
Great Pyramid of Egypt 86
Grocer, The 89
Grocery, List of 91
Gun money, James II.'s 17

Home again 89
How to bring the powdered ore into continual contact with mercury . 73
How to maintain the quickness of the mercury 73
Hungary and Bohemia, Gold washing in 49
Hydrogen-Amalgam process, The 72

Igneous and aqueous rocks 32
Imperfections picked out 79
Increased quantity of gold extracted 74
Ingottsville, John Smith's visit to 81
Intrinsic value 20
Invented about 900 B.C., Coins 14

PAGE
Inventor of Hydrogen-Amalgam process 72
„ „ weighing machine 79
Ironmongery, List of 90
Iron money 15

John Smith's definition of "Value and Price" 95
„ „ commission 107
„ „ gives the exchange value of British coins 8

Land rising 34
„ subsiding 34
Lead money 15
Leather money 12
Legal tender 22
Limestone 33
Loss of gold 73

Machinery, &c. 26
Machines at work, Hydrogen-Amalgam 74
Manchester, Visit to 87
Marking machines 77
Melting department, The 75
Metamorphic rocks 35
Metal easily divided and sub-divided 21
Metal points 103
Metals hidden in earthy or mineral ore 40
Metals in use now 18
Mineralogy and chemistry 25
Miners' tricks 43
Mining companies 28
„ contracts 30
„ John Smith's ideas of 28
„ officers 30
Mint, A visit to the 75
Mono-metallists and bi-metallists 23
Monetary system does not affect principles of barter 96
Money of account 83

Nickel 17
Norman's single grain system 83
Norman's single grain standard of measure 87

Order of strata always the same 34
Ordinary methods of working foreign exchanges 109
Origin of metal money 13
Origin of mountains 33
Ornaments 12
Oxidise, To 54

Palace Hotel, San Francisco 45
Paper money 24
„ „ Intrinsic value of 24
Pattinson's process 56
Perfect coins 79
Platinum 17
Pony's feed 92

PAGE
Press room 78
Price of a British sovereign in India 99
Price of a grain of gold in a silver standard country 99
Price of a grain of silver in a gold standard country 98
Primitive forms of metal money 14
Professor Piazzi Smyth and Major Tracey, R.A. 86
Proportion established between gold and silver in a gold standard country 100
Proportion established between silver and gold in a silver standard country 101
Proposed practical lessons 82
Proposed trip to New York 52
Pyx, Trial of the 79

Quarters, Mr. Bullion and John Smith's. 45
Quartz 36
Quartz rocks. Gold and silver mining in 46
Queen's chamber, Standard of measure 86

Refining 58
Refractory ores cause mercury to sicken. 72
Rent of ground 29
Report of examination 124
,, on commissions 108
Representative money 23
Ring money 15
Rough lumps 14
Route from California to New York 60
,, ,, Land's End to Panama. 27
,, ,, Panama to California 45

Separating gold from the amalgam 51
Separation of gold and silver. 68
Series of conversations, This leads to a 9
Shopping in Manchester. 83
Silver bars 76
Silver bars per mil fine 71
Silver for coinage 71
Silver island 60
Silver ores 53
Single grain system—Comparative weights seen at a glance 109
Sinking shafts 46
Sixty days' sight 112
Small cost of treatment by this process 74
Smelting 53
Soil in which the precious metals are found 28
Specific gravity of liquids 37
,, ,, solids 39
Standard money 22
Success of our present system due to certain points 18
Sulphurets 50
Supply and demand 96
Systems sometimes missing 34

Tailor, The 88
Tin 16

PAGE
Tin mines . . . 44
,, money . . . 16
,, never found native . . . 44
,, used in coinage . . . 71
Tizzy, Mr. . . . 63
Tizzy's invitation, Mr. . . . 62
Tobacco . . . 13
Token money . . . 23
Treatment of gold granulations . . . 68
,, powdered ores . . . 48
,, silver granulations . . . 69
Tribute work . . . 29
Tut work . . . 29
Twenty-third street, New York . . . 67

Unit of value . . . 82
Unstratified and stratified rocks . . . 32
Use of reservoirs . . . 48
,, single grain system . . . 93

Value and price . . . 94
Value in English money of foreign moneys of account . . . 94
Value of coins, On the . . . 8
,, money, On the . . . 9
Various uses of gold and silver . . . 64
Vegetable productions, Other . . . 13
Veins and lodes . . . 36
Verdigris at the mining district, Mr. . . . 45
,, Good-bye to Mr. . . . 71
Volcanic eruptions . . . 35

Weighing the coins . . . 78
Weight of gold ingots . . . 75
What is money? . . . 7
Will's commission . . . 105
,, definition of value and price . . . 94
,, manner of reckoning corrected . . . 92

For Contents of Appendix, see pages 127 to 130.

WATERLOW AND SONS LIMITED, PRINTERS, LONDON WALL, LONDON.

To be pasted into "COIN OF THE REALM: What Is It?" and to be digested by the Reader.

THE EXCHANGES

UPON A SCIENTIFIC BASIS;

ALSO

THE MODES OF EFFECTING EXCHANGES.

BY

JOHN HENRY NORMAN.

Reprinted from "Bankers' Magazine" for February, 1889.

PRICE ONE PENNY.

LONDON:
WATERLOW & SONS LIMITED, PRINTERS, LONDON WALL.

1889.

THE EXCHANGES UPON A SCIENTIFIC BASIS, &c.

Tens of thousands of persons throughout the world who are in the habit of working colonial and foreign exchanges never think of definite weights of standard gold or silver indicated by the denominational expressions with which they are working. Even the chain rule, which is so widely used in effecting arbitrations of exchanges, to a large extent embraces denominational expressions for weights of gold and silver instead of the weights themselves. These rules and examples are found ready to hand, and the mind goes no further than the mechanical work to reach the correct answer. If this is the practice of merchants, bankers and exchange dealers, is there any cause for surprise that rulers, statesmen, legislators, scientists and political economists fail of having "a masterly skill in bullion and coin," and are as rudderless ships at sea in "delicate emergencies," and when most important monetary problems have to be nationally discussed and settled? Trade in countries, and between countries possessing effective standards of gold or silver, the denominational expressions for weights of which are prices and rates of exchange, is carried on in precisely the same way as when Abraham weighed his silver out in payment for his burial cave. For the effigy certifying the weight of fine metal in the standard coin ensures that weight counted out in coin as though the metal were weighed out. The receipt of any recognised token of the standard metal is as effective a discharge of debt as though the standard metal were weighed out for it. This paper will show the force of metal prices and exchanges between countries possessing effective metal standards.

The working of exchanges upon denominational expressions for weights has introduced confusion which even practical exchangers are occasionally entangled in. This is manifest in calling a rise a fall and a fall a rise, a premium a discount, and a discount a premium in exchange. For instance, in the exchange between the British Isles and India compare 1*s*. 10½*d*. with 1*s*. 4½*d*. per rupee. In the British Isles we should say the exchange with India has fallen 6*d*. per rupee, and it would be right. Because in the one case 10·6 grains of fine gold are given for 165 grains of fine silver, and in the other 7·8 grains of fine gold are given for 165 grains of fine silver. But in India, speaking of the difference between the same rates, the rate would be said to have fallen, which is wrong. Because in the one case 165 grains of fine silver would command 10·6 grains of fine gold, and in the other 165 grains of fine silver would command only 7·8 grains of fine gold; showing that the Indian rate had risen in consequence of the same weight of silver commanding a less weight of gold. There never could have been any confusion if a more scientific system had been followed. We see in the present method of quotations of exchanges that between two countries, say, for instance, the British Isles and India, one expression is invariably a constant, in this case the rupee. The quotation both in the British Isles and in India is more or less pence per rupee.* The following suggestion is made as defining a scientific method and one free from obscurity and not leading to confusion. *The variable expression or weight in the country originating the transaction for the constant expression or weight in the country with which the comparison is made or upon which the bill is drawn.*

Of the quotations of the British Isles on other countries, and of other countries on the British Isles, the sixteen following are specimens of those in use. The countries having at present inconvertible paper currencies are treated as if they possessed effective metal standards.

TABLE I.

FG—Grains of Fine Gold. FS—Grains of Fine Silver.

	British Isles on.	On British Isles.
France . .	Francs *f* 25·22 or 113·0016 FG for £1 or 113 0016 FG.	*f* 25·22 or 113·0016 FG for £1 or 113·0016 FG.
Germany . .	Marks *m* 20·43 or 113·0016 FG for £1 or 113·0016 FG.	*m* 20 43 or 113·0016 FG for £1 or 113·0016 FG.
Russia. . .	Pence *d* 26·21 or 12·34 FG for 1 rouble or 277·7224 FS.	*d* 26·21 or 12·34 FG for 1 rouble or 277·7224 FS.
Austria-Hungary	Florins *f* 14·83 or 2542·54 FS for £1.	*f* 14·83 or 2542·54 FS for £1.
India . . .	Pence *d* 15·56 or 7·33 FG for 1 rupee 165 FS.	*d* 15·56 or 7·33 FG for 1 rupee or 165 FS.
United States of America . .	Dollar $ 4·86 or 113·0016 FG per £.	$ 4·86 or 113·0016 per £1.
Chili . . .	Pence *d* 32·87 or 15·48 FG per peso or 347·228 FS.	*d* 32·87 or 15·48 FG per peso or 347·228 FS.
Argentine Republic	Pence *d* 49·16 or 23·148 FG per peso or 23·148 FG.	*d* 49·16 or 23 148 FG per peso or 23·148 FG.

*Additional confusion in this instance arises from the statement that the par of exchange with India was 2*s* per rupee. This was not so. For 2*s*. per rupee is the equivalent of 64·58 pence per standard ounce of silver, and between this present time and 1833 the highest yearly average price was 62¼ pence in 1859. Under this term 2*s*., the one-tenth of a pound, or 11·30003 grains of fine gold has been lost sight of.

There is no system in these. If you start with the idea that between the British Isles and silver standard countries the quotations will be pence for the moneys of account of these countries, you find the conditions with Russia and Austria-Hungary, both professedly silver standard countries, throw you out, with Russia pence per rouble, with Austria-Hungary florins per £1. Again Chili, with a professedly silver standard, and the Argentine Republic, with a professedly gold standard, both are quoted pence per their moneys of account. A scientific system of quotations of exchanges would be the following for the sixteen quotations of the eight countries named as examples for the whole.

TABLE II.

FG—Grains of Fine Gold. FS—Grains of Fine Silver.

	British Isles on.	On British Isles.
France . .	Pence *d* 9·51 or 4·48 FG per franc or 4·48 FG.	Francs *f* 25·22 or 113·0016 FG per £1 or 113·0016 FG.
Germany . .	Pence *d* 11·75 or 5·5313 FG per mark or 5·5313 FG.	Marks *m* 20·43 or 113 0016 FG per £1.
Russia . . .	Pence *d* 26·21 or 12·34 FG per rouble or 277·7224 FS.	Rouble *r* 9·15 or 2542·53 FS per £1.
Austria-Hungary	Pence *d* 16·18 or 7·62 FG per florin or 171·470 FS.	Florin *f* 14·83 or 2542·53 FS per £1.
India . . .	Pence *d* 15·56 or 7·33 FG per rupee or 165· FS.	Rupee *r* 154·09 or 2542·53 FS per £1.
United States of America . .	Pence *d* 49·31 or 23·22 FG per dollar or 23·22 FG.	Dollar $ 4 866 or 113·0016 FG per £1.
Chili . . .	Pence *d* 32·87 or 15·48 FG per peso or 347·228 FS.	Peso *p* 7·35 or 2542·53 FS per £1.
ArgentineRepublic	Pence *d* 49·16 or 23·148 FG per peso or 23·148 FG.	Peso *p* 4·881 or 113·0016 FG per £1.

Since it is not to be expected that there will be any alteration in quoting and working the exchanges of the world, it might serve to keep the mind free from error to be careful when quoting a rate to put the coin of the country originating the transaction first in the formula. Thus in India, instead of quoting pence per rupee, quote rupee per pence. If a rupee, or 165 grains of fine silver, is given for a less number of pence or a smaller weight of gold, the exchange in India on the British Isles has risen. If fewer pence are given in the British Isles for a rupee, the exchange in the British Isles on India has fallen.

With regard to the effect of the exchanges, let it be thoroughly grasped that every grain of wheat and oil seed, each bank of jute and skein of silk, every pound of indigo and ounce of tea which come from India and are used in the British Isles, have silver and gold as good as weighed out against their weights more than once between the production and consumption of these commodities. Follow a spoonful of tea, with which you are about to make your afternoon cup of this refreshing beverage. The planter, who is a friend of yours, has sent it to you from his factory in Assam. He has paid silver against it to the labourer for his work and for other necessaries in Assam. He has sent it to his agent in London for transmission to you. You do not know either the cost price or the sale price of the tea, and you can only tell your friend who likes it, and desires to know its price, that you think it better than some you recently bought at a first-class shop at 2*s*. 6*d*. per lb. Suppose that you have bought that spoonful of tea, and the tea planter has dealt with it in the ordinary commercial manner. He would send the tea to his agent at the seaport, with instructions to sell it there. The buyer would pay silver for it, having ascertained upon what terms *silver in India could be exchanged for gold in the British Isles*. He sends the tea to London, and sells it at auction in the Mincing Lane tea market to a tea dealer, the buyer paying gold for it. At length it comes into your possession, you having paid gold for the same. The tea might have passed through more hands than those mentioned before it came into yours, both in India and in the British Isles, but the possessor of it each time practically weighed out either silver or gold for it. It should be particularly noticed that the purchaser in India first ascertained at what rate he could exchange silver for gold, before he parted with his silver for the tea. It may be asked why he did this? he had parted with his silver and got the tea instead: he would have nothing more to do with silver in the transaction. True. *But he has bought the tea for the purpose of selling it for gold in the British Isles.* Assume that your spoonful of tea is part of one pound, which has cost you 2*s*. 6*d*. per lb., of which 6*d*. was for duty. Assume that the purchaser of the tea in India has to do with the remaining 2*s*. We have to account for his anxiety to know at what rate he could exchange silver for gold before he purchased the tea. Say that his position in India was 10 lbs. of tea for 10·96 rupees, or 1,808 grains of fine silver. He is going to sell the tea for gold in the British Isles, and he must ascertain how much fine gold embodied in pounds sterling are equal to 1,808 grains of fine silver. He finds that the rate of exchange is 21·88 pence per rupee, or 10·31 grains of fine gold for 165 grains of fine silver; so that his 10·96 rupees are worth £1, or 113·0016 grains of fine gold. On this exchange, by selling to you one pound of the tea at 2*s.* per lb. he makes nothing. But assume that exchange has altered in India, and has become 15·56 pence per rupee, or 165 grains of fine silver for 7·33 grains of fine gold, whilst the price of the tea in India has remained the same, viz., 1,808 grains of fine silver, or 10·96 rupees per 10 lbs. Under these conditions the cost price of the tea stands at 14*s.* 3*d.*, or 80·36 grains of fine gold, and could be sold at a trifle more than 1*s.* 5*d.* per lb. The difference between 1*s.* 5*d.* and 2*s.* is 41 per cent. It is hardly necessary to state that the competition among producers, merchants of tea and others, would reduce profits to the ordinary level, and the consumer would get the immediate benefit of the reduced cost of the tea in the British Isles.*

When we examine into the cause of the diminished gold price of the tea, we do not find it to be the diminished cost of production or over-production of the tea, nor the diminished supply of gold and the consequent increased purchasing power of that metal in the British Isles: but we trace it distinctly and solely to the increased silver price of gold. The altered relation of silver to gold in the proportion of 15½ to 16 parts of silver to 1 of gold in 1873, to 22½ parts of silver to 1 of gold now, has not been produced by the gold but by the *fact that silver can be obtained from the earth at vastly less cost value* than in the proportion which formerly existed, when some mints of the world were open to the unlimited reception of that metal at a fixed relation of 15½ to 16 parts of silver to 1 part of gold. All the time these mints were open on these terms, the market price of silver was bound to be at the same relation, and marvellous profits were assured to silver miners.

Modes of effecting Exchanges.

The definition of a rate of exchange for business between two countries which possess effective metal standards may mean one of three things—I. The weight of fine metal forming the standard in one country, for a weight of fine metal form-

* The testimony of traders with India in this country confirms this. It is also *a direct necessary result* upon the first principles of competition. Consider this collateral evidence. The gold price of Indian Government rupee securities has fallen 30 per cent. in the British Isles since 1873. There has been no such fall in India, nor has there been a rise in their silver price in the least corresponding with the rise in the silver price of gold. The cause of the decline in price in the British Isles is not the damaged credit of the Indian Government, the quantity of this class of securities, nor the diminished supply of gold, but the fall in the gold price of silver. The same motive actuates both the dealers in Indian commodities, such as cotton and wheat, and in Indian Government securities—namely, profit measured in grains of gold or grains of silver. Surely the same cause equally affects the gold prices of both classes of property.

ing the standard in another country, resulting from the transmission of the metal. The metals may be gold for gold, silver for silver, gold for silver, or silver for gold. II. The weight of fine metal which has to be given in one country for a bill upon another country, which bill is a legal obligation to pay a definite weight of fine metal in that country. III. The weight of fine metal which could be obtained in one country by the sale of a bill upon another country, which bill is a legal obligation to pay a definite weight of fine metal in that country. The limitation to the fluctuation of exchange in the three cases would be the cost of carriage and coinage of the metal. Assume the following, a domestic case:—A person in London has funds in India which he desires to possess in London. There are three methods open to him whereby he could accomplish this—I. Order the rupees home and sell them in London. II. Have his silver invested in a bill on London for gold. III. Sell his bill in London for gold for his rupees in India. The best of the methods would depend upon whether India is indebted to the British Isles, or the British Isles are indebted to India, considered in connection with the probabilities of the future. The transmission of silver keeps the operation open until the sale of it, but this method is independent of the risk of a bill of exchange being dishonoured. This mode, however, owing to the uncertainty of the gold price of silver in the British Isles and the trouble connected with the business, would not be thought of unless the ordinary dealers in bills of exchange declined to buy bills in London upon India or to sell bills in India upon London. If India is receiving metal—her normal condition—the best mode would be by sale of a bill here for the silver in India. If India is sending silver to London, there would be little difference between selling a bill in London on India or buying a bill in India upon London.

The normal state of the exchange between the British Isles and India necessitating the remittance of silver to the latter country, a closer investigation into the reasons for the rate for a bill of exchange in London on India being for so much, may be interesting and instructive. Take the market price of silver in London at the proportion of 22½ parts of silver to 1 of gold, or 41·88 pence per standard ounce. The par of exchange between London and India at this price would be 15·56 pence per rupee. The par being 15·56 pence, why should a seller of a bill for rupees in London get a higher price than this? Because the bank or dealer in bills who is desirous to remit money to India would have to pay 2⅕ per cent for coinage of his silver in India and ⅘ of 1 per cent. for charges on the transmission of it, in all 3 per cent. more if he was compelled to resort to the shipment of silver. A bill which gives him rupees in India causes him less trouble and suits him as well in other respects. So the seller of a bill obtains 1*s.* 4·15*d.* for a rupee. But if the state of India's indebtedness to the British Isles necessitates the shipment of silver, then upon the the same gold price of silver the person desiring the equivalent of his rupees in London would obtain no more than 1*s.* 3·44*d.* because ⅘ of 1 per cent., being charges on the transmission of the silver home, must be deducted.

The same laws would operate in connection with the exchanges of standard metal or metals between all countries of the world as those described in the exchange between the British Isles and India, and the object of the latter part of this paper is to bring them in a simple manner before your readers.

The world has no science of money. Not a day should be lost in preparing a science primer of money. I would that I could assist to stimulate the scientific men whose vision is not distorted by credit instruments, who possess an aptitude for the subject and could easily acquire "a masterly skill in bullion and coin," in my own country, in the United States of America, in Germany and in France, to accomplish this. Within ten years of the subject being taught with geography in the schools of the world and the issue of this primer, the utmost astonishment would be expressed at the present all but universal darkness which is over the subject and the gross errors which flourish therein.

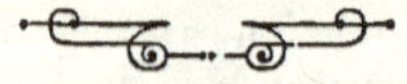

www.ingramcontent.com/pod-product-compliance
Lightning Source LLC
Chambersburg PA
CBHW021817230426
43669CB00008B/787

* 9 7 8 3 7 4 4 7 5 9 4 3 4 *